LETTERS TO A MORMON ELDER

James R. White

BETHANY HOUSE PUBLISHERS
MINNEAPOLIS, MINNESOTA 55438

D0062819

Elder Hahn and the Mission President are fictional characters based upon the author's wide experience and interaction with LDS people. They are not meant to represent any particular person in any way.

Published by Bethany House Publishers
A Ministry of Bethany Fellowship, Inc.
11300 Hampshire Avenue South
Minneapolis, Minnesota 55438

Printed in the United States of America

Library of Congress Cataloging-in-Publication Data

White, James R.
    Letters to a Mormon elder / James R. White.
       p. cm.
    Originally published: Southbridge, MA : Crowne Publications, ©1990.
    1. Church of Jesus Christ of Latter-Day Saints—Controversial literature.
2. Mormon Church—Controversial literature.   3. Missions to Mormons.
4. Imaginary letters.   I. Title. [BX8645.W49 1993]
289.3—dc20   93-25153
ISBN 1-55661-344-X (pbk.)   CIP

LETTERS
TO A
MORMON
ELDER

BHP Books by James R. White

9708

ACKNOWLEDGMENTS

There are simply too many people who have had a hand in making this work a reality to thank them all, but that isn't going to stop me from thanking some of them. To the folks of Alpha and Omega Ministries, who have allowed me to study, work, and write, I say thank you. Rich Pierce, Benny Diaz, Larry and Debby Vondra, Whitney Lynch, Barry Ladden, and everyone else—you are a part of this work. I thank Jeff Niell, who has believed in this book for years, and D.L., who has proven that the theology in this book works. Also, to the co-founder of Alpha and Omega, Michael Beliveau and his wife, Linda— we finally got around to that book, didn't we?

I dedicate this book to my wife of eleven years, Kelli. You have given up so much for our ministry together. This book would not exist except that God has given you to me as a helpmate. Patience is a virtue in which you lack nothing, and in which you have helped me so much. I hope you see this work as yours. Thank you for being my wife.

James White
Phoenix
April 1993

JAMES R. WHITE is the Director of Ministries for Alpha and Omega Ministries, a Christian apologetics and counter-cult ministry. He has earned a B.A. from Grand Canyon University and an M.A. from Fuller Theological Seminary. He and his wife have two children and make their home in Arizona.

FOREWORD

Nearly everyone likes to read someone else's mail. James White allows us to look over his shoulder as he writes a series of friendly and penetrating letters addressed to a Mormon elder who might be any one of the many he has met. He draws upon hundreds of hours of discussions with Mormon missionaries and dedicated members of the Mormon Church encountered through his work with Alpha and Omega Ministries.

He addresses in a very personal and loving way the charges that Mormonism brings against true Christianity, and tactfully shows the falseness of some of Mormonism's own teachings. Both Christians and Mormons can see clearly how really defenseless and self-contradictory the Mormon position is, yet the material is presented not in a combative spirit, but out of caring and concern for each Mormon's ultimate welfare.

We urge you to peek over James's shoulder and follow the vital truths he presents.

Reverend Wesley P. Walters
August 1990

(Reverend Wesley Walters, one of the foremost researchers into Mormon history, pastor of the Marissa Presbyterian Church, passed away shortly after writing this foreword. His great service to the cause of Christ shall be remembered by those of us who knew him.)

CONTENTS

Please note these abbreviations I've used in this book:

D&C	*Doctrine and Covenants*
BoM	*Book of Mormon*
DHC	*Documentary History of the Church (7 volumes)*
JoD	*Journal of Discourses (26 volumes)*
PGP	*Pearl of Great Price*

INTRODUCTION

I had been married only a few months when I received a phone call from my sister-in-law. Two young Mormon missionaries had come to her door, and she had made an appointment to talk with them the next Monday. Could I come over and help her?

At the time, I knew little about the Church of Jesus Christ of Latter-day Saints, or Mormonism. I had read one book on the subject, and had run into an LDS lady while making an outreach visit for my church a few years before. I had a few days to "bone up," so I reread my one book on Mormonism and went back over my list of memory verses.

On the appointed day two young gentlemen came to the door of my sister-in-law's home. Elders Reed and Reese, both nineteen years of age, introduced themselves and sat down. I don't recall many of the specifics of the conversation that day. I know we talked about grace and works, baptism—the normal areas of discussion about salvation that come up. I remember being impressed with the honesty of the missionaries, for they even came right out and said "we are not Bible scholars, and we will have to look into that verse you just quoted and get back to you on that." The conversation was friendly, and they agreed to come back in three days—on Thursday afternoon.

When they left, my wife, her sister, and I sat down and sort of looked at one another. I had some firm convictions as a result of our talk: first, that I didn't know nearly enough about Mormons or their beliefs to effectively share the gospel with them. Second, I didn't know my own faith well enough to accurately and succinctly express it to someone such as a Mormon missionary. I had a lot of work to do.

In the intervening days I read three or four more books on Mormonism. I was amazed at what I found. I began making extensive notes on the differences between what I saw as biblical teaching and that of the LDS Church. I visited my first LDS bookstore and bought my first Book of Mormon. I read of the supposed visit of Jesus to the Americas in Third Nephi, and was immediately struck by the differences between the Bible and the Book of Mormon.

I also began to realize that in our first discussion we had been speaking different languages. That is, they were speaking Mormonese and I was speaking Christianese—using the same terms, but meaning very different things. I began to see how confusing the whole situation could be for those with less biblical background than I. When I met again with Elders Reed and Reese, I felt a little better prepared. This time I understood more of what they were trying to say and was better able to communicate with them in their own language. We spoke of God, and their concept that He was once a man over against the Bible's clear teaching that He had always been God and would always be God. I do remember clearly how that meeting finished. With every ounce of concern and love in my heart I spoke to them of the vast difference between salvation offered by the unchangeable, eternal, and omnipotent God, and the salvation they presented, based as it was upon a being who changed and evolved, and might do so again tomorrow. With that we parted company.

Elders Reed and Reese don't know how much they impacted my life. Of course I now see the providential hand of God in that meeting, but at the time I had absolutely no idea how important those two meetings would be. Of course, they had no intention of spurring me on to found Alpha and Omega Ministries and to produce many tracts and materials for sharing the gospel with Mormons. But that is exactly what happened. God put a fire in my heart for sharing with Latter-day Saints that burns brightly to this day.

I soon discovered that there were many opportunities for witnessing to Mormons. One of the best was at the Mormon Easter Pageant held each spring on the front lawn of the Arizona Temple in Mesa, Arizona. Over 70,000 people attend the pageant during the week-long performance. Beginning in 1983, I too began attending the pageant, not to watch but to share with those who would stop and talk about the faith on the sidewalks surrounding the Temple. Since then Alpha and Omega Ministries has passed out over 100,000 tracts and spent many hundreds of hours sharing with Mormons and non-Mormons during the Easter Pageant.

Every six months, on the first weekend in April and the first weekend in October, the Mormon Church holds its semi-annual General Conference. Tens of thousands of Mormons pack into the Temple Square to hear the "Prophet" and the "Apostles" speak. And nearly every single one of those folks has to walk across public-access sidewalks and through one of three gates to get in. The first time we witnessed at the General Conference, we had all of three people.

That was the first of what to this date has been eighteen consecutive trips to the General Conference of the Mormon Church in Salt Lake City. Every time the LDS Church has met for the past nine years, I have been present to share with them. We have had as many as eighteen people in Salt Lake, quite a sufficient number to adequately cover all three gates and then some. I have had long, intense conversations with individuals, and have had loud, difficult conversations with entire crowds of Mormon missionaries, numbering over twenty-five at a time. I've spoken with young and old, men and women. The people who attend the conference can be some of the hardest people with whom to speak. Many are former missionaries, and almost all of them think that we poor souls outside the gates are utterly unaware of even the first thing about the LDS Church. Despite the obviously volatile situation, we have been blessed of God in our work, and have had the wonderful opportunity of meeting people who have come up to us and said, "I took one of your tracts two years ago just to prove you wrong. Once I started studying, though, I found out you were right, and I am now a member of a local Christian church."

Why this short history of Alpha and Omega Ministries and my own involvement in missions work to the Mormons? My extensive experience in sharing with LDS people one-on-one on the street corner forms an important part of the basis upon which this book, and the letters it contains, is written. Over the past few years I have spoken with well over 1,400 Mormon missionaries in Arizona and Utah, and an equal number of plain Mormon folk. I have corresponded with many, many Mormon elders as well. I am not a newcomer to the field, simply applying high-sounding theology learned in seminary to a problem of cult evangelism—I have taken what is in this book right to the gates of the Temple in Salt Lake City and have tested and proven it there. The information contained in the following pages is drawn not simply from the theological classroom or from the reading of this book or that; it comes as well from hundreds and hundreds of hours of witnessing to

Mormon people and listening closely to their responses.

The need for Christians to be prepared to answer the challenges of the LDS Church hardly needs to be emphasized. Most real believers know the danger presented to the Christian Church by the counterfeit Christianity that is Mormonism. The average Mormon is far better prepared to deal with the Christian than vice versa. It is hoped that this work will help countless believers fulfill their longing to be prepared to give an answer for the hope that is within, yet with gentleness and reverence.

A word concerning the format of this work. Most works on Mormonism address each of the various doctrinal or historical issues in a chapter-by-chapter format. I have chosen not to repeat what has been done by others. Rather, by placing the information concerning Mormonism into the form of letters, I hope to also provide help in knowing how to present the information when the opportunity arises. This way the information is presented in a practical way, one that, it is hoped, will provide needed encouragement and direction to those who will share this information with LDS friends, relatives, and acquaintances.

Also, there are a number of excellent works on Mormonism that do a tremendous job addressing the many historical issues relevant to the LDS faith. It is not my intention to attempt to reinvent the wheel when people such as Jerald and Sandra Tanner have put so much time, and so much effort, into providing the Christian community with well-researched, solid information that is presented with the highest level of integrity. The reader is directed to their many, many fine works for in-depth material on the history and practices of the LDS Church. Therefore, only three letters will deal with specific historical issues such as the Book of Mormon or the false prophecies of Joseph Smith. The primary thrust of this work is to fill in where many other works do not—that being to provide a *theological response* to the LDS Church.

James White

What Is Truth?

Monday, May 21

Dear Elder Hahn,

I wanted to write and thank you for the time you spent with my wife and me last Friday evening. We enjoyed your company. Given that you indicated that your partner, Elder Young, would be transferring out this past weekend, I decided to write to you specifically. If you get a chance, please feel free to forward our correspondence to Elder Young, as he seemed interested in the topics we discussed.

We touched on quite a number of different things Friday evening, many of which I wanted to expand upon but could not, given the time constraints we were under. If you are willing, I would like to go into some of those areas with you by mail, as I realize that your busy schedule will not allow you to spend a great deal of time visiting me in my home. I would like to say, however, that I would be more than willing to travel to meet with you, if you would like. Just let me know a convenient time.

Before I go into any particular doctrines or teachings that were considered that evening, I wanted to talk with you about the last thing you said as we were saying goodbye. As I recall, it went something like this:

> Despite all we've discussed, Mr. White, I want to bear you my testimony that I know that the Church of Jesus Christ of Latter-day Saints is the true Church, that Jesus is the Christ, and that Joseph Smith was a prophet of God. Further, I bear you my testimony that

Ezra Taft Benson is a prophet of God. I have prayed about the Book of Mormon and have received a testimony of the Holy Ghost that it is true.

At that time I just quickly mentioned to you the importance of comparing one's *feelings* to the clear, inspired revelation of God, the Bible. At that point you had to leave. I would like to pick up with your testimony, if you don't mind.

First, I want to say that I respect you immensely for what you do. Not many young people today would be willing to give two years of their lives to the work of their church. Even beyond this, you have obviously studied your faith and seem to honestly desire to share that faith with others. In our world today, that is a rare attitude indeed.

But, as we discussed, I do not believe that what you are preaching is the true gospel of Jesus Christ. We both know people who are honest, kind, and moral, but who teach falsehood about Jesus Christ and His gospel. For example, we both have encountered Jehovah's Witnesses as they go door-to-door preaching *their* version of the truth. You and I agree that the Witnesses are wrong in their teaching—they believe that Jesus is actually Michael the Archangel, Jehovah's first creation. You and I agree that that is in error. Therefore, no matter how honest or sincere the Witnesses at my door might be, *they are in error!* In the same way, you believe me to be in error, though I would hope that you would admit my honesty and sincerity with regard to my religious faith. And, from my perspective, you too are in error, though I freely admit your sincere feelings regarding your beliefs.

So what I am saying is this: You can be sincere, but be sincerely *wrong.* I know sincere Buddhists, sincere Muslims, even sincere atheists—but they are wrong, no matter how sincere they might think themselves to be. Truth exists, and we are responsible for how we relate to that truth. If we deny the truth, even if we have been taught from childhood to do so, we are wrong all the same. What is right is right, what is wrong is wrong. Truth exists independently of either you or me. You do not define truth, and I do not define truth. And let us flee quickly from the all-too-common thinking of the world today, "Well, you have your truth, and I have my truth. . . . " Such is nonsense. Truth is truth, and it will be true whether I believe it to be true or not.

But, I doubt we disagree about that. We both share the belief that truth exists, and that it can be known. Where we disagree is exactly *what that truth is.*

In your testimony, you mentioned that you had prayed about the Book of Mormon and "knew" that it was true. Elder Hahn, may I point out to you that I too have a testimony, and my testimony is in direct conflict with yours! I believe that the Spirit has testified to me that there is but *one* God, and this is out of harmony with your beliefs. How, then, are we to decide who is right? You honestly say that you have experienced feelings that you interpret to be the testimony of the Holy Ghost. I say the same thing. Yet, what we feel has been revealed by the Holy Ghost is in contradiction. If we leave it at this, no one can ever say "this is true, this is not" since we are back to saying that each person has his or her own truth. So how can we know?

> There is a way which seemeth right unto a man, but the end thereof are the ways of death. (Proverbs 14:12)

If we trust in our feelings, Elder Hahn, in that which we *feel* is right, we can find ourselves in grave danger. Many a man has felt that this or that belief or path was right, but the end of that path proved to be nothing but death and destruction. We cannot trust in our feelings to guide us properly. The writer of Proverbs said, "He that trusteth in his own heart is a fool" (Proverbs 28:26), and Jeremiah said, "The heart is deceitful above all things, and desperately wicked: who can know it?"(Jeremiah 17:9).

Any man who thinks his heart a faithful and safe guide knows very little about the evil and wickedness that lurks in its dark recesses. You know how easily you can rationalize evil behavior, and how simple it is to convince yourself that what you are doing is right, when in fact, it is wrong. If you are honest with your own heart, you know this to be the case. So, how can you possibly trust your feelings with reference to the truth of your church? What if your feelings are wrong? How can you know one way or the other?

Thankfully, the Bible gives us the answer. There is something that is unchanging, unlike our feelings. There is something that tells us the truth at all times, again, unlike our feelings. That something is the Word of God. Listen to these passages from the Bible:

> Every word of God is pure: he is a shield unto them that put their trust in him. Add thou not unto his words, lest he reprove thee, and thou be found a liar. (Proverbs 30:5–6)

> Whoso despiseth the word shall be destroyed: but he that feareth the commandment shall be rewarded. (Proverbs 13:13)

> The grass withereth, the flower fadeth: but the word of our God shall stand for ever. (Isaiah 40:8)

And we should not forget the words of the Lord Jesus, where He spoke the same truth by saying, "Heaven and earth shall pass away, but my words shall not pass away"(Matthew 24:35). The sure, unchanging Word of God provides us with the basis and definition of truth itself. While we may feel one way one day, and totally different another, the Bible does not change. Its message is not altered by the changing, shifting moods of man.

When Paul and Silas entered into the city of Berea (as recorded in Acts 17), they preached the gospel. The Bereans had never heard this message before—it was totally new to them. How, then, did they determine whether it was true or false? Does the Bible tell us that they dropped to their knees and prayed about it, seeking some kind of *feeling* to help them know? Did they trust in their feelings and believe on that basis? Certainly not. Listen to what the Bible says:

> These were more noble than those in Thessalonica, in that they received the word with all readiness of mind, and searched the scriptures daily, whether those things were so. (Acts 17:11)

Note what these Bereans did. They "searched the scriptures daily." Rather than looking to their feelings, they looked to the Scriptures, and compared the message preached by Paul and Silas with what was in the Holy Writings. By doing this, they discovered that the gospel was true, and believed in the Lord Jesus Christ. They did just as Paul exhorted the Thessalonians in his first letter, chapter 5, verse 21: "Prove all things; hold fast that which is good." The Bereans *proved* the message of Paul and Silas by comparing it with the Scriptures.

Note well, Elder Hahn, that the Holy Ghost will never give a testimony that is in conflict with that which He has inspired to be written in the Scriptures. The Holy Ghost is a consistent being, is He not? Is He not called the "Spirit of Truth" in John 16? Yes, He is. Then, if anyone claims that they have received a testimony from the Holy Ghost that such-and-such is true, and that belief is contradictory to that which we find in Scripture, then we can be sure of this one thing: *The spirit that testified to that individual is not the Spirit of God!* For example, the Holy Ghost will not testify to one person that "there is only one God" and to another, "there are many Gods." That would involve a contradiction, an inconsistency, on the part of the very Spirit of Truth. This is important, Elder, because I believe that the teachings of Joseph Smith are in direct contradiction to the inspired writings of the Bible. If we say that the Holy Ghost inspired the teachings of the Bible, and Joseph Smith contradicted those writings, then the Holy Ghost would never give anyone, *including you,* a testimony that Joseph Smith was a prophet of God.

Before I close, allow me to answer what has, in my experience, been a very common objection to what I have just said. James wrote,

> If any of you lack wisdom, let him ask of God, that giveth to all men liberally, and upbraideth not; and it shall be given him. (James 1:5)

Many Latter-day Saints feel that this passage teaches them to pray about what is true, and what is not true. They believe that it gives them warrant to trust in certain feelings that have been theirs, certain experiences that they have had. Yet, is this really what James said?

You might note first, Elder Hahn, that the verse, as it is written in the original language of Greek, assumes that it is true that men lack wisdom. It could even be translated, "Since a man lacks wisdom, let him ask of God. . . . " We all lack wisdom, do we not? But, is wisdom the same as knowledge of what is true and false? Not necessarily. First, wisdom and knowledge are two different terms in the Greek language, in which the book of James was written. One must have knowledge to use wisdom; wisdom is the use of knowledge. They are related, but they are not the same thing. This passage from James does *not,* then, teach us to trust in our feelings over what the Bible teaches. The Bible gives us true and clear *knowledge* of what is true about God and salvation. If we are *wise,* we will accept that truth, and will not pray to God and ask Him to repeat what He has already said.

Elder Hahn, I do not presume to know the exact nature of your testimony, nor the depth of the feelings that come with it. I know the feelings that are mine, the testimony of the Spirit that I have. But, as I've said, my feelings, no matter how special they are to me, do not make the message that I proclaim right and true. Just so, your feelings, no matter how much they mean to you, cannot be allowed to stand in the way of your examination of God's Word and your own beliefs. We must not fall into the trap of molding the Word of God to our feelings; our feelings must be molded by the Word of God.

In light of this, Elder, I hope you will join with me in examining what the Bible says about who God is, how He has revealed himself, and how He has provided for salvation in Jesus Christ. Shall we begin by looking at the truth about God? I look forward to hearing from you.

Sincerely,

James White

But It *Is* Translated Correctly!

Friday, June 1

Dear Elder Hahn,

Thank you for your letter of May 26th. I appreciate the swift response, as well as the kind attitude with which you wrote.

I realized in writing to you originally and suggesting that we begin with a discussion of the Bible's teaching about God that we might have to hold off long enough to deal with the subject of the Bible. I have met a few Mormons with whom such a diversion was not necessary, but that is the exception rather than the rule. The vast majority of LDS, in my experience, harbor some doubts concerning the accuracy of the Bible, some going so far as to reject the Bible, for all intents and purposes, as a book that can be trusted. Indeed, Mormon Apostle Orson Pratt once wrote:

> What shall we say then, concerning the Bible's being a sufficient guide? Can we rely upon it in its present known corrupted state, as being a faithful record of God's word? We all know that but a few of the inspired writings have descended to our times, which few quote the names of some twenty other books which are lost. . . . What few have come down to our day have been mutilated, changed, and corrupted in such a shameful manner that no two manuscripts agree. Verses and even whole chapters have been added by unknown persons; and even we do not know the authors of some whole books; and we are not certain that all those which we do know were written by inspiration. Add all this imperfection

to the uncertainty of the translation, and who, in his right mind, could, for one moment, suppose the Bible in its present form to be a perfect guide? Who knows that even one verse of the whole Bible has escaped pollution, so as to convey the same sense now that it did in the original? . . . There can be no certainty as to the contents of the inspired writings until God shall inspire someone to rewrite all those books over again. . . . No reflecting man can deny the necessity of such a new revelation. (*Orson Pratt's Works*, "The Bible Alone an Insufficient Guide," pp. 44–47)

I have met a number of Mormons who were that radical in their view. But, I've also met others who would disagree with Orson Pratt; even Brigham Young, who, in response to comments such as those above by Pratt, said:

. . . why I make this particular remark is because this congregation heard brother O. Pratt scan the validity of the Bible, and I thought by the time he got through, that you would scarcely think a Bible worth picking up and carrying home, should you find one in the streets. . . . The Bible is good enough as it is, to point out the way we should walk, and to teach us how to come to the Lord of whom we can receive for ourselves. (Brigham Young, *Journal of Discourses*, 10/8/1855, 3:116)

As you can see, there are a lot of different attitudes toward the Bible among Latter-day Saints. Your objections to the accuracy of the Bible, Elder Hahn, are common in my experience, and I will do my best to answer them.

In my previous letter I noted a few passages from the Bible, such as Isaiah 40:8 and Proverbs 30:5–6. It seems obvious to me, Elder Hahn, that the Lord Jesus believed that the Scriptures were truly and really the words of God, and this is perfectly in line with the views expressed in those Scriptures I just cited. In fact, in disputing with the Jews, Jesus said, "Have you not read what God spoke to you saying, 'I am the God of Abraham and the God of Isaac and the God of Jacob?' " (Matthew 22:31–32). Here the Lord Jesus refers to the written words of Scripture as the very words of God himself. You will not find the Lord Jesus ever "correcting" the Old Testament Scriptures. Each time He quotes the Old Testament writings, He accepts what they say without question and expects all others to have the same attitude. A high view of the Bible is surely Jesus' belief. Do you believe that what you find in the Bible is actually *God's words*, Elder Hahn? Or have you been taught that the Bible is not fully trustworthy, not fully accurate?

There are two scriptures that clearly present my belief in the *nature* of the Bible as God's Word. The first is 2 Timothy 3:16–17, the second is 2 Peter;1:20–21. Let me briefly review these passages with you.

Paul wrote to Timothy, "All Scripture is God-breathed, and is profitable for doctrine, for reproof, for instruction, for training in righteousness, in order that the man of God might be complete, fully equipped for every good work." Yes, I know, that is not the King James translation—it is my own translation of the Greek in which Paul wrote to Timothy in the first place. I will discuss the topic of translation a little later, if I might ask your indulgence till then. Paul describes the Scriptures as "God-breathed." The term itself that is commonly translated as "inspired" literally means that the Scriptures find their origin, their source, in God himself. They are like the breath of God himself, coming forth from His mouth. Note, too, that the Bible is not here speaking of *how* the writers were led by God to write what they did, but that *what they wrote* was inspired or "God-breathed." God used men to write His Word, but He did so in such a way as to insure that what was written was word-for-word what He had intended from eternity past. The God of the Bible is big enough to use men to write His message, yet at the same time see to it that the resultant revelation is not mixed with error or untruth.

The Apostle Peter did address the manner in which the holy men chosen by God wrote the Scriptures. In 2 Peter 1:21–22 we read, "Knowing this first of all, that no Scriptural prophecy ever came about by the prophet's own personal interpretation, for no prophecy ever was borne by the will of man, rather, while being carried along by the Holy Spirit, men spoke from God." Again, this is my own translation of the original Greek. Peter is discussing not the *interpretation* of the text, but the *origin* and *fidelity* of the text. He asserts that the prophecies of Scripture (and he is not speaking simply of prophecies in the sense of predictions of future events, but the whole proclamation of the truth of God) never came about simply by human impulse or through human thinking. God's revelation has never found its origin in the will of man. Instead, these men spoke from God while being carried along by the Holy Spirit of God. What they said came *from* God, and as they spoke these things, they were being carried along by the Spirit of God. Obviously, then, the Spirit of God would not have led these men into error in what they said as they spoke from God, would He? We see, then, that the apostles, just as the Lord Jesus, believed in the *inerrancy* of the biblical text—that what they wrote contains no errors, no untruths.

We might agree to this point. You might be willing to say, "Yes, as the Bible was *originally* written it was the perfect and complete Word of God." But, then you'd be quick to add, "Things have changed—the Bible has been changed, things have been lost. We can no longer say that the Bible is fully and completely the Word of God." That really seems to be your main objection if I am interpreting your last letter correctly. If so, you seem to be in line with a majority of LDS today. However, you might note that one of your own LDS scholars, James Talmage, was not quite as strident in his criticism of the Bible. Rather, he knew enough of the Bible itself to be much more moderate in his words:

> The Latter-day Saints believe the original records to be the word of God unto man, and, as far as these records have been translated correctly, the translations are regarded as equally authentic. The English Bible professes to be a translation made through the wisdom of man; in its preparation the most scholarly men have been enlisted, yet not a version has been published in which errors are not admitted. However, an impartial investigator has cause to wonder more at the paucity of errors than that mistakes are to be found at all. (James Talmage, *Articles of Faith*, pp. 236–37)

He also noted,

> The New Testament must be accepted for what it claims to be; and though, perhaps, many precious parts have been suppressed or lost, while some corruptions of the texts may have crept in, and errors have been inadvertently introduced through the incapacity of translators, the volume as a whole must be admitted as authentic and credible, and as an essential part of the Holy Scriptures. (*Articles of Faith*, p. 248)

It is interesting that Talmage would say "perhaps many precious parts have been . . . lost" and "some corruptions of the texts may have crept in" in light of the clear teachings of many of the early LDS teachers (such as Orson Pratt) as well as the direct statements of the Book of Mormon about the Bible:

> Neither will the Lord God suffer that the Gentiles shall forever

remain in that awful state of blindness [the Book of Mormon originally read "awful state of woundedness"], which thou beholdest they are in, because of the plain and most precious parts of the gospel of the Lamb which have been kept back by that abominable church, whose formation thou hast seen. (1 Nephi 13:32)

Of course, this passage only says that these "plain and precious truths" are withheld by the "abominable church," and not that they have been removed from the Bible, but many, many LDS believe this to be the case. 1 Nephi 14:10 says:

And he said unto me: Behold there are save two churches only; the one is the church of the Lamb of God, and the other is the church of the devil; wherefore, whoso belongeth not to the church of the Lamb of God belongeth to that great church, which is the mother of abominations; and she is the whore of all the earth.

It is clear that the "all churches other than the LDS Church" must be actively "keeping back" many "plain and precious truths" of the Bible. How this is done is not stated by the Book of Mormon; but, popular belief among Latter-day Saints says that the Catholic Church removed whole sections of the Bible during the Middle Ages. You stated in your letter:

But, you must know that the Bible has been translated over and over and over again. We can't know exactly what the Bible said originally, because it has been translated so often. As the Eighth Article of Faith says, "We believe the Bible to be the word of God as far as it is translated correctly; we also believe the Book of Mormon to be the word of God."

You are about the four hundredth Mormon missionary who has said this to me, I can assure you of that! But, your assertion is simply not correct. Let me explain.

Transmission Versus Translation

We need to define some terms, Elder Hahn, so that we can properly understand how we received the Bible as it is today. You made the statement that the Bible has been "translated over and over and over again." In one sense, that is true, but I doubt you are thinking of translation in the proper sense. Most Mormons, when they say this, mean that the Bible was translated from one language into another, and then from that language into another, and then into another, and so on. Often the example is used of the child's game where one person whispers a phrase to one person, and then on to the next, around the circle, and each time the phrase is changed by the time it gets to the end of the process. But, this is not what happened with the Bible.

When we speak of the history of the Bible, and how it came to us, we are speaking of the *transmission* of the text over time. For the first fifteen hundred years of the Christian era, the text of the Bible was transmitted by hand-copying, from one manuscript to another. We have today over 25,000 handwritten manuscripts of the New Testament alone, and over 5,000 of these are written in Greek, the original language of the New Testament. Most of the time, when Mormons speak of the Bible being "mistranslated" in terms of the Eighth Article of Faith, they are not referring to its actual translation, but rather they are alleging that there have been errors made in the transmission of the text. Normally it is believed that passages, and even whole books, have been lost in the process of *transmission*, not in *translation*.

Translation is the process whereby one renders a passage in one language into the words of another language. For example, above I gave you my own translation of both 2 Timothy 3:16–17 and 2 Peter 1:20–21. That is, I had before me a text of the New Testament written in Greek, and I translated those passages from Greek into English, and put that translation down on paper for your benefit. Each of the various versions of the Bible that are available today—the King James Version, the New American Standard Bible, the New International Version—each is simply a different translation of the one Bible, which was written in Hebrew, Aramaic, and Greek. There is only one Bible, while there are many translations of that Bible into the many languages of mankind, including our own English versions. I enjoy reading the Bible in Greek and Hebrew, and have other translations in languages I have studied such as German and French. I am not reading different Bibles when I read in these different languages—I am reading different *translations* of the *one* Bible, originally written in Greek and Hebrew.

I hope the difference between transmission and translation is now clear to you. When we speak of supposed errors in rendering the original Hebrew or Greek texts, we are speaking of translation. When we speak of the allegation that passages of the Bible, even entire books, have been "removed," or that the text of the Bible has been corrupted over time, we are speaking of transmission. In light of these definitions, allow me to address your statements.

You said that the Bible had been "translated over and over again." Yes, that is true in the sense that each time I open my Greek New Testament, I am "translating" it over again. But, I don't believe you meant it in that way. Rather, you seem to be saying that the Bible has gone through a process whereby it has been translated from one language into another, sort of like this:

Hebrew ◊ Greek ◊ Latin ◊ French ◊ German ◊ Spanish ◊ English

Obviously, if that is how it happened, you would be right in saying that by the time it got to English, much of what it originally said would have been lost in translation. But, that is not how it happened. Each of the English versions is based directly upon the original languages, and there is but one step between the original Hebrew and Greek texts to the English translation thereof. So, as you can see, we *can* know what the Bible originally said with reference to its translation from the original languages into English.

So, in a sense, I can say that I agree that the Bible is the word of God as far as it is translated correctly, in the sense that a purposeful and malicious attempt to *mis*translate the Bible would not produce a result that I would feel obliged to call "the word of God." For example, the Watchtower Bible and Tract Society (Jehovah's Witnesses) produces what they call *The New World Translation*. This, I believe, is not truly "the word of God" for it purposefully mistranslates a number of passages that are relevant to the person of Jesus Christ, in an attempt to "smuggle" the doctrines of Jehovah's Witnesses into the text of the Bible. I feel no obligation to follow this mistranslation as if it were the Word of God. In the same way, Elder Hahn, I do not follow Joseph Smith's "translation" of the Bible, for it has no basis in the manuscripts of the Bible that we have, and, in the case of his substantial addition to the fiftieth chapter of Genesis, he was obviously attempting to insert a prophecy about himself in something that was written a full 3,000 years earlier.

I have often had LDS people say, when confronted with a passage that contradicted their own beliefs, "Well, that must be mistranslated." I ask, "Do you know what the correct translation is, then?" "No," they reply. "Have you examined this passage in the original Hebrew or

Greek?'' ''No, I have not,'' they say. ''Then how do you know it is mistranslated?'' I ask. ''Because it contradicts what the LDS Church teaches,'' they reply. Only a handful of times have I met anyone who has done even a small amount of study on a passage that they alleged to be mistranslated. If you ask me, Elder Hahn, James Talmage *knew* that the Bible was translated accurately in the English versions, and he also knew that the charges of gross corruption of the biblical text, made so often by Latter-day Saints, have no basis in fact. That is why he was so reticent in his statements that I cited above.

So the next question, obviously, is this: Has the text of the Bible been changed and corrupted, as many allege? Or do we know what the original authors of the Scriptures wrote? We can speak all we wish of being able to translate the texts of the Bible accurately (and we can do so), but if the text has not been transmitted correctly over time, what does it matter?

Recently, I heard a Christian talk-show host and a Mormon speaking about the Bible on a nationwide talk program. The Mormon said, ''Well, the Bible has been translated many times, and we no longer know what it originally said because it has been changed.'' Sadly, the talk-show host responded not with accurate information about the biblical text, but rather said, ''Well, the Book of Mormon has been changed, too!'' While he is correct that the Book of Mormon has undergone a good deal of specific, purposeful editing (the Doctrine and Covenants even more so!), that is not the point. Two wrongs don't make a right. The host should have responded by refuting the charge of corruption that was lodged against the Bible.

It is impossible, of course, for me to attempt a full discussion of the history of the text of the Bible in a letter. Besides, many fine scholars have put pen to paper in the description of this very thing. Two fine, more basic works come to mind that I would like to recommend to you. F. F. Bruce's *The New Testament Documents: Are They Reliable?* and J. Harold Greenlee's *Scribes, Scrolls and Scripture*. Both should be readily available to you. But I shall not simply direct you to others without giving you a basic reply to your contentions.

While it may be true that none of the 5,000 Greek manuscripts (as an example) of the New Testament read *exactly* like another, this in itself is not a very meaningful fact. That *any* handwritten document of the length of even one of the Gospels should read exactly like another would be quite remarkable, for the probability of misspelling even one word, or skipping one "and" in a whole book is quite high. Despite this, at least seventy-five percent of the text of the New Testament is without textual variation; that is, three out of four words in the New Testament are to be found without variation in all the manuscripts we have. Ninety-five percent of the remaining twenty-five percent of the text is easily determined through the process of textual criticism. Textual criticism is the process whereby, knowing the propensities of scribes in making errors and utilizing the incredibly rich amount of evidence available to us (the New Testament, for example, has far more manuscript evidence available for study than any other document of antiquity), the most likely original reading is determined from the possibilities presented by the manuscripts. That leaves but a little less than 1½ percent of the entire text—less than two out of every one hundred words—where serious doubt as to the exact wording of the original exists. But note this well, Elder: One thing certain is we do have the original readings available to us in the possibilities given to us by the manuscript tradition. What I mean is this: Every reading that has entered into the manuscripts of the New Testament has remained there. While some might think that this is bad, it is not, for what it also means is that since no readings "drop out" of the text, the original reading is still there as well! Our task is not, then, impossible, for the original readings are still there—we just need to recognize which of two or three possibilities it is.

This tenacity of the New Testament text (that is, the fact that readings "stick around" even if they look to be obviously in error) also helps us to see why another favorite LDS accusation against the Scriptures is wrong. Many believe that large sections of the Bible have been removed or have been lost over time. Seemingly, given what the Book of Mormon says as cited above, this "editing" was done by the Roman Catholic Church, which, it is alleged, removed that which was not in harmony with its own beliefs. Aside from the fact that there remains much in Scripture that is not in harmony with Roman Catholic teaching (which, I guess, would mean they did not do a very good job in their editing), what is obvious is the fact that such a task of editing would have been simply impossible to do! Why? There are thousands of copies of the Scriptures, spread out all across the Roman Empire, from Spain to Egypt. How could any one man, or any one organization, gather up all these copies, including many buried under the sands in Egypt or in clay pots in Palestine, change all of them, and then replace all of them?

Some may wish that God had not allowed for all these copies of the manuscripts to exist with their minor variations, but, in reality, we can see that this was a wonderful way of protecting the text! Any change in one manuscript shows up like a sore thumb when compared with the others! For example, if one person took a manuscript and attempted to rewrite it so as to teach a completely new doctrine, this one manuscript would be vastly different than those manuscripts found a thousand miles away. The change would be obvious to all.

So I hope you can see, Elder Hahn, that many of the things you have been taught regarding the Bible are, actually, *myths* rather than reality. When we read the New Testament, we can *know* that Paul wrote "For by grace you have been saved through faith . . ." (Ephesians 2:8); we can know what was originally written and can build our faith upon the sure revelation of God in Scripture.

I have waxed long, but I feel it is important. Please feel free to ask further questions about the Bible, as it will be vitally important to any discussions we might have later on. I hope you are feeling well, and I hope to hear from you again soon.

Sincerely,

James White

LETTER 3

Errors in God's Word?

Friday, June 8

Dear Elder Hahn,

Thank you for your prompt reply. I have to note in passing that your letter did not directly respond to much of what I said before regarding the Bible's claims concerning itself. That is not really unusual, but I feel that it should be pointed out to you that providing a list of supposed "contradictions" is not the same as dealing with the direct claims of Scripture. Your approach, instead, is to deny the teachings of the Bible by providing examples of alleged errors that would, by their presence, *disprove* the words of Scripture. I hope you will consider further the Bible's own teachings about itself.

The list of "contradictions" you have provided me is a common one—at times I think that this list, or one very similar to it, is a part of the "missionary training packet" that is passed out to every new missionary before being sent out into the field. I say that because of the fact that these same passages keep coming up over and over again as I speak with representatives of the LDS Church. In fact, the very first time anyone at all attempted to prove to me that the Bible was contradictory to itself was when I met with my first pair of Mormon missionaries—and, interestingly enough, the passage they threw at me was the first one you listed in your letter.

Before I address these particular passages, I would like to point something out to you, Elder Hahn. Have you ever thought about the fact that you have to join hands with atheists and other enemies of the Christian faith in your attacks upon the Bible? I have spoken with, and corresponded with, many, many atheists over the past few years, and the supposed contradictions they speak about are the same as those you have provided me. Surely your reasons are a little different than theirs, but, in the final analysis, may I suggest to you that you *have* to attack the validity and accuracy of the Bible *in order to find a way to establish your "other" scriptures?* If the Bible is what it claims—the inspired, sufficient revelation of God—then there is no need for any other writings, including yours. Not only this, but I believe the attacks made upon the accuracy of the Bible by the LDS Church are necessary so that the *clear and evident contradictions between the teaching of the Bible and LDS theology can be dismissed with as little difficulty as possible.* Hopefully, we shall be able to get into those particular biblical teachings in a short time.

Your list of contradictions in the Bible is actually very well suited for my purposes. The passages you cite provide me with good examples of various kinds of errors made by those who attack the accuracy of God's Word. (I'm sorry if that description offends you, but, you must admit it is an accurate representation.) Let's look at the passages you listed:

Acts 9:7/Acts 22:9, and the alleged discrepancies in the story of Paul's meeting Jesus Christ on the road to Damascus. This seems to be the classic example of a contradiction for many LDS, and it provides me with a good example of how people fail to do their homework when reading the Bible. We shall spend most of our time here.

Matthew 27:9–10/Zechariah 11:12–13, and Matthew's citation of the prophecy of Zechariah as being the prophecy of Jeremiah.

Matthew 27:45/Mark 15:25/Luke 23:44/John 19:14, and the time of the Lord's death on the cross. Was He crucified at the "third hour" and died in the "ninth hour" as Matthew, Mark, and Luke indicate, or is John right in giving a different time?

Matthew 4:18–20/John 1:40–42, and whether Andrew went and got Peter, or did Jesus just call them from their nets by the seashore?

Mark 6:8/Luke 9:3, and the question, were the disciples to take a staff on their journey or not?

I am sure that you could multiply your examples, as I surely could. I have *reams* of lists of supposed contradictions in the Bible. But those you have provided me will function well to help us see the various kinds of allegations that are made against the Bible. Let's start with the first, and seemingly most popular of them all, Acts 9:7 and Acts 22:9. In these two passages the story of Paul's encounter with the risen Lord Jesus Christ is given, first by Luke, then in Paul's own words as he stands before the mob in Jerusalem. In the King James Version of the Bible we read,

> Acts 9:7—And the men which journeyed with him stood speechless, hearing a voice, but seeing no man.

> Acts 22:9—And they that were with me saw indeed the light, and were afraid; but they heard not the voice of him that spoke to me.

The alleged contradiction is, of course, easy to see. Acts 9:7 says the men heard the voice, and Acts 22:9 says they did not hear the voice. Clearly the question is, did the men hear the voice or not? To answer that question, we must, obviously, deal with the text as written by Luke in its original languages. This is an excellent example of a situation where the original words must be allowed to be heard in the argument, for we could be charging Luke with a simple mistake that he did not make. These passages will also serve well, Elder Hahn, to demonstrate how "doing one's homework" can save one from making errors in attacking the Bible. In providing the following information to you, I am not attempting simply to bury you under a mountain of citations and quotes; I am, however, attempting to show you how important in-depth Bible study is. There are precious few who have objected to my belief in the inerrancy of the Bible and have demonstrated their position on the basis of real, solid research.

We need to notice that some modern versions translate the passage differently. For example, the New International Version reads as follows:

> 9:7—The men traveling with Saul stood there speechless; they heard the sound but did not see anyone.

> 22:9—My companions saw the light, but they did not understand the voice of him who was speaking to me.

Note that in the NIV the contradiction no longer exists; in the first passage the men hear a sound; in the second they do not understand the voice of the one speaking to Saul. Critics would assert that the NIV has translated in accordance with interpretation and convenience rather than according to language and usage. But is this so? Let's examine these passages and see.

First, before going into the text itself, we must address the issue of "what is a contradiction?" The law of contradiction, stated briefly, would be that you cannot have *A* and *non-A* simultaneously. You cannot have a chair in a room and outside the room at the same time. That would be a contradiction. But, is this what we have in this case in Acts?

The answer can only be no, we do not have a contradiction here. First, let's transliterate the passages from the original language of Greek so that their differences can be seen:

9:7—*akouontes men tes phones*
22:9—*ten de phonen ouk ekousan tou laluntos moi*

It would be good to list the differences between the passages:

1. In 9:7 *akouo* is found as a nominative plural participle; in 22:9 it is a plural aorist verb.
2. In 9:7 *phone* is a singular genitive noun; in 22:9 it is a singular accusative noun.
3. In 9:7 *akouo* precedes its object; in 22:9 it follows its object.
4. In 9:7 the phrase is not modified; in 22:9 it is modified by "of the one speaking to me."
5. In 9:7 Luke is narrating an event in Greek; in 22:9 Paul is speaking to a crowd in Hebrew (or Aramaic).

Clearly the critic is placed in an impossible position of forcing the argument here, for the differences between the two passages are quite significant. Hence the argument must proceed on the grounds of contradictory meanings only, for the grammar of the two passages will not support a clear *A* vs. *non-A* proposition.

We then must answer the question, are the differences between these passages significant enough to warrant the NIV's translation? Do we have a solid basis upon which to assert that what Paul meant was that the men heard a sound but did not understand what the voice was saying? Following are some of the comments made by some eminent Greek scholars about these passages:

> Thus in Acts 9:7, "hearing the voice," the noun "voice" is in the partitive genitive case [i.e., hearing (something) of], whereas

in 22:9, "they heard not the voice," the construction is with the accusative. This removes the idea of any contradiction. The former indicates a hearing of the sound, the latter indicates the meaning or message of the voice (this they did not hear). "The former denotes the sensational perception, the latter (the accusative case) the thing perceived." (Cremer). In John 5:25, 28, the genitive case is used, indicating a "sensational perception" that the Lord's voice is sounding; in 3:8, of hearing the wind, the accusative is used, stressing "the thing perceived." (W. E. Vine, *Expository Dictionary of New Testament Words*, pp. 204–205)

Instead of this being a flat contradiction of what Luke says in 9:7 it is natural to take it as being likewise (as with the "light" and "no one") a distinction between the "sound" (original sense of *phone* as in John 3:8) and the separate words spoken. It so happens that *akouo* is used either with the accusative (extent of the hearing) or the genitive (the specifying). It is possible that such a distinction here coincides with the two senses of *phone*. They heard the sound (9:7), but did not understand the words (22:9). However, this distinction in case with *akouo*, though possible and even probable here, is by no means a necessary one for in John 3:8 where *phonen* undoubtedly means "sound" the accusative occurs as Luke uses *ekousa phonen* about Saul in Acts 9:4. Besides, in Acts 22:7 Paul uses *ekousa phones* about himself, but *ekousa phonen* about himself in Acts 26:14, interchangeably. (Dr. A. T. Robinson, *Word Pictures in the New Testament*, Vol. III, pp. 117–18)

The fact that the maintenance of an old and well-known distinction between the acc. and the gen. with *akouo* saves the author of Acts 9:7 and 22:9 from a patent self-contradiction, should by itself be enough to make us recognize it for Luke, and for other writers until it is proved wrong. (James Hope Moulton, *A Grammar of New Testament Greek*, Vol. I, p. 66. Robertson quotes this approvingly in *A Grammar of the Greek New Testament in Light of Historical Research*, pp. 448–49)

The partitive genitive occurs in NT with verbs of perception, especially with a personal object. For *akouo*, the class(ical) rule is that the person whose words are heard is in the genitive . . . but the thing (or person) about which one hears is in the accusative, and *akouo* c. accusative may mean to understand. . . . We have to ask whether the class. distinction between genitive and accusative has significance for exegesis in NT. There may be something in the difference between the gen. in Ac. 9:7 (the men with Paul heard the sound) and the accus. in Ac. 22:9 (they did not understand the voice). (Nigel Turner, *A Grammar of New Testament Greek*, Vol. III, p. 233)

Basically, these writers are referring to the possibility that the difference in the case of the term *akouo* would in this instance (9:7, 22:9) point to a difference in *meaning*. However, as Dr. A. T. Robertson said above, this distinction cannot be written in stone. Why then do we feel that we are correct in asserting this difference as the "answer" to this supposed contradiction? *Context*, Elder Hahn, *context*. Though none of the above authors went deeply into the subject, an examination of the context of the passages in question here makes it very clear that Luke meant a difference to be understood in what he was writing.

The key element in this investigation is pointed out by R. J. Knowling (*Expositor's Greek Testament*, ed. W. Robertson Nicoll, Vol. 2, pp. 231–33) and by John Aberly (*New Testament Commentary*, ed. H. C. Alleman, p. 414). In Acts 22:9 Paul is speaking to a crowd in Jerusalem. According to Acts 21:40 Paul addressed the crowd in Hebrew (NIV says Aramaic—exactly which dialect it was is not very relevant). He mentions to his Hebrew listeners that when Jesus called him, he called him in their own language—Hebrew. How do we know this? In both Acts 9:4 and in Acts 22:7 Saul is not spelled in its normal form, but is spelled in its Hebrew (or Aramaic) form *Saoul*. What does this tell us? It tells us that the "voice" spoke in Hebrew. Therefore, Acts 22:9 would be referring to the fact that the men who accompanied Paul did not understand what was said for they could not understand Hebrew! The text supports this very strongly, for Paul modifies his saying "they did not hear (understand) the voice" by adding the vital phrase, "of the one speaking to me (*tou lalountos moi*)." The emphasis is on the speaking of the voice, which would indicate comprehension and understanding. Now, given the above scholars' quotations, and the context of the passages, can anyone seriously deny that there is a perfectly plausible explanation for this supposed contradiction? I think not.

Finally, it must be stated that part and parcel of dealing with almost any ancient or even modern writing is the basic idea that the author gets the benefit of the doubt. It is highly unlikely that a writer will contradict himself within short spans of time or space. Luke was a careful historian, and it is sheer speculation that he would be so forgetful as to forget what he wrote in Acts 9 by the time he wrote Acts 22. Some critics of the Bible seem to forget the old axiom "innocent until proven guilty." The person who will not allow for the harmonization of the text (as we did above) is in effect claiming omniscience of all the facts surrounding an event that took place nearly two millennia ago. Most careful scholars do not make such claims. The above presented explanation is perfectly reasonable, it coincides with the known facts, and does not engage in unwarranted "special pleading." If you wish to continue to claim that Acts 9:7 contradicts Acts 22:9, Elder Hahn, there is little I or anyone else can do about that. But realize that (1) your position cannot be proven; (2) you are operating on unproven assumptions (Luke was not intelligent enough to notice a contradiction in his own writing); and (3) there is a perfectly logical explanation, based on the original languages and contexts.

I hope that you do not mind, Elder, that I took a good bit of time and space to answer the first of your alleged contradictions. I do hope that if you desire to do so, you will look into the sources I cited and discover the truth for yourself. I want you to see, however, that attacking the accuracy of the Bible *on the basis of our own misunderstanding of a translated text* (i.e., our understanding of the English translation) is not a wise, nor correct, procedure. The King James Version's translation is not a *mis*translation in and of itself; if we wish to ask "what does it mean to 'hear' a voice" then we need to ask that question of the *original text* as well as the translated one.

At this point, in the past, I have had many LDS say, "Hey, you are getting real complicated here, and I think you are just trying to hide something. You don't need to know all this Greek stuff—the apostles were simple men who were unlearned and untrained." While the apostles (with the notable exception of Paul) may have been unlearned and untrained, that has little if anything to do with the current topic, that being supposed errors in the Bible. Unlearned and untaught men can receive great truth from God. But they are also unlikely candidates to be *attacking* the veracity and accuracy of God's revelation as well. You won't find the apostles doing that! So, when others, such as yourself, Elder Hahn, come against the Scriptures and accuse them of error, that is far different than an untrained, unlearned, humble man receiving grace and knowledge from God. You must demonstrate that you have truly examined the issues, and done your homework, before making allegations such as these. The issues we must deal with—Greek, Hebrew, translation, transmission, history, grammar—all of these are "scholarly" issues, requiring study and work.

Let's move on to your other "contradictions." The next on your list was Matthew 27:9–10 in comparison with Zechariah 11:12–13. Matthew writes,

> Then was fulfilled that which was spoken by Jeremiah the prophet, saying, And they took the thirty pieces of silver, the price of him that was valued, whom they of the children of Israel did value; And gave them for the potter's field, as the Lord appointed me.

The cited passage is clearly from Zechariah 11:12–13, not from the specific book of Jeremiah. So was Matthew wrong in his citation? Seemingly you believe either he was, or, sometime over the many years since Matthew wrote this, someone "changed" it. But is this necessarily the case?

No, it is not. Let's look at some of the possibilities. When we look back to the time period in which this was written, we remember that the normal form of writing for the Jewish people was the *scroll*. If you will think about the form of a scroll, you will realize that a scroll would be constructed in such a way that you would have to start in one book, "scroll" through it to the next, and so on. You could not just open it up to a particular passage without going through what came before. Now, if a particular prophet's book appeared in the beginning spot in the scroll, the entire scroll would be identified with that prophet's name. One tradition holds that Jeremiah was the first in the order of the prophets, and, therefore, one could easily cite *anything* in that scroll as being "in Jeremiah." This is a possibility as to why Matthew cites this passage as being from Jeremiah.

But there is more. Other scholars point out that this passage in Matthew is a "conflation" of two passages from the Old Testament—one from Zechariah, the other from passages in Jeremiah, specifically Jeremiah 18:2, 19:2–11 and 32:6–9. They point out that Zechariah nowhere mentions the field that Matthew is actually talking about; Jeremiah, however, does in these passages. Therefore, Matthew put together the prophecies from both Jeremiah and Zechariah into one statement about the Lord Jesus. Since Jeremiah is the "major" prophet, and

Zechariah his "junior," then the major prophet's name is used. A similar thing happens in Mark 1:2–3, where prophecies from both Isaiah and Malachi are put together in one quotation. So, as we can see, there are at least two plausible explanations as to why Matthew would cite this passage the way that he did, and not be in error for having done so. Surely it can be said that it is not possible to prove that Matthew was in error and made such an obvious mistake for no purpose. Is there any particular reason why the biblical writers should be given less credit for their knowledge of the Scriptures than a modern writer? Why should we believe Matthew to be so ignorant of the Old Testament? The idea that there was a *purpose* to his words is logical and rational.

Let's look next at another issue that will again illustrate the accuracy of the Bible over against the charges made against it—that being your question concerning the time of Jesus' crucifixion and death as given to us by Matthew, Mark, and Luke, seemingly in opposition to John. Mark 15:25 says, "And it was the third hour, and they crucified him." Then, in Mark 15:33–34, we read:

> And when the sixth hour was come, there was darkness over the whole land until the ninth hour. And at the ninth hour Jesus cried with a loud voice, saying, "Eloi, Eloi, lama sabachthani?" which is, being interpreted, My God, my God, why hast thou forsaken me?

This same information is given by Matthew 27:45 and Luke 23:44. All three of the Synoptic Gospels (Matthew, Mark, and Luke) agree that Jesus was (1) crucified at the third hour and (2) that darkness was over the land from the sixth to the ninth hour, at which time the Lord Jesus gave up His spirit.

But, as you pointed out, John says in John 19:14, "And it was the preparation of the passover, and about the sixth hour; and he saith unto the Jews, Behold your King!" Here Jesus is still before Pilate in the sixth hour while the Synoptic Gospels are unanimous in saying that Jesus was on the cross at the sixth hour, at which time darkness came over the land. Is this not a clear error?

During the days of Christ there were two different systems of keeping time. The Jewish system began at sunrise and went to sunset. For them, the day would begin about 6 A.M., and the sixth hour would be high noon, the ninth hour about 3 P.M. The Romans, however, did not reckon time in this way. Rather, they followed a system more like our own, where the times started at midnight and at noon. For them the sixth hour would be 6 A.M. in the morning or 6 P.M. in the evening, depending on whether you are speaking of daytime or nighttime.

It seems very clear that the Synoptic Gospels are using Jewish time in their recording of the events of the crucifixion. Therefore, they record that Jesus was crucified at the third hour, which would be nine in the morning. Darkness was over the land from the sixth to the ninth hours, corresponding to noon till 3 P.M., at which time the Lord Jesus gave up His spirit.

John, on the other hand, is not using the Jewish reckoning of time. He is not writing to Jews, and, in fact, most probably wrote this Gospel after Jerusalem was destroyed in A.D. 70, and therefore would have no reason to use that system of time-keeping. Tradition states that John lived in Ephesus, which would have used the Roman system of time-keeping. When this difference is taken into consideration, John is "right on time" with his figures. He says that Jesus was before Pilate during the sixth hour, which, in Roman thinking, would be around 6 A.M. This is perfectly in line with Matthew, Mark, and Luke, for they say He was crucified three hours later, at 9 A.M. So, we see again that there is no error here—the only error is made by those who fail to allow the writers the freedom of expressing themselves differently; here, John using a different time system than was used by the other writers.

The next example you provided, Elder Hahn, I feel shows clearly how *unwilling* most critics of the Bible are to allow the authors to tell their story in their own way, without necessarily being in "error" in what they say. The *assumption of error* on the part of the modern reader is far too quickly made. You brought up Matthew 4:18–20, which speaks of Jesus calling Peter and Andrew to follow Him. They immediately leave their nets and follow Him. Then, you cite John 1:40–42 and the fact that here Andrew, being a disciple of John the Baptist, went and found his brother Peter and said, "We have found the Messiah!" You asked, "Which account is true?" I say, *both* are! See, you don't have to take one to the exclusion of the other, as long as you don't make one very *big* assumption—that the encounter of Jesus with Peter and Andrew on the beach was the *first* time they had ever met. What is wrong with allowing for harmony here, and understanding it as follows? Andrew is a follower of John the Baptist. He goes and gets his brother Peter, and he meets Jesus. Then a period of time elapses—whether Peter and Andrew are with Jesus during the whole of this period of time or not is difficult to say—but at some point Peter and Andrew are back at their business, that of fishing. Jesus comes along and calls them away *permanently* from their work, calling them to the life of a full-time disciple, and later, of an apostle. Dr. A. T. Robertson, in his work *A Harmony of the Gospels*, separates the original meeting of Jesus with Andrew and Peter and the eventual calling of them by the seashore with quite an amount of material (see pages 23–33 of his work).

Has it ever caused you to wonder, even a little, why Peter and Andrew would just drop their nets, leave their families and businesses, and walk off with a man they had never even met before? If the incident of Matthew 4:18–20 was the *first* time they had ever met Jesus, that would indeed be strange. But, taking the whole of Scripture into account, we see that it is in full harmony with itself—this *wasn't* the first time they had met. I might add in passing, Elder Hahn, that you are not alone in not doing your "homework" on this one—I've heard many a sermon preached about the "incredible faith" of Peter and Andrew, who just dropped everything and followed Him without knowing a thing about Christ. Makes good preaching, but lousy theology, and bad Bible study!

Next you brought up the seeming discrepancy between Mark 6:8 and Luke 9:3. The passages read,

> And [Jesus] commanded them that they should take nothing for their journey, save a staff only; no scrip, no bread, no money in their purse. (Mark 6:8)

> And he said unto them, Take nothing for your journey, neither staves, nor scrip, neither bread, neither money; neither have two coats apiece. (Luke 9:3)

Were they to take a staff (stave) or not? It would be nearly impossible to resolve this situation if these were the only two passages that mention Jesus' words. But, though I am sure it was not intentional on your part, Elder Hahn, you neglected to mention the *third* passage that gives us Jesus' instructions to the disciples, that being Matthew 10:9–10.

> Provide neither gold, nor silver, nor brass in your purses, nor scrip [bag] for your journey, neither two coats, neither shoes, nor yet staves: for the workman is worthy of his meat.

Here we find an instance, Elder Hahn, where the provision of *three* witnesses to the same event shows us how, if we had but one or two, we would not have a full understanding of the real situation. If we had but Mark and Luke, it would be difficult to understand how this is not in error.

The Lord Jesus is sending His disciples out in ministry. Matthew gives the fullest account, and in doing so provides the obvious explanation as well. Jesus is instructing the disciples to go out with the *barest* of necessities, not looking to "provide" (Matthew 10:9) or to "acquire" (the translation given by the New American Standard Bible, and which best brings out the meaning of the original term) anything *extra* for the trip. When the Lord tells the disciples to not take shoes, do we really think that He means that they are to go barefoot? Of course not—rather, they are not to take *an extra pair* of shoes along. In the same way, if a disciple *had* a staff, he would not be prohibited from taking one along; but, if he did not, he was not to "acquire" one just for the journey— he was to go as he was.

So what we have in Luke and Mark is *part* of what we have in Matthew. Luke records the prohibition given against *acquiring* yet another staff, while Mark communicates the implicit *permission* to take along the staff that one already had. No actual contradiction is found to exist, but we are again impressed by the fact that we must allow for harmonization of the texts. What do I mean by this, Elder Hahn? What if we had only Luke and Mark, without Matthew's additional information, and you attacked Luke and Mark, accusing either the authors of error, or someone later of making errors in copying (though, as I explained in my earlier letter, the original reading would be found no matter what happened during the period of copying)? We can see how they are not contradicting each other, but are rather giving *complementary* information. In fact, one is referring to a prohibition of acquiring a *new* staff while the other is referring to one *already owned*. They are not even talking, specifically, about the same thing. Yet, without Matthew's information, if I suggested this resolution of the difficulty, would you not be tempted to say, "Well, you are just pleading the case, and not really dealing with the text"? Are there not *many* other passages in the Gospels, and throughout the Bible, where we encounter similar situations? Is it not the wiser course to admit we don't know all of the backgrounds and contexts, and to give the authors the benefit of the doubt? It would certainly seem so to me.

As you can see, Elder, each of the instances you have provided to me has a logical and rational explanation. As I mentioned, you could quite easily find many, many more alleged errors such as those above—but I hope you now realize that the vast majority of these allegations fall into the categories we saw above. When (1) the original languages are allowed to have their say, (2) the historical contexts are examined, (3) harmonization between different accounts of the same event is allowed, (4) the authors are recognized to be intelligent, cognizant beings who were not given to contradicting themselves in every other word, the vast majority of commonly presented "contradictions" are shown to be based more upon a desire to *prove* the Bible wrong than they are upon any defect in the Bible itself.

There is one more item from your letter that I must address, that being your list of "missing books." It was quite an impressive list! Let's look at some of them you mentioned:

Exodus 24:7—"the book of the covenant"
Numbers 21:14—"the book of the wars of the LORD"
Joshua 10:13—"the book of Jashar"
1 Kings 11:41—"the book of the acts of Solomon"
1 Chronicles 29:29—the chronicles of Samuel, Gad, and Nathan
2 Chronicles 9:29—records of Nathan the prophet, prophecy of
    Ahijah the Shilonite, visions of Iddo the seer
2 Chronicles 33:19—records of the Hozai
Colossians 4:16—the letter to the Laodiceans

I know of a few others as well, but your list is fairly representative. Now, you wrote,

> Clearly these books have been lost from the Bible. How can you say the Bible is complete when all these books are missing? Might they not teach things that are important? This is why we need latter-day revelation to restore that which is missing in the Bible.

Aside from the fact that the Book of Mormon itself refers to records that are not contained in it (like the "prophecies of Zenos" mentioned in 1 Nephi 19:10 and elsewhere), I have to ask why every person who has made the allegation that the Bible is missing books thinks that the Bible cannot mention the existence of any other writing without making that writing a part of the canon of Scripture? Many of the books mentioned above were obviously secular in nature; that is, they were public or royal records. Why do you say these books were *supposed to be* part of Scripture? Why cannot the Bible even *mention* the existence of secular writings without making those writings part of the Scriptures? If the Bible were being written today, and the Bible were to mention, for example, a national newspaper, would that automatically make the newspaper part of Scripture? For example, let's say that a prophet of God was attacked in an editorial written in a particular newspaper. The writer of Scripture mentions this. Does this mean that the newspaper becomes part of the inspired Word of God? If so, for what reason? So, when 1 Kings 11:41 mentions the "book of the acts of Solomon," it would be similar to mentioning the Congressional Record or something of that kind. But why do you believe that these books were *ever* considered to be Scripture by the people of God?

Some of the books mentioned in the Bible were clearly of a religious nature, such as the records of Nathan the prophet or the prophecy of Ahijah the Shilonite. But again, why believe that these were ever meant to be part of the Bible? The same example as used above is relevant here. If the Bible were being written today, and a particular religious leader was mentioned, and, rather than listing everything that this particular person did, the writer of Scripture were to say, "now, the rest that this person did is written in this book . . . ," does that book automatically become inspired because the Scripture writer refers someone to it for further information, if they desire it? I don't believe so, do you?

Finally, you mentioned the "epistle from Laodicea" in Colossians 4:16. Again, I see no reason to call this a "lost book" if God never intended it to be in the Bible in the first place. Surely, if God wishes a book to be in His Word, He can manage to get it there. But, in this particular instance, we probably do have this letter. Which one, you ask? Well, the book of Ephesians seems to have been written as a "circular letter" that was intended to be read in various churches in different places. Many Bible scholars feel that the letter we know as Ephesians is actually the same letter referred to in Colossians, and, if it is, then we *do have* the letter mentioned here.

I've gone longer than I expected, and I hope you will continue our conversation. Shall we move on to talk about the God of the Bible? I stand ready.

Sincerely,

James White

The Doctrine of God: One God or Many?

Friday, June 15

Dear Elder Hahn,

The August 15, 1844 edition of the *Times and Seasons* contained the remarks made by the president of the Mormon Church, Joseph Smith, at the April conference of the Church the preceding spring. Since delivering that sermon, Joseph Smith had been murdered in the jail in Carthage, Illinois.

The sermon printed in those pages, and which is also to be found in various other LDS publications such as the *Journal of Discourses,* Volume 6, pages 1–11, and in Joseph Fielding Smith's *Teachings of the Prophet Joseph Smith*, pages 342–62, has come to be absolutely *foundational* to LDS doctrine and thought, for in it Joseph Smith laid out what was to be his final doctrine of God and man before his death. I mentioned to you in our original meeting, Elder Hahn, my belief that Joseph Smith's doctrines "evolved" over the period of time between the publication of the Book of Mormon in 1830 and his death in 1844. The doctrines set forth in this sermon by Smith, known as the "King Follett Funeral Discourse" (as it was given at the funeral of Elder King Follett) are not only *not* to be found in the Book of Mormon, but are completely contradictory to the teachings of the Bible as well. Below I will review some of Smith's comments in this sermon, for I feel it is *vital* that we both know exactly what he stated and believed about God. I know you are probably familiar with most of this material, but I have met many LDS who were not, so I feel thoroughness would be advisable at this point.

I have been requested to speak by [King Follet's] friends and relatives, but inasmuch as there are a great many in this congregation who live in this city as well as elsewhere, who have lost friends, I feel disposed to speak on the subject in general, and offer you my ideas, so far as I have ability, and so far as I shall be inspired by the Holy Spirit to dwell on this subject.

My first object is to find out the character of the only wise and true God, and what kind of being he is; and if I am so fortunate as to be the man to comprehend God, and explain or convey the principles to your hearts, so that the Spirit seals them upon you, then let every man and woman henceforth sit in silence, put their hands on their mouths, and never lift their hands or voices, or say anything against the man of God or the servants of God again.

. . . If I show, verily, that I have the truth of God, and show that ninety-nine out of every hundred professing religious ministers are false teachers, having no authority, while they pretend to hold the keys of God's kingdom on earth, and was to kill them because they are false teachers, it would deluge the whole world with blood.

I will prove that the world is wrong, by showing what God is. I am going to enquire after God; for I want you all to know him, and to be familiar with him. . . .

God himself was once as we are now, and is an exalted man, and sits enthroned in yonder heavens! That is the great secret. If the veil were rent today, and the great God who holds this world in its orbit, and who upholds all worlds and all things by his power, was to make himself visible,—I say, if you were to see him today, you would see him like a man in form—like yourselves in all the person, image, and very form as a man; for Adam was created in the very fashion, image and likeness of God, and received instruction from, and walked, talked and conversed with him, as one man talks and communes with another.

In order to understand the subject of the dead, for consolation of those who mourn for the loss of their friends, it is necessary we should understand the character and being of God and how he came to be so; for I am going to tell you how God came to be God. We have imagined and supposed that God was God from all eternity. I will refute that idea, and take away the veil, so that you may see.

These are incomprehensible ideas to some, but they are simple. *It is the first principle of the Gospel to know for a certainty the*

Character of God, and to know that we may converse with him as one man converses with another, and that he was once a man like us; yea, that God himself, the Father of us all, dwelt on an earth, the same as Jesus Christ himself did; and I will show it from the Bible. . . .

Here, then, is eternal life—to know the only wise and true God; and you have got to learn how to be Gods yourselves, and to be kings and priests to God, the same as all Gods have done before you, namely by going from one small degree to another, and from a small capacity to a great one; from grace to grace, from exaltation to exaltation, until you attain to the resurrection of the dead, and are able to dwell in everlasting burnings, and to sit in glory, as do those who sit enthroned in everlasting power.

. . . What is it? To inherit the same power, the same glory and the same exaltation, until you arrive at the station of a God, and ascend the throne of eternal power, the same as those who have gone before. What did Jesus do? Why; I do the things I saw my Father do when the worlds came rolling into existence. My Father worked out his kingdom with fear and trembling, and I must do the same; and when I get my kingdom, I shall present it to my Father, so that he may obtain kingdom upon kingdom, and it will exalt him in glory. He will then take a higher exaltation, and I will take his place, and thereby become exalted myself.

Yes, I know, Elder Hahn, that the above sermon is not a part of "Mormon Scripture." However, I believe that it is (1) foundational to the theology of the LDS Church, (2) fully supported by not only the early prophets and apostles of the Mormon Church but by modern-day leaders as well, and (3) fully in line with the teachings of such passages as D&C 130:22, and all of Section 132. It is *not* in line with the teachings of the Book of Mormon, mainly because Joseph Smith's beliefs *evolved* so during the period between the writing of the Book of Mormon and his final beliefs in 1844. When Smith wrote the Book of Mormon, he was still *monotheistic* in his beliefs, and had not yet developed the concept of multiple gods (yes, I know about the First Vision, but, as we shall see, Smith did *not* claim to have seen God the Father until well *after* the writing of the Book of Mormon).

The first LDS belief that we can derive from these comments by Smith, that of an open and direct *polytheism*, a belief in multiple gods, was reiterated just a matter of weeks later by Smith himself:

I have always declared God to be a distinct personage, Jesus Christ a separate and distinct personage from God the Father, and the Holy Ghost was a distinct personage and a Spirit: and these three constitute three distinct personages and three Gods. If this is in accordance with the New Testament, lo and behold! we have three Gods anyhow, and they are plural; and who can contradict it?. . . .

The head God organized the heavens and the earth. I defy all the world to refute me. In the beginning the heads of the Gods organized the heavens and the earth. (*Teachings of the Prophet Joseph Smith,* pp. 370, 372)

In fact, Smith went so far as to ridicule the doctrine of the Trinity, which, if Mosiah 15:1–4 in the Book of Mormon means anything, he once at least *attempted* to teach by saying,

Many men say there is one God; the Father, the Son and the Holy Ghost are only one God. I say that is a strange God anyhow— three in one, and one in three! It is a curious organization. "Father, I pray not for the world, but I pray for them which thou hast given me." "Holy Father, keep through thine own name those whom thou has given me, that they may be one as we are." All are to be crammed into one God, according to sectarianism. It would make the biggest God in all the world. He would be a wonderfully big God—he would be a giant or a monster. (*Teachings of the Prophet Joseph Smith,* p. 372)

While many modern Mormons like to say that they believe in "one God," they mean this solely in the sense of one God *in purpose,* not one God in *being* as Smith makes clear above. Elder Hahn, there is no more basic element of a religious teaching than whether it is *monotheistic* and teaches that there is but one God, or if it is *polytheistic* and teaches that there is more than one god, or that there are many gods. Christianity is *monotheistic* to the core, despite what many of its enemies say. Christians believe that there is only one God who has eternally been God. Over against this, listen to what early Mormon Apostle Orson Pratt said,

This explains the mystery. If we should take a million worlds like this and number their particles, we should find that there are more Gods than there are particles of matter in those worlds. (*Journal of Discourses,* 2:345)

The same apostle also said,

> We were begotten by our Father in Heaven; the person of our Father in Heaven was begotten by a still more ancient Father and so on, from generation to generation, from one heavenly world to another still more ancient, until our minds are wearied and lost in the multiplicity of generations and successive worlds, and as a last resort, we wonder in our minds, how far back the genealogy extends, and how the first world was formed, and the first father was begotten. (*The Seer,* p. 132)

Some modern LDS writers seem to blush at the openness of the early Mormons. They would much rather say that they believe there is only one God, but, in reality, what they mean is that there is one "Godhead" in purpose, made up of three gods. Mormon Apostle Bruce R. McConkie wrote,

> Three separate personages—Father, Son, and Holy Ghost—comprise the Godhead. As each of these persons is a God, it is evident, from this standpoint alone, that a *plurality of Gods* exists. To us, speaking in the proper finite sense, these three are the only Gods we worship. But in addition there is an infinite number of holy personages, drawn from worlds without number, who have passed on to exaltation and are thus gods. (*Mormon Doctrine*, pp. 576–77)

But, at the same time, and in the same book, he can say,

> *Monotheism* is the doctrine or belief that there is but one God. If this is properly interpreted to mean that the Father, the Son, and Holy Ghost—each of whom is a separate and distinct godly personage—are one God, meaning one Godhead, then true saints are monotheists.

I think it is very clear that Apostle McConkie is playing word games with us here, for he clearly believes in a multitude of gods, yet, wishes to be called a monotheist. Such simply will not work. Christians are monotheists in that they believe that there is one God, eternal and unchangeable. There were no gods before Him, none will be gods after Him. He is the only God there is. So we see the first major difference between Mormonism and Christianity—monotheism versus polytheism.

Next, we note Smith's teaching that God was once a man who lived on another planet: "God himself was once as we are now, and is an exalted man, and sits enthroned in yonder heavens!" Mormon Prophet Lorenzo Snow, it is said, developed the one-line description of this LDS belief which runs, "As man is, God once was; as God is, man may become." God is an exalted man, who at some point in the past was a limited, finite being such as you and I. In fact, early Mormon teachers, following Smith's concepts as found in this sermon, even went so far as to directly say that God the Father, (or, you might specifically identify him as "Elohim") was in a *fallen state* during his "mortal existence" just as you and I, and that Elohim needed to be redeemed before he could become an exalted being, a "god." Orson Pratt said,

> The Gods who dwell in the Heaven from which our spirits came, are beings who have been redeemed from the grave in a world which existed before the foundations of this earth were laid. They and the Heavenly body which they now inhabit were once in a fallen state. Their terrestrial world was redeemed, and glorified, and made a Heaven: their terrestrial bodies, after suffering death, were redeemed, and glorified, and made Gods. And thus, as their world was exalted from a temporal to an eternal state, they were exalted also, from fallen man to Celestial Gods to inhabit their Heaven forever and ever. (*The Seer,* p. 23)

This teaching gives rise to what is known as the "Eternal Law of Progression" with which I would imagine you are familiar, and to which I will turn in just a moment. For now, I wish to emphasize that in Mormonism, God the Father is an "exalted man," an *anthropomorphic god,* or, as one LDS acquaintance of mine put it, a *"theomorphic man."* Whatever the case, God the Father was once a man and has "progressed," or, to use a term that might today carry with it some negative connotations, "evolved" to his present position. Apostle George Q. Canon did not seem to object to that description:

> Men talk about evolution. This is the true evolution—being such as we are and developing and advancing and progressing in that upward and onward career until we shall become like Him, in truth, until we shall possess the powers that He possesses and exercise the dominion that He now exercises. This is the promise that is held out to us. (*Gospel Truth,* 1:131)

He also noted,

TRUE EVOLUTION. We hear considerable about evolution. Who is there that believes more in true evolution than the Latter-day Saints?—the evolution of man until he shall become a god. . . . That is the Gospel of Jesus Christ, believed in by the Latter-day Saints. That is the kind of evolution we believe in, but not the evolution of man from some low type of animal life. (*Gospel Truth*, 1:9)

So we are taught by Mormonism that God the Father was once a man, just like you or me, who lived on another planet. He was in a fallen state. He walked and talked like you and me. We should think that he worshiped the "god" of that world as well, who himself, it would seem, was a man as well. And so it goes back into time. Not only was God once a man, but, as Smith said, He continues in that form, for "if the veil were rent today, and the great God who holds this world in its orbit . . . was to make himself visible,—I say, if you were to see him today, you would see him like a man in form—like yourselves in all the person, image, and very form as a man." This is echoed in the Mormon Scriptures, *Doctrine and Covenants* 130:22:

The Father has a body of flesh and bones as tangible as man's; the Son also; but the Holy Ghost has not a body of flesh and bones, but is a personage of Spirit. Were it not so, the Holy Ghost could not dwell in us.

And so we see the first two elements of Smith's teaching: (1) the concept of polytheism, and (2) the concept that God was once a man who lived on another planet, and who continues to exist in a physical form.

The third concept to be derived from Smith's sermon given above is the doctrine of Eternal Progression. Mormon Apostle Bruce R. McConkie described it as follows:

Endowed with agency and subject to eternal laws, man began his progression and advancement in pre-existence, his ultimate goal being to attain to a state of glory, honor, and exaltation like the Father of spirits. During his earth life he gains a mortal body, receives experience in earthly things, and prepares for a future eternity after the resurrection when he will continue to gain knowledge and intelligence (D&C 130:18–19). This gradually unfolding course of advancement and experience—a course that began in a past eternity and will continue in ages future—is frequently referred to as a course of *eternal progression.*

. . . In the full sense, eternal progression is enjoyed only by those who receive the fulness of the Father; they have all power, all knowledge, and all wisdom; they gain a fulness of truth, becoming one with the Father. All other persons are assigned lesser places in the mansions that are prepared, and their progression is not eternal and unlimited but in a specified sphere. . . .

Those who gain exaltation, having thus enjoyed the fulness of eternal progression, become like God. (*Mormon Doctrine,* pp. 238–39)

Basically, the doctrine teaches that man begins the "cycle" when he is born as a spiritual son or daughter of celestial parents. This "pre-existence" is something that all of us—you and I—experienced. We had celestial parents—in our case, Elohim (God the Father) and one of his celestial wives. Elohim and his wives have physical bodies (as we saw above in D&C 130:22), but have *spiritual* offspring. From the point of this pre-existence, these spirits are placed into physical bodies on a planet, to be "tested" during their "mortal probation." Somehow, in the process of entering into physical existence, the memory of the pre-existence is lost.

During the mortal probation, man is faced with the choice to do right and return back to God the Father, or go his own way and reject what is good and proper. If man is faithful, and follows all the commandments of God, he will be resurrected and exalted to the position of a god himself, then to begin the "cycle" all over again, becoming celestial parents of further spiritual offspring. So, the process seems to be:

Spiritual Children ◊ Mortal Probation (if faithful) ◊ Exaltation

Obviously, that is a simplified version, for as McConkie pointed out, many, if not most, of mankind will not attain to full exaltation, but will end up receiving a "lesser" position after death.

You, then, Elder Hahn, believe that if you were to be "faithful" during this life, including receiving your endowments in the temple, being sealed to your wife, etc., you could gain "exaltation" and become, as D&C 132:20 puts it, a god. So, we see the third concept from Smith, the doctrine of eternal progression; man and God are of the same kind of being; God is simply further "advanced" than man in his present state. Indeed, Apostle McConkie stated that "man is of the same race as Deity" (*The Promised Messiah*, p. 305). And if Elder McConkie's words are not sufficient to establish the point, please note the words of the *Encyclopedia of Mormonism*, published in 1992:

> Latter-day Saints perceive the Father as an exalted Man in the most literal, anthropomorphic terms. They do not view the language of Genesis as allegorical; human beings are created in the form and image of a God who has a physical form and image. . . . Latter-day Saints deny the abstract nature of God the Father and affirm that he is a concrete being, that he possesses a physical body, and that he is in space and time. They further reject any idea that God the Father is "totally other," unknowable, or incomprehensible. . . . Gods and humans represent a single divine lineage, the same species of being, although they and he are at different stages of progress. . . . The important points of the doctrine for Latter-day Saints are that Gods and humans are the same species of being, but at different stages of development in a divine continuum, and that the heavenly Father and Mother are the heavenly pattern, model, and example of what mortals can become through obedience to the gospel. (Stephen Robinson, "God the Father," *Encyclopedia of Mormonism*, pp. 548–49)

There is one more concept that comes from Smith's teachings that is disputed by LDS people themselves. It is the concept of the *continuing progression of God*. Early Mormon writers spoke much of God's continuing development and advancement. Smith directly said as much above, and he was followed by many of the prophets and apostles of Mormonism after him. But, in our century, this concept has changed. Today it is more fashionable to say that God's "progression" is now limited solely to the expansion of his "dominions and kingdoms." Note the following two quotations that show how clearly LDS teaching in this point has changed:

> If there was a point where man in his progression could not proceed any further, the very idea would throw a gloom over every intelligent and reflecting mind. God himself is increasing and progressing in knowledge, power, and dominion, and will do so, worlds without end. (Wilford Woodruff, *Journal of Discourses,* December 6, 1857, 6:120)

> . . . It should be realized that God is not progressing in knowl-

edge, truth, virtue, wisdom, or any of the attributes of godliness. (Bruce R. McConkie, *Mormon Doctrine*, 1966, p. 239)

Is God progressing in knowledge or not? Wilford Woodruff said he was, Bruce McConkie said he wasn't, and Joseph Fielding Smith said the same thing. Some Mormons today say he is, more say he isn't. It is not consistent, I believe, to accept Smith's teachings and say that God is *not* progressing, but many LDS today, realizing the problems attendant with the concept of a changing God, prefer to hold to a different belief.

So the Mormon view of God, as seen above, includes (1) polytheism, the belief in more than one God; (2) the concept that God was once a man who lived on another planet, and who progressed to the status of God; (3) the eternal law of progression, whereby, it is said, men can become gods.

While the number of quotations in support of the above concepts could be multiplied indefinitely, I see no reason to do so, as you obviously hold to these concepts, given your comments in your last letter. But, is the above teaching *true*? Please continue on and read carefully.

Hear, O Israel! The LORD our God is one LORD! (Deuteronomy 6:4)

So wrote Moses long, long ago. Deuteronomy 6:4 is called the *Shema*. It is the beginning of the central "confession of faith" of the Jewish people. Every Jewish prophet believed what Deuteronomy 6:4 says. Every morning the pious Jew would pray a prayer that began with those words, "Hear, O Israel! The LORD our God is one LORD!" Surely the Lord Jesus, and His apostles, also prayed the *Shema*. It underlies all that the Bible teaches.

The most basic revelation that God has made about himself, Elder Hahn, is that He is *unique*. Something that is *unique* is "one of a kind." Something that is unique is an "only" thing. There are not multiple copies of something that is unique. God has revealed himself to be utterly unique, the only God in all of heaven and earth.

One of the most basic sins of man is idolatry. Man seems to have buried deep within his heart a bent toward worshiping that which is *not* God. Though God had revealed himself to the people of Israel, they still engaged in idolatry, the worship of other gods. They would bow down before Baal and offer sacrifices to statues in his image. The peoples around them believed in many gods, and they seemed to so quickly abandon the one true God for the false gods of their neighbors. Though God warned them over and over again of the tragic consequences of this kind of action, they often went their own way, and ended up in bondage and defeat.

During the ministry of the prophet Isaiah, God deemed it fitting to reveal through Isaiah more about himself than He ever had before. He did this in the form of challenges to the false gods, the idols to which the people of Israel were in danger of turning. For example, in Isaiah 41:4 we read,

> Who hath wrought and done it, calling the generations from the beginning? I, the LORD, the first, and with the last; I am he.

The question has only one answer: God is the one who has called forth the generations, not any idols or false gods. And he continues in Isaiah 41:22–24,

> Let them bring them forth, and show us what shall happen; let them show the former things, what they are, that we may consider them, and know the latter end of them; or declare us things to come. Show the things that are to come hereafter, that we may know that ye are gods; yea, do good, or do evil, that we may be dismayed, and behold it together. Behold, ye are of nothing, and your work of nought; an abomination is he who chooseth you.

Here God challenges the idols to tell us the future. Can they do it? No, only the true God of the universe can tell us the future, since He is the one who "calls forth the generations from the beginning." Idols cannot say what is going to happen in the future because they have no control over it! God also challenges the idols to tell us what has happened in the past (the "former things"). Why? Because God can not only tell us *what happened,* but, because He is the sovereign God of the universe, He can say just *why* those things took place! Idols cannot do that. God mocks the idols, and says, "Well, do *something* so that we may be frightened of you!" They can't do anything, because they are nothing more than blocks of stone or wood.

Throughout Isaiah chapters 40 through 48 God "throws down the gauntlet" so to speak, challenging man's idols to do what only God can do. In Isaiah 45:2 (and in many other places in this section) God identifies himself as the one who "created the heavens, and stretched them out; he who spread forth the earth, and that which cometh out of it; he who giveth breath unto the people upon it, and spirit to them that walk in it" (see also 44:24). Did the idols create the heavens? No, they themselves are created things, not the Creator. The true God created all that exists and is the Author of all life as well. Similarly, Jeremiah wrote,

> But the LORD is the true God; he is the living God, and an everlasting king; at his wrath the earth shall tremble, and the nations shall not be able to abide his indignation. Thus shall ye say to them, The gods that have not made the heavens and the earth, even they shall perish from the earth, and from under these heavens. (Jeremiah 10:10–11)

It is in the midst of this "trial of the false gods" in Isaiah that the clearest, most unambiguous statements of absolute *monotheism* are to be found. But, before reviewing these passages (and I choose them as being representative of a teaching that is to be found throughout the Bible), allow me to address the immediate objection that is made by LDS apologists. "But, these passages are simply teaching that, *for this world,* there is only one God. God is just telling the Israelites that they are to worship only Him, not any others. This does not mean that there are not other Gods in the universe." I hope you do not mind my anticipating your answer, but when the same reply has been given to you by a hundred different missionaries, you become accustomed to it.

There are a number of reasons why this objection does not hold up to scrutiny. First, as I noted above, in these passages God describes himself in ways that are utterly inconsistent with the concept that He is simply claiming to be the God of this planet only. He describes himself as the Creator of all things, not *just* this planet but all the heavens as well. If God actually once lived on a planet as a man, just like you and me, then there must have been a "Creator" of that planet as well, right? That would mean that there are worlds that God did *not* create, prior to his own "rise to godship." But such is not what these passages say. Secondly, God describes himself as the very Creator of time itself, both past, present, and future. How could God be the Creator of time if, in fact, He had "progressed" through time to attain the status of God? Finally, we shall see that God directly asserts that there are no gods *like* Him to which people can turn—in fact, He will assert that He himself knows of no other gods.

We begin by looking at what is probably the most "popular" verse that Christians use in sharing with Mormons relevant to the doctrine of God—Isaiah 43:10. We hear God speaking,

> Ye are my witnesses, saith the LORD, and my servant whom I have chosen: that ye may know and believe me, and understand that I am he: before me there was no God formed, neither shall there be after me.

Here God calls Israel as His "witnesses." They are to testify to the truth of what He has said. And what are they to give testimony to? *"Before me there was no God formed, neither shall there be after me."* No gods before, none after. None preceded Him, none shall take up where He leaves off. Many have said, "Well, He is just talking about false gods," but can we really accept this reasoning? There were no false gods before Him, and there shall be no false gods after Him? No, certainly not. The meaning is clear and unambiguous. He is the Self-Existent One, the Eternal One. There was no one to "create" Him, and there will be no one who will "take His place" in eternity to come. He is the only God there is. He does not follow after any others (over against Joseph Smith's direct teachings, as we shall see later), and none will follow after Him. One God, one Creator. No others.

Please note as well, Elder Hahn, how this passage cuts the "eternal law of progression" right down the middle. God denies that He is in reality but one god in a long line of gods stretching back into eternity by denying that there has ever been any other God but Him. And, He denies that any "god" could ever arise in the future, denying that men can indeed become gods as He is God.

But this is certainly not all God has to say about this subject. In fact, the claim that He is the only God becomes downright repetitious as one reads through these passages. It certainly seems God wanted to make His point clear! In Isaiah 44:6–8 we read,

> Thus saith the LORD the King of Israel, and his redeemer the LORD of hosts; I am the first, and I am the last; and beside me there is no God. And who, as I, shall call, and shall declare it, and set it in order for me, since I appointed the ancient people? and the things that are coming, and shall come, let them show unto them. Fear ye not, neither be afraid: have not I told thee from that time, and have declared it? ye are even my witnesses. Is there a God beside me? yea, there is no God; I know not any.

The God of Israel is the "first and the last." Can the god described by Joseph Smith in King Follet's funeral sermon make that claim, Elder Hahn? Can he say, "Beside me there is no God"? When the true God of the Bible asks, "Is there a God beside me?" He can answer without hesitation: "Yea, there is no God; I know not any." Please remember that God's understanding is infinite (Psalm 147:5), and His knowledge knows no limits (Romans 11:33). Surely, *if* God was once a man who lived on another planet, and *if,* as Joseph Smith taught, the Father, Son, and Holy Ghost are separate and distinct personages, and separate and distinct gods, would God not have knowledge of these other gods? How could God the Father have become exalted without knowledge of the god of the planet upon which He lived? Surely, if there are indeed many gods in the heavens who have progressed to their status of godhood over ages and ages of time, Elohim, the God of this world, would know of them, would He not? If Joseph Smith knew they existed, how could God not know they existed? Yet, here God says plainly, "I know not any other God." How can this be, except that there are *no* other Gods? Surely this is His point. In fact, God makes this point clear over and over again in the following verses:

I am the LORD, and there is none else, there is no God beside me: I girded thee, though thou hast not known me: That they may know from the rising of the sun, and from the west, that there is none beside me. I am the LORD, and there is none else. (Isaiah 45:5–6)

For thus saith the LORD that created the heavens; God himself that formed the earth and made it; he hath established it, he created it not in vain, he formed it to be inhabited: I am the LORD; and there is none else. (Isaiah 45:18)

. . . and there is no God else beside me; a just God and a Savior; there is none beside me. Look unto me, and be ye saved, all the ends of the earth: for I am God, and there is none else. (Isaiah 45:21b–22)

Remember the former things of old: for I am God, and there is none else; I am God, and there is none like me, declaring the end from the beginning, and from ancient times the things that are not yet done, saying, My counsel shall stand, and I will do all my pleasure. (Isaiah 46:9–10)

It seems inarguable, then, that God made the fact of His utter uniqueness as the only God painfully clear through the prophet Isaiah. But, of course, that is not the only way in which God has revealed this truth. It is all through the Bible, underlying every statement about God to be found. Everyone who believes the testimony of the Bible can say with the Psalmist, "For all the gods of the nations are idols: but the LORD made the heavens" (Psalm 96:5).

So we see that the first of Smith's concepts is directly contrary to the Word of God. There is only one God. The second concept I listed was the idea that God was once a man who lived on another planet, and, I might add to that, the concept that God is a man, that He shares the very same kind of being as mankind, that He is of the "same species." Let's now examine this in the light of the Scriptures.

> I will not execute the fierceness of mine anger, I will not return to destroy Ephraim: for I am God, and not man; the Holy One in the midst of thee: and I will not enter into the city. (Hosea 11:9)

In this passage, God indicates that He will not come upon the people in wrath. Why? Because He is God, and not man. There is a basic, foundational difference between man, who is the creation of God, and God, who is the Creator of all things. God is not man, but the Creator of man. He is utterly different.

> God is not a man, that he should lie; neither the son of man, that he should repent: hath he said, and shall he not do it? or hath he spoken, and shall he not make it good? (Numbers 23:19)

God is different than man. He is not changeable, as man is. He is not liable to sin, as man is. In fact, in reproaching the wicked in the fiftieth psalm, God said,

> These things hast thou done, and I kept silence; thou thoughtest that I was altogether such an one as thyself: but I will reprove thee, and set them in order before thine eyes. (Psalm 50:21)

Man likes to attempt to make God in *man's* image. It is much more comfortable to "cut God down to size" so to speak, and think of Him as just a "super-man," and this is nowhere as clearly seen as it is in the doctrines and teachings of the LDS Church. Bruce R. McConkie wrote,

> . . . Man and God are of the same race, and it is within the power of righteous man to become like his Father, that is to become

a holy Man, a Man of Holiness. (*Mormon Doctrine,* pp. 465–66)

The same concept is to be found in the D&C, where, in section 93 we read,

> Man was also in the beginning with God. Intelligence, or the light of truth, was not created or made, neither indeed can be. (v. 29)

But the God of the Bible will not allow himself to be put into human categories. He directly denies the idea that He is like a man, and surely He is not a changeable being like man is. He will reprove those who would make the mistake of thinking that He is "altogether such an one as thyself." Indeed, the LDS concept of God is well described, and refuted, by Scripture, as we see in Isaiah 29:16 (NIV):

> You turn things upside down, as if the potter were thought to be like the clay! Shall what is formed say to him who formed it, "He did not make me"? Can the pot say of the potter, "He knows nothing"?

Rather than the changing, evolving God of Mormonism (even if one believes that He is not *now* evolving, He was, at some point in the past, a changing being), the Bible presents the eternal and unchanging God:

> Before the mountains were brought forth, or ever thou hadst formed the earth and the world, even from everlasting to everlasting, thou art God. (Psalm 90:2)

The Jews would frequently refer to God simply as "the Eternal One." They had good reason to do so. God has always been God, He has never been anything else. Elder Hahn, I have had many LDS people ask me, "Who created God?" I reply, "No one created God, as God is uncreated and eternal—He is the Creator of everything else, and that includes everything in the universe, including time itself! Pretty incredible, isn't He?" Some laugh, some scoff, but the Bible teaches it. "I am the LORD, I change not" (Malachi 3:6). That is the confession of God. He is not changing, He has always been what He is today, the Sovereign King of all the universe. While Joseph Smith might have desired to refute the concept that God has been God from all eternity, to do so he would have to remove just about every description of God from the Bible, and would have to close God's own mouth when He says,

. . . And I am God. Even from eternity I am He; And there is none who can deliver out of My hand; I act and who can reverse it? (Isaiah 43:12b–13, NASB)

Most LDS do not believe that God is omnipresent, but rather believe that He is limited in time and space. Obviously, if God has a body of flesh and bone, it is easy to understand how this would be. But the Bible presents a very different teaching about God. Listen to what God said to Jeremiah:

Can any hide himself in secret places that I shall not see him? saith the LORD. Do not I fill heaven and earth? saith the LORD. (Jeremiah 23:24)

The physical universe is the creation of God and therefore God cannot be limited by that which He created, can He? The God of Mormonism did not, in reality, create *all things,* for there obviously were "worlds without number" that existed long before Elohim became a god. And, in fact, Joseph Smith taught that matter itself is eternal, and therefore uncreated, and went on to say that "God never had the power to create the spirit of man at all" (*Teachings of the Prophet Joseph Smith,* p. 354). But this is just another difference between the God of the Bible and the God of Joseph Smith. The *true* God is the Creator of *all things,* and He is not limited by His creation, for, as He himself said, "Do not *I* fill heaven and earth?" (Jeremiah 23:24).

So we see that God is not, in His true and absolute nature, a man. He is the eternal God, the Creator of all things, including mankind. He is not limited by the physical universe, so He is not limited to one place at one time. We also see that the third concept taught by Smith, the idea that man can become a god, is false as well; if there is but one infinite and eternal God, it is impossible for a second infinite and eternal god to arise. Men were created to be men, Elder Hahn, not gods. The Bible says that God has always been God, so unless you have always been god, you cannot *become* a god. Not only this, but remember what Jeremiah recorded for us in Jeremiah 10:10? Any "god" who is not the Creator will perish, for they are all false gods who are not the Creator. There is only one Creator, the true God of the Bible.

Before I close this letter, and allow you to reply, let me deal with a few passages that almost *always* come up when this particular doctrine is addressed. In fact, the one you mentioned when we first met at my home, Elder Hahn, was John 10:34.

> Jesus answered them, Is it not written in your law, I said, Ye are gods?

As I said earlier, the first thing to do when approaching any passage of Scripture is to determine the context—what was being said, and to whom? John 10:1–18 presents Jesus as the Good Shepherd who lays down His life for the sheep. Verse 19 tells us that the Jews were divided over the issue of who Jesus was, some saying He had a demon, others pointing to His works and saying that demonized individuals don't do things like that. In verses 22–25 the Jews surrounded Jesus in Solomon's porch and asked Him directly if He was the Messiah. Jesus' answer in verses 25–30 represents one of the greatest Christological passages in John. Christ finishes the brief discourse with the words, "I and my Father are one." The Jews' reaction to this statement was natural and quick—they picked up rocks to stone Him. Jesus asks them for a reason for their action in verse 32, and in verse 33 the Jews respond by saying, "For a good work we stone thee not; but for blasphemy; and because that thou, being a man, makest thyself God." Again John points out the real problem of the Jews—they would not accept Jesus Christ for whom He revealed himself to be. Jesus had earlier addressed this problem in John 8:24 by saying, "I said therefore unto you, that ye shall die in your sins: for if ye believe not that I am he, ye shall die in your sins."

At this point we encounter Jesus' words in John 10:34. A few brief comments need to be made on the passage itself. First, Jesus says, "Is it not written in your law?" This is found in Psalm 82:6. This is vital to the understanding of the passage. Jesus often quoted from the Old Testament to demonstrate a truth to the Jews. I will look at that passage in a moment.

Second, the word "are" is in the present tense—if someone claims that this passage teaches that men can become gods, why is it that Jesus said the Jews were *right then* "gods"? However He meant it, it certainly cannot be taken in reference to eventually being exalted to the status of a true "god."

Jesus went on from verse 34 to claim that He was sanctified and sent into the world by the Father, and that they should believe in Him if for no other reason than the works He had done before them.

And so we come back to the original question, this time in a better position to answer it. The key to understanding John 10:34 is found in Jesus' use of the Old Testament quotation from Psalm 82. What is Psalm 82 about? The answer is found by reading this brief eight-verse Psalm. Verse 2, in reference to the "gods," says, "How long will ye judge unjustly, and accept the persons of the wicked?" Psalm 82 is about unrighteous judges of Israel. These judges were called "elohim" (gods) because of their position of judging Israel in the place of God. Yet Psalm 82 indicates that many of these judges did not act righteously, causing the Psalmist to lament this condition. Notice what verses 6 and 7 say: "I have said, Ye are gods; and all of you are children of the most High. But ye shall die like men, and fall like one of the princes." The psalm itself contains the prophecy of the doom of these unrighteous judges. Obviously, therefore, the psalm is not about eternal, infinite gods (infinite, true gods don't "die like men") but rather applies the term *gods* to men in a figurative way due to their position as judges in Israel.

Realizing that the Jews would know this background, what was the significance of Jesus' quotation of Psalm 82:6? As can be seen, Jesus was, in effect, calling His accusers *false judges* by applying this passage to them. He then goes on to point out the error of accusing Him of blasphemy despite the Father's clear approval of the Son (John 10:36). Then in verse 38 He asserts the inter-penetration of the Father and the Son ("the Father is in me, and I in him"), which is followed again by the attack of the Jews (vs. 39), which causes Jesus to withdraw from Judea (vs. 40). Any kind of interpretation of John 10:34 that ignores the Old Testament background of the passage is bound for error. The interpretation you provided to me in my home, Elder Hahn, is certainly incorrect, is it not?

A favorite of many LDS is Matthew 5:48:

Be ye therefore perfect, even as your Father which is in heaven is perfect.

Many LDS assume that this means that men can become gods, yet, is this what Jesus is saying? This text comes from the Sermon on the Mount. In this section Jesus is laying out the "kingdom standards" for the people of God. This section is *ethical* in nature, and the standard of perfection to which He calls us is ethical and moral. The Lord is not addressing the vast chasm that separates the creature, man, from the Creator, God, but is instead calling us to the moral perfection that is

God's. Such is hardly a solid basis for teaching that creatures can cease being creatures and become gods!

Another passage that is very often presented as evidence of polytheism in the Bible is 1 Corinthians 8:5. However, to get the full context, let's look at verses 4–6:

> As concerning therefore the eating of those things that are offered in sacrifice unto idols, we know that an idol is nothing in the world, and that there is none other God but one. For though there be that are called gods, whether in heaven or in earth, (as there be gods many, and lords many), but to us there is but one God, the Father, of whom are all things, and we in him; and one Lord Jesus Christ, by whom are all things, and we by him.

This passage opens a discussion by the Apostle Paul on the sensitive topic of behavior among believers, and the matter of each person's conscience. He is answering a question that must have been included in a letter sent to him by the congregation at Corinth ("now concerning the eating of those things sacrificed to idols . . ."). Idols were a very common sight in Corinth, as in many ancient cities of the time (though Corinth was notorious for its idolatrous behavior). Some of the believers, having been involved in idol worship, could not with a clear conscience partake of meat that they knew had been sacrificed to idols. This was a serious problem, because nearly every bit of the meat in the city may have been involved in such practices.

Paul addresses the problem by first saying that idols "are nothing in the world." An idol has no power over the Christian. It has no reality other than the demonic power that would cause someone to worship it. There was no real Diana, or Jupiter, or any of the other false gods of the age. He then puts forth the fact that though things or people may be called "gods," to the Christian there is only one God, the Father, and one Lord, Jesus Christ (obviously connecting them in a supernatural way). In the process, Paul says that "there are gods many, and lords many." Obviously what he meant by this is that there are many false gods and false lords being worshiped by nonbelievers, but these are simply idols of man's own making. One can make a god out of almost anything: As someone put it—some people get up in the morning and shave their god in the mirror, others get into their god and drive it to work, while others sit in front of their god for hours each night and simply watch it. Idolatry is alive and well today.

The fact that Paul is alluding to false gods is brought out more clearly in some modern translations:

> For even if there are so-called gods whether in heaven or on earth, as indeed there are many gods and many lords . . . (NASB)

> For even if there are so-called gods, whether in heaven or on earth (as indeed there are many "gods" and many "lords") . . . (NIV)

As we saw above, the Bible says that "all the gods of the peoples are idols . . ." (Psalm 96:5). In context, then, Paul is not saying that he believed in polytheism, but rather he was a monotheist—he believed in only one God.

Now in light of this, Elder Hahn, it is amazing to read the words of Joseph Smith in regards to this verse. He said,

> . . . You know and I testify that Paul had no allusion to the heathen gods. I have it from God, and get over it if you can. I have a witness of the Holy Ghost, and a testimony that Paul had no allusion to the heathen gods in the text. (*Teachings of the Prophet Joseph Smith,* p. 371)

Given that it was the Spirit of God who inspired the writing of Paul's admonitions in 1 Corinthians 8:4–6, and we can see that the passage itself indicates that Paul is indeed speaking of idols—the "heathen gods"—how can we accept Joseph Smith's testimony when it is flatly contradictory to the Bible?

Another passage that is frequently presented is from Acts 7:55–56:

> But he, being full of the Holy Ghost, looked up stedfastly into heaven, and saw the glory of God, and Jesus standing on the right hand of God, and said, Behold, I see the heavens opened, and the Son of man standing on the right hand of God.

Often I have heard LDS people say, "See, Stephen saw Jesus standing on the right hand of God. God, then, must have a right hand at which Jesus can stand." Even some LDS have gone so far as to make this a literal right hand, which, it seems, Jesus was standing *upon.* In reply, let me note a few items:

> He shall cover thee with his feathers, and under his wings shalt thou trust: his truth shall be thy shield and buckler. (Psalm 91:4)

If we take this passage in the way that many LDS take Acts 7:55–56, we have to be consistent and say that God not only has a hand big enough for Jesus to stand on it (that's a BIG hand!), but He also has wings and feathers. In Hebrews we are told that our God is a consuming fire, so should we need to somehow fit a blast furnace into the whole anthropomorphic picture we are making here? No, of course not.

God is spirit, and a spirit does not have flesh and bones (John 4:24; Luke 24:39). So what does "right hand" mean? The "right hand" is a common idiomatic expression in Semitic thinking, Elder, and it refers to the position of power and authority. But, you don't need to take my word for it, look these up for yourself: Exodus 15:6, 15:12; Deuteronomy 33:2; Job 40:14; Psalm 16:8, 16:11, 17:7, 18:35, 20:6, 21:8, 44:3, 45:4, 45:9, 48:10, 60:5, 63:8, 73:23, 77:10, 78:54, 80:15, 80:17, 89:13, 98:1, 108:6, 109:6, 109:31, 110:1, 118:15–16, 138:7; Proverbs 3:16; Ecclesiastes 10:2(!); Isaiah 41:10, Isaiah 48:13; Habakkuk 2:16, and Matthew 26:64, where it is specifically the "right hand *of power*."

The vast majority of the rest of the times it is used it refers simply to a direction, or is used in the phrase "do not turn to the right hand or to the left" in following God's law. There is much more that I would like to share with you about the God of the Bible, Elder Hahn, but I will allow you to respond to this material first. I look forward to hearing from you soon. Your continuing willingness to deal with these issues is very commendable, and I hope that we will again have an opportunity to meet and discuss some of these things in person. I want you to know that you are in my prayers. I am praying that you will listen to the words of the Spirit as He has spoken in the Scriptures.

Sincerely,

James White

LETTER 5

Elohim and Jehovah: One God

Thursday, June 21

Dear Elder Hahn,

Welcome to summer in Phoenix! Predicted high today? Yes, 115°! But, as they say, it is a *dry heat*, right? As if that made any difference! I hate to tell you this, but last summer we had over 140 days that were over 100° and that was a new record! Not only that, but on two occasions it reached our all-time record, 118°. Aren't you happy about *that!* I surely hope you have access to an air-conditioned car these days.

I received your message on my answering machine last evening, and I understand your inability to get around to a full rebuttal of my last letter. I appreciate your invitation to go ahead and address the other issues mentioned in my letter. Your Bible dictionary in the back of the 1981 edition of the King James Version of the Bible, on pages 710–11, says,

> JEHOVAH. The covenant or proper name of the God of Israel. It denotes the "Unchangeable One," "the eternal I AM" (Ex. 6:3; Ps. 83:18; Isa. 12:2; 26:4). The original pronunciation of this name has possibly been lost, as the Jews, in reading, never mentioned it, but substituted one of the other names of God, usually Adonai. Probably it was pronounced Jahveh, or Yahveh. In the KJV, the Jewish custom has been followed, and the name is generally denoted by LORD or GOD, being printed in small capitals.
>
> Jehovah is the premortal Jesus Christ and came to earth being born of Mary.

68

I made a special effort, in my preceding letter, to avoid addressing the issue that I now present to you because it is somewhat complicated at first glance. However, I also made a special effort to accurately cite the Bible and indicate when the KJV utilized the special form of the word "lord" that is printed like this: LORD. Note the small capitals used to inform the English reader that, as your Bible dictionary said above, the Hebrew term that is being translated as LORD is *YHWH*, or *Yahweh*, or, as you would probably put it, *Jehovah*. You will find that form of LORD all through your Old Testament, Elder Hahn. Each time you see that, you will know you are actually seeing the name of Yahweh, or Jehovah.

Why is this small bit of information important? Well, as you know, in Mormon belief, the Father and the Son are separate and distinct individuals, and separate and distinct gods. LDS doctrine has identified the Father by the term *Elohim,* as I mentioned in my earlier letter. The word is from the Hebrew language, and is, as you are aware, normally rendered simply as "God" in the KJV. While Joseph Smith was right to point out that the term *Elohim* is plural in Hebrew, he was just as *wrong* to say that it should then be translated as "gods." While it is translated "gods" in some contexts, the number of the verb with which it is used, as well as the context of the passage, is the determinative factor. When it is used with a singular verb, it should be translated singularly, not as a plural.

Be that as it may, in Mormonism the Father is "Elohim." Now, the Son, Jesus Christ, is identified as Jehovah by the LDS Church. Therefore, since the Father and Son are separate and distinct gods, then Jehovah and Elohim also are separate and distinct gods. Mormon scholar James Talmage, in his book *Articles of Faith,* in Appendix 2, presents a discussion of this very issue, and in doing so presents "The Father and the Son: A Doctrinal Exposition by The First Presidency and the Twelve." Below I quote from this work:

1. *"Father" as Literal Parent*—Scriptures embodying the ordinary signification—literally that of Parent—are too numerous and specific to require citation. The purport of these scriptures is to the effect that God the Eternal Father, whom we designate by the exalted name-title "Elohim," is the literal Parent of our Lord and Savior Jesus Christ, and of the spirits of the human race. Elohim is the Father in every sense in which Jesus Christ is so designated, and distinctively He is the Father of spirits.

. . . . Jesus Christ is the Son of Elohim both as spiritual and bodily offspring; that is to say, Elohim is literally the Father of the spirit of Jesus Christ and also of the body in which Jesus Christ performed His mission in the flesh, and which body died on the cross and was afterward taken up by the process of resurrection. . . .

. . . With this meaning, as the context shows in every case, Jehovah who is Jesus Christ the Son of Elohim. . . .

. . . None of these considerations, however, can change in the least degree the solemn fact of the literal relationship of Father and Son between Elohim and Jesus Christ. Among the spirit children of Elohim the firstborn was and is Jehovah or Jesus Christ to whom all others are juniors. . . . (James Talmage, *Articles of Faith*, pp. 466–72)

Lord willing, Elder Hahn, I shall return to the subject of Jesus Christ being the *literal* offspring of God the Father in the flesh, and what this means with regards to the virgin birth, etc. But for now, I am attempting to set this point firmly before us: In Mormon belief, the Father is Elohim; the Son, Jesus Christ, is Jehovah. Since the Father and the Son are separate and distinct gods, then Elohim and Jehovah are, in Mormonism, names of separate and distinct gods. Now I recognize that many LDS have said, "Well, Jehovah can be called 'Elohim' in the sense that Jehovah is *a god.*" I recognize this fact. However, what is clear is that Jehovah can not be said to *be* Elohim, and certainly, if we find the Lord Jesus identifying the Father as Jehovah, we find a real problem in LDS theology. If I might allow Elder McConkie to address the issue:

Being thus aware of how far astray the religious intellectualists have gone in defining their three-in-one God, it comes as no surprise to learn that they thrash around in the same darkness in trying to identify Elohim and Jehovah and to show their relationship to the promised Messiah. Some sectarians even believe that Jehovah is the Supreme Deity whose Son came into mortality as the Only Begotten. As with their concept that God is a Spirit, this misinformation about the Gods of Heaven is untrue. The fact is, and it too is attested by Holy Writ, that Elohim is the Father, and that Jehovah is the Son who was born into mortality as the Lord Jesus Christ, the promised Messiah. (*The Promised Messiah*, p. 100)

I was "biting my lip" so to speak in my previous letter, as so often

I wanted to bring out the underlying identification of Jehovah as the *only* "elohim" that is made so often in the passages I quoted to you. If you would, go back now and, realizing that whenever you see the word "LORD" in those passages in Isaiah (or elsewhere), you are reading about Jehovah, and almost always when you see the word "God" you are reading about Elohim, reread those passages and see how often LDS belief is contradicted by the words of the Bible. Note some of the more obvious passages:

> Isaiah 43:10b—"before me there was no God [*El,* the shortened form of Elohim] formed, neither shall there be after me." [*Note that it is Jehovah who is here speaking.*]

> Isaiah 45:5—"I am the LORD, [Jehovah], and there is none else, there is no God [Elohim] beside me." There is no Elohim beside Jehovah? That is what the Bible says.

How can it be that Jehovah can say that there is no Elohim beside Him? Of course, I believe that the only God anywhere is Jehovah God, so that is easy for me to answer. But you must be asking why the Bible does speak of "Elohim" as God as well, right? The answer is pretty clear:

> Deuteronomy 4:35, 39—Unto thee it was shown, that thou mightest know that the LORD [Jehovah] he is God [Elohim]; there is none else beside him. . . . Know therefore this day, and consider it in thine heart, that the LORD [Jehovah] he is God [Elohim] in heaven above, and upon the earth beneath: there is none else.

You see, Elder Hahn, *Jehovah IS Elohim.* Both names refer to the one God of the Bible, not to two different gods. In fact, the compound name "Jehovah Elohim" occurs over 500 times in the Old Testament, all referring to the one God of Israel, Jehovah. It is Jehovah who created all things, Jehovah who has eternally existed as God.

Let me point out a few specific things in the above quotation from Deuteronomy 4. First, note that the fact that Jehovah *is* Elohim is repeated twice—the same truth is to be seen in such passages as 1 Kings 18:39 and Psalm 100:3. The term *Elohim* is definite in the Hebrew language; that is, it has the definite article before it. This is *the* Elohim about which we are speaking, which would indicate that this is not just a description of Jehovah as "a god" as in a title. If the LDS Church is going to say that there is a separate God named "Elohim," then that is the God under discussion here. Next, note that if Jehovah and Elohim were separate gods, the passage would say "there is none other besides *them.*" But, of course, it doesn't say that. It says there is none else beside *him.* Yes, the term is singular in the Hebrew. *It is utterly impossible, on the basis of the Bible, to distinguish between Jehovah and Elohim.* The Bible simply will not allow for it. There is only one God, "Jehovah Elohim."

Let's look at another passage, Exodus 34:14:

> For thou shalt worship no other god; for the LORD, whose name is Jealous, is a jealous God.

Elder Hahn, *if* there are indeed three separate and distinct gods for this planet—Elohim, Jehovah, and the Holy Ghost—which one do we worship? Do we worship Elohim only? Do we worship Jehovah? Who? Apostle Bruce R. McConkie addressed this issue in a talk he gave at Brigham Young University in March of 1982. In this speech (in which he declared that people "should not strive for a special and personal relationship with Christ") he addressed the question of whom we should truly worship. Here is what he said:

> We worship the Father and him only and no one else. We do not worship the Son and we do not worship the Holy Ghost. I know perfectly well what the scriptures say about worshipping Christ and Jehovah, but they are speaking in an entirely different sense—the sense of standing in awe and being reverentially grateful to Him who has redeemed us. Worship in the true and saving sense is reserved for God the first, the Creator.

Apostle McConkie said that his words were "doctrine of the Church," and he said that "everyone who is sound spiritually and who has guidance of the Holy Spirit will believe my words and follow my counsel." In this talk we are told that "Christ worked out his own salvation by worshipping the Father." How strange this sounds to the person who understands the monotheism of the Bible! Indeed, how absurd it is to think of Jehovah worshiping someone higher than himself! Psalm 97:9—"For thou, LORD, art high above all the earth; thou art exalted far above all gods." Psalm 135:5—"For I know that the LORD is great, and our Lord is above all gods." There is none above Jehovah, there is none beside Him. Jehovah worships none, but is to be worshiped by all, for He is the one true God.

This takes us back to the Scripture at hand, Exodus 34:14. Here we are told that worship—and who can doubt that this means worship in its highest sense, for the context is that of worshiping gods—belongs solely and completely to Jehovah. We are to worship no other God than Jehovah. Jesus expressed this in Matthew 4:10 when He rebuked Satan by saying, "Worship the Lord your God, and serve him only." Since Jesus is worshiped in the Bible, it is clear that both the Father and the Son along with the Spirit are the one Jehovah. Worship is due to none else.

You are left with a dilemma, then, Elder Hahn. Whom shall you worship? Since Mormons are polytheistic and believe that there are true gods other than Jehovah, they are left in a situation where there is no solution. Worship, true worship, demands strict monotheism. Mormonism does not have a proper knowledge of the true God, hence true worship is impossible. Therefore, when you worship a god other than Jehovah, Elder Hahn, you are doing so in violation of not only Exodus 34:14, but also of the first commandment as recorded in Exodus 20:2–3, which states,

> I am the LORD [Jehovah] thy God, which have brought thee out of the land of Egypt, out of the house of bondage. Thou shalt have no other gods before me. (See also Deuteronomy 5:6–7)

You have a god before Jehovah, Elder Hahn! Your Mormon beliefs are causing you to break the very first commandment of God himself! Is there a more *basic* truth of God than this, that He alone should be worshiped? No, there is not. Yet, when you attempt to make the Bible into a polytheistic book, in the process you end up creating such a mess that you have to break the very first commandment! As I said before, the fact of God's *uniqueness* is the most basic truth revealed in Scripture. It is central to properly worshiping God, wouldn't you agree? And can you see how very *dangerous* it is to be in error on this issue, Elder? If these passages of Scripture are correct, you have been led into a grave error—the sin of idolatry itself.

The fact that Jehovah is the *only* God acknowledged by the Bible is to be found all through the Old Testament. Jehovah is the Creator of all that is. Remember the passages from Isaiah that we saw in my previous letter? Look at this one from Isaiah 44:24:

Thus saith the LORD [Jehovah], thy redeemer, and he that formed thee from the womb, I am the LORD [Jehovah] that maketh all things; that stretcheth forth the heavens alone; that spreadeth abroad the earth by myself.

I realize how sensitive the subject of the endowment ceremony in the Mormon temple is to you, Elder, and I shall not ask you to comment on this issue, as I know you would feel uncomfortable doing so, but I wanted to point out to you that in the LDS temple ceremonies Elohim, the Father, is portrayed sending Jehovah and Michael down to "organize" the earth. How can you reconcile this teaching with the statements made by Jehovah here in Isaiah 44:24? Jehovah claims to have stretched out the heavens "alone" and to have spread abroad the earth by himself! Wasn't Elohim involved? What about Michael? Of course, as we have seen, Jehovah *is* Elohim, and that is the explanation of this passage. Jehovah is the only Creator there is, since He is the only God there is. Making two gods out of the one God of the Bible can only lead you to confusion and error.

Above I mentioned the fact that some LDS have attempted to avoid the clear difficulties attendant with their belief in two separate gods, Elohim and Jehovah, by asserting that Jehovah can indeed be called Elohim, and not compromise their theology. But, upon pressing them further, I have asked, "could then the Father ever be identified as Jehovah?" "No!" was the consistent reply. Jehovah is a name reserved solely and completely for the Son. However, I would like to point out, Elder Hahn, that the Bible clearly teaches that the name "Jehovah" is connected with the Father, the Son, and the Holy Spirit as well. You do not object to the identification of the Son as Jehovah, of course, and I will not here delve into the issue of the identification of the Spirit as Jehovah other than to simply point you to such passages as Isaiah 6:9; Acts 28:25–26; Exodus 4:11; 1 Corinthians 12:10–11. The main issue here is the identification of the Father as Jehovah.

The popular LDS booklet *What the Mormons Think of Christ* quotes Matthew 22:41–46, and in so doing *twists* the Scriptures to hide the clear fact that here Jesus identifies the Father as Jehovah. How is this done? Below I give you the quotation *exactly* as it appears in the pamphlet, including the brackets (you can check this against the copies that were in your Book of Mormon the evening you were at my home):

"While the Pharisees were gathered together, Jesus asked them,

Saying, What think ye of Christ? whose son is he? They say unto
him, The Son of David. He saith unto them, How then doth David
in spirit call him Lord, saying, the Lord [Elohim, the Father] said
unto my Lord [Jehovah, the Son], Sit thou on my right hand, till I
make thine enemies thy footstool? If David then call him Lord,
how is he his son? And no man was able to answer him a word,
neither durst any man from that day forth ask him any more questions." (p. 6 in the 1976 and 1982 editions)

The Mormon authors of this pamphlet have added the information
that the quotation Jesus gives of Psalm 110:1 identifies the Father speaking to the Son, which is correct, as far as it goes. *Incorrect* is the
information added—that being that the first "Lord" is "Elohim," and
the second "Lord" is "Jehovah." Is this true? Does Psalm 110:1 say
that Elohim spoke to Jehovah as if there were two different gods here,
one Elohim and one Jehovah?

No indeed! Let's look at Psalm 110:1 from the KJV: "The LORD
said unto my Lord, Sit thou at my right hand, until I make thine enemies
thy footstool." Note, Elder Hahn, that the passage says that "Jehovah
said unto my Lord (Hebrew: *Adonai*)" *not* "Elohim said to Jehovah."
The name "Elohim" does not even appear in the passage. If this is
indeed the Father speaking to the Son, as the pamphlet says (and I
agree), then what we have here is Jehovah (the Father) speaking to the
Son (Adonai, "Lord"). Clearly, then, the Father is here identified as
Jehovah, the one speaking to the Son. Since it is also clear that the
Bible *also* says Jesus is Jehovah, then we must conclude, as the Christian Church always has, that Jehovah is *tri-personal;* that is, that three
persons (Father, Son, and Holy Spirit) share the one being that is Jehovah God. I realize that for a person raised in LDS teaching, who is
accustomed to believing in a finite god, this could be confusing. What
you need to realize is that the God of the Bible is infinite—that is, he
is unlimited. His being, therefore, can be shared by more than one
person, just as the Bible teaches.

There are other references that identify the Father as Jehovah. For
example, when Jesus was tempted by Satan, Satan demanded worship
from Christ. Jesus replied by stating that one is to worship God alone.
In doing so he quoted Deuteronomy 6:13 and 10:20 (passages specifically about Jehovah God) in reference to the Father. No one who listened
to the Lord Jesus speak and preach doubted that when He spoke of the
Father, He was speaking of Jehovah God.

I hope you will think about this and find the time to respond. I realize, however, that you may be very confused, especially about the relationship of the Father, the Son, and the Spirit, considering what I have written. So, in closing, I would like very quickly to make *sure* you understand what Christians believe about the doctrine of the Trinity. If you would like to discuss it further at another point, that is fine with me. I have met so many Mormons who have a very *flawed* understanding of the Trinity that I would like to attempt to head off any problems we might have right now.

For me, simplifying the doctrine of the Trinity to its most basic elements has been very important and very useful. When we reduce the discussion to the three clear biblical teachings that underlie the Trinity, we can move our discussion from the abstract to the concrete biblical data, and can help individuals such as yourself understand why Bible-believers such as myself believe in the Trinity, despite the fact that the word *Trinity* does not appear in the text of Scripture.

We must remember that very few have a good idea of what the Trinity is in the first place—hence, accuracy in definition will be very important. The doctrine of the Trinity states that there is one eternal being of God—indivisible, infinite. This one being of God is shared by what we call three co-equal, co-eternal persons—the Father, the Son, and the Spirit. It is good here to distinguish between the terms *being* and *person*. It would be a contradiction to say that there are three beings within one being, or three persons within one person. So what is the difference?

We clearly recognize the difference between being and person every day. We recognize *what* something is, yet we also recognize individuals within a classification. For example, we speak of the *being* of man— human being. A rock has *being*—the being of a rock, as does a cat, a dog, etc. Yet, we also know that there are personal attributes as well. The Bible tells us there are three classifications of personal beings— God, men, and angels. What is personality? The ability to have emotion, will, to express oneself. Rocks cannot speak. Cats cannot think of themselves over against others, and, for example, work for the common good of "catkind." Hence, we are saying that there is one eternal, infinite *being* of God, shared fully and completely by three *personal* self-distinctions: Father, Son, and Spirit. I use the phrase "personal self-distinctions" rather than "persons" simply because you, as a Mormon, would be highly likely to attach to that term a physical form, which would be an incorrect assumption. When I speak of a "divine Person" I am *not* referring to a physical human being, but to a Person who is *personal*—that is, who speaks, loves, wills, etc. The term, for me, does *not* refer to a physical manifestation. And note this as well, Elder Hahn: I am *not* saying that the Father is the Son, or the Son the Spirit, or the Spirit the Father. It is very common for people to misunderstand the doctrine to mean that we are saying Jesus is the Father. The doctrine of the Trinity does not in any way say this!

The three biblical doctrines that flow directly into the river that is the Trinity are as follows: (1) There is one and only one God, eternal, unchanging. (2) There are three eternal Persons described in Scripture— the Father, the Son, and the Spirit. These Persons are never confused with one another—that is, they are carefully differentiated as Persons. (3) The Father, the Son, and the Spirit, are identified as being fully deity—that is, the Bible teaches the deity of the Father, the Son, and the Holy Spirit. One could possibly represent this as follows:

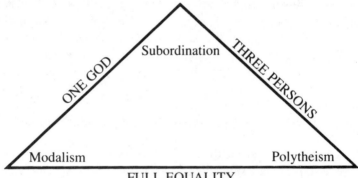

The three sides of the triangle represent the three biblical doctrines, as labeled. When one denies any of these three teachings, the other two sides point to the result. Hence, if one denies that there are Three Persons, one is left with the two sides of Full Equality and One God, resulting in the "Oneness" or "modalistic" teaching of the United Pentecostal Church and others. If one denies Full Equality, one is left with Three Persons and One God, resulting in "subordinationism" as seen in Jehovah's Witnesses, the Way International, and others (though to be perfectly accurate the Witnesses deny all three of the sides in some way—they deny Full Equality [i.e., Jesus is Michael the Archangel], Three Persons [the Holy Spirit is an impersonal, active "force" like electricity] and One God [they say Jesus is "a god"—a lesser divinity than Yahweh; hence they are in reality not monotheists but henotheists, believers in one "major" deity, as well as other "minor" deities]). And, if one denies One God, one is left with polytheism, the belief in many gods, as seen clearly in the Mormon Church.

I truly hope, Elder Hahn, that you will look into God's Word and examine these issues. I am more than happy to provide you with this information, but I want you to realize that you are now responsible for it. You cannot simply ignore the clear teaching of the Bible as you have now seen it. You must deal with what God's Word says. I reiterate my offer—if you wish to sit down and talk about these things, please feel free to contact me. May God bless you as you seek His will.

Sincerely,

James White

LETTER 6

Latter-Day Revelation?

Tuesday, June 26

Dear Elder Hahn,

I almost have to apologize for the weather. Since I moved here in 1974, it has *never* been this hot—in fact, it has simply never been this hot *ever* before—at least not as long as anyone has kept records! But, to me, 122° doesn't feel much worse than 118°—after a while, I guess it just doesn't matter.

Your letter arrived with this morning's mail. Somehow, as I held the unopened letter in my hand, I *knew* what you were going to say. Any kind of rebuttal of what I had written to you would require more than two sheets of paper, but I could tell your letter contained no more than that. I believe that your response can be summarized under two topics: (1) the concept of *latter-day revelation*, and (2) the *priesthood authority*. Your letter provides the basis for my summary:

> Mr. White, while I appreciate all the biblical information you provided to me, and while I admit that I am not a Bible scholar, I must point out to you that since you do not accept all that God has revealed—that is, since you do not accept latter-day revelation— you are not in a position to be able to make the sweeping and final judgments that you do. When *all* that God has said is taken into consideration, your position is found to be incorrect.

And then later,

> Your interpretation of these passages of the Bible lacks the

proper authorization, the proper authority. God has restored the priesthood authority upon the earth, and since God has always operated through this means, and you do not have this authority, you lack the proper means of interpretation, and, therefore, the proper understanding of the Bible. Your interpretation is at odds with the teachings of those who hold God's priesthood authority.

I am going to ask you to allow me to address the *priesthood authority* issue in two stages—the first, relevant to the history of the teaching, when I discuss Joseph Smith, and the second, regarding the theology of the "priesthood" at a later point, Lord willing. For now, I wish to address the concept of *latter-day revelation* and the Mormon understanding of it, especially as that relates to our current discussion.

I would like to point out a few things that I believe are relevant to your claims concerning latter-day revelation and the discussion in my letters concerning the doctrine of God. First, even if such a thing as latter-day revelation existed, it would not in any way supersede, or contradict, what the Bible says in the passages we have examined. God is a self-consistent being, is He not, Elder Hahn? Does God contradict himself? Certainly not. While God may change the ways in which He works in the world, at one time through the theocracy of the nation of Israel, now through the instrumentality of the Spirit in the Church, He does *not* change His truth! God does not change, and the truth about God does not change. We can learn *more* about God over time; for example, with the coming of Jesus, much, much more was revealed about God than had ever been revealed before. But what Jesus revealed about God does not *contradict* what God had revealed before!

Now in the case of the teachings of the LDS Church, we do not encounter a *greater* revelation of the being of God as we find in the coming of Christ, but a direct and obvious contradiction of what God has already revealed concerning himself. We find D&C 130:22 ("The Father has a body of flesh and bones as tangible as man's") in direct contradiction to the Bible's teachings concerning God (Hosea 11:9, 2 Chronicles 6:18, Jeremiah 23:24, John 4:24, etc.). Smith's teachings concerning a plurality of gods are in direct contradiction with Isaiah 43:10, 44:6–8, and Deuteronomy 6:4. It seems that you take "latter-day revelation" to be superior to all else, and, if there is a contradiction, you simply dismiss the teachings of the Bible in favor of LDS doctrine.

Elder Hahn, I ask you to consider for a moment the wisdom of this course of action. Obviously, the Bible and its teaching of one eternal and infinite God, and the Mormon Scriptures (primarily the *Doctrine and Covenants*, as well as the teachings of the LDS prophets and apostles) and their teaching of a plurality of finite gods, are in contradiction with one another. Therefore we *cannot* say that the Holy Spirit of God inspired the writing of *both* of these sources of religious teaching, for to do so is to say that the Holy Spirit can contradict himself. I believe, as Jesus did, that the Bible is the inspired Word of God—one will search in vain in the Lord's words for even a hint of doubt as to the complete accuracy *and consistency* of the Old Testament revelation of God. Since this is the case, then anything that is contradictory to the plain precepts of the Bible *cannot,* by definition, come from the Holy Spirit of God. By taking the LDS position as an *a priori* assumption, and then *forcing* the Bible into the mold created by Mormon teaching, you are doing great injustice to the teachings of the Bible. I note you did not do what many LDS have done by alleging that the Bible must be in error in those passages, as we have already discussed that issue and demonstrated the inherent accuracy of the biblical text. So, instead of this course of action, you allege that my interpretation is "incomplete" because I lack something you have—in this case, further revelation from God. And I reply, if you have further revelation from God, it will be in perfect harmony with what God has already revealed! As is plain to see, that which you call revelation from God is *not* in harmony with the Christian Scriptures, the Bible.

The Mormon claim of latter-day revelation can be approached from many different angles. We could enter into the seemingly never-ending debate about what books are and are not to be included in the Bible, that is, the canon of Scripture—is it "open" with more Scripture being revealed, or is it "closed" with what has already been revealed being sufficient for God's people. Obviously, I would take the latter position, you the former. We could, with profit, discuss the *sufficiency* of the revelation of the Bible, in light of Peter's teaching that God has "given unto us all things that pertain unto life and godliness, through the knowledge of him that hath called us to glory and virtue" (2 Peter 1:3). I could point you to the "faith which was once delivered unto the saints" (Jude 3). But I have learned that, for purposes of discussion, this is not the best avenue at first. As long as you think the Mormon "revelations" consistent, harmonious, and true, the truth of the *sufficiency* of the biblical revelation will be lost to you.

To examine the LDS claims to latter-day revelation, we compare those revelations with what we find in the Bible, assuming that, as I have said, if the Holy Spirit, who is called "the Spirit of truth," is a consistent being, what He says in one portion of Scripture will be in harmony with what He says in another portion of Scripture. I have done this, Elder Hahn, and find the Mormon revelations to be lacking the stamp of divine inspiration. They are inconsistent, as we have seen already, with the truths of the Bible, and they are, in fact, inconsistent with themselves as well.

Latter-day revelation is based, primarily, upon the teachings and prophecies of Joseph Smith, Jr., the founder and first president of the Church of Jesus Christ of Latter-day Saints. Most would agree with my assessment. In fact, Joseph Fielding Smith wrote,

> CHURCH STANDS OR FALLS WITH JOSEPH SMITH. Mormonism, as it is called, must *stand or fall on the story of Joseph Smith.* He was either a prophet of God, divinely called, properly appointed and commissioned, or he was one of the biggest frauds this world has ever seen. *There is no middle ground. (Doctrines of Salvation,* 1:188)

If Joseph Smith was not what he claimed to be, then the LDS faith is built upon smoke and mirrors—it has no basis, no foundation. The whole claim of latter-day revelation will stand or fall with Joseph Smith.

I have no great desire to spend time discussing Joseph Smith, Elder Hahn. I realize that you may have the idea that those who oppose your teaching derive great enjoyment and pleasure out of "tearing down" the Mormon faith, primarily in "attacking" Joseph Smith. Some may, but I most certainly do not. I would much rather spend my time talking positively about the gospel of Jesus Christ, and the magnificent God who has revealed himself in the Word, or about the tremendous grace of God that brings salvation to men. But sometimes we have to discuss that which is not pleasant for good to come about. That is the situation we find ourselves in now.

You believe that Joseph Smith, Jr., was a prophet of God. That belief, and the beliefs that flow from it (your "testimony" of the truthfulness of the Book of Mormon, your acceptance of the teachings of the *Doctrine and Covenants* and the *Pearl of Great Price*, and your allegiance to the continuing teaching authority of the LDS Church), stands in the way of your acceptance of the true gospel of Jesus Christ. Anything that stands between a person and the gospel must be dealt with—it must be exposed by the light of truth. If this means "tearing down" falsehoods, then so be it. If I care for you, Elder Hahn, I will do whatever is necessary to present the gospel to you. Sometimes that calls for drastic measures, measures that we otherwise would not find expedient. Paul struck a man blind when he stood in the way of the proclamation of the gospel of Christ (Acts 13:6–13). If your belief in Joseph Smith stands in your way of finding a real relationship with Jesus Christ, I will do whatever is necessary to remove that stumbling block, *simply because I care about you*. I do not enjoy the task—but tough love often demands that we do that which we do not like.

Mormons often cry "persecution!" when someone such as I begins to point out the false teachings, the *deceptions*, of Mormon leaders such as Joseph Smith. But, Elder Hahn, such is hardly the case. Persecution is attack without cause; what I do in pointing out the danger of belief in Joseph Smith is attack *with* cause. It is done, I assure you, out of a deep love for the LDS people, and a real concern for their eternal welfare. I have often been challenged by LDS people, "If you really loved us, you would leave us alone! Christ would never do such a thing!" When I have replied that I do what I am doing simply because I really do care, and I have love in my heart for the Mormon people, I normally encounter rude retorts and statements of, "You do not! You are lying!" I ask, "If you saw that I was in a situation where I was deceived, and was in eternal danger, would you not care enough for me to warn me, even if you knew I would probably, due to my blindness, be offended at you?" I've received a *wide* variety of answers to that question!

So I take up the pen against Joseph Smith, Elder Hahn, not because I want to, or like to, but because I *must*! I hope my comments on these issues will be read with these words in mind.

There is one more statement I must make before I delve into the subject of Joseph Smith and the claims made by him, and about him. One could write for a very, very long time on these subjects. Others have done so, and I do not feel it would be a proper stewardship of your time, or mine, to repeat their noble efforts. So I will keep my comments as brief as possible, while doing my best not to sacrifice clarity in the process. And, to allow you to dig more deeply into these historical topics, I have purchased two books at the Christian bookstore I mentioned to you when we first met—the one that is less than a mile from your apartment. The book clerk is holding them in your name right now—all you have to do is go in and ask for them, and they are yours. Actually, you will only need one of them—let me explain. Both books are by Jerald and Sandra Tanner. You may have heard of them. In my opinion, their books are the best available on the history and practices of Mormonism. Their research is top-notch, and their ministry is conducted with a great deal of *integrity*. One of the two books is their largest work entitled *Mormonism: Shadow or Reality?* This is a *big* book, Elder Hahn, and may discourage you from reading it simply by the huge mass it carries. So, the other book is a condensation of the first in paperback entitled *The Changing World of Mormonism.* If you would like them both, that's fine with me. They are both yours, *if you will honestly read them.* I will bring up a number of topics in the rest of this letter, and probably in the following letters, that you could do further research into with the aid of these fine resources. I hope you will stop by and pick them up.

To be perfectly honest with you, having heard many Mormon testimonies, I would have to say I've heard the name of Joseph Smith at least as often, if not *more* often, than the name of Jesus Christ. At the very least, it can be said that Mormons view Joseph Smith as about the most important person short of Jesus who has ever walked the earth—and I include in that comparison Moses, Isaiah, Peter, and Paul. I note, for example, the words of Brigham Young as he spoke on August 31, 1871:

> Well, now, examine the character of the Savior, and examine the characters of those who have written the Old and New Testaments; and then compare them with the character of Joseph Smith, the founder of this work—the man whom God called and to whom he gave the keys of the Priesthood, and through whom he has established his Church and kingdom for the last time, and you will find that his character stands as fair as that of any man's mentioned in the Bible. We can find no person who presents a better character to the world when the facts are known than Joseph Smith, jun., the prophet, and his brother, Hyrum Smith, who was murdered with him. (*Journal of Discourses,* 14:203)

A number of years earlier President Young spoke about the *importance* of Joseph Smith in God's scheme of things:

> Joseph Smith holds the keys of this last dispensation, and is now engaged behind the vail in the great work of the last days. I

can tell our beloved brother Christians who have slain the Prophets and butchered and otherwise caused the death of thousands of Latter-day Saints, the priests who have thanked God in their prayers and thanksgivings from the pulpit that we have been plundered, driven, and slain, and the deacons under the pulpit, and their brethren and sisters in their closets, who have thanked God, thinking that the Latter-day Saints were wasted away, something that no doubt will mortify them—something that, to say the least, is a matter of deep regret to them—namely, that no man or woman in this dispensation will ever enter into the celestial kingdom of God without the consent of Joseph Smith. From the day that the Priesthood was taken from the earth to the winding-up scene of all things, every man and woman must have the certificate of Joseph Smith, junior, as a passport to their entrance into the mansion where God and Christ are—I with you and you with me. I cannot go there without his consent. He holds the keys of that kingdom for the last dispensation—the keys to rule in the spirit-world; and he rules there triumphantly, for he gained full power and a glorious victory over the power of Satan while he was yet in the flesh, and was a martyr to his religion and to the name of Christ, which gives him a most perfect victory in the spirit-world. He reigns there as supreme a being in his sphere, capacity, and calling, as God does in heaven. Many will exclaim—"Oh, that is very disagreeable! It is preposterous! We cannot bear the thought!" But it is true.

I will now tell you something that ought to comfort every man and woman on the face of the earth. Joseph Smith, junior, will again be on this earth dictating plans and calling forth his brethren to be baptized for the very characters who wish this was not so, in order to bring them into a kingdom to enjoy, perhaps, the presence of angels or the spirits of good men, if they cannot endure the presence of the Father and the Son; and he will never cease his operations, under the directions of the Son of God, until the last ones of the children of men are saved that can be, from Adam till now.

Should not this thought comfort all people? They will, by-and-by, be a thousand times more thankful for such a man as Joseph Smith, junior, than it is possible for them to be for any earthly good whatever. It is his mission to see that all the children of men in this last dispensation are saved, that can be, through the redemption. You will be thankful, every one of you, that Joseph Smith, junior, was ordained to this great calling before the worlds were. (*Journal of Discourses*, 7:289)

And, with regards to the authority of his own teaching, the same Brigham Young said,

> I know just as well what to teach this people and just what to say to them as what to do in order to bring them into the celestial kingdom, as I know the road to my office. . . . I have never yet preached a sermon and sent it out to the children of men, that they may not call Scripture. Let me have the privilege of correcting a sermon, and it is as good Scripture as they deserve. The people have the oracles of God continually. (*Journal of Discourses,* 13:95)

I realize, Elder, that the sermons contained in the *Journal of Discourses* are not considered Scripture by modern LDS—my point is simply to demonstrate the *high view* of Joseph Smith that prevailed in early days, and it is hardly any less true of the Latter-day Saints today.

Joseph Smith is hardly to be surpassed in his own view of himself. Note these words, uttered barely a month before he was murdered (*not* martyred, for martyrs do not die with a pistol in their hands fighting back—see the *Documentary History of the Church,* 6:618):

> God is in the still small voice. In all these affidavits, indictments, it is all of the devil—all corruption. Come on! ye prosecutors! ye false swearers! All hell, boil over! Ye burning mountains, roll down your lava! for I will come out on the top at last. I have more to boast of than ever any man had. I am the only man that has ever been able to keep a whole church together since the days of Adam. A large majority of the whole have stood by me. Neither Paul, John, Peter, nor Jesus ever did it. I boast that no man ever did such a work as I. The followers of Jesus ran away from Him; but the Latter-day Saints never ran away from me yet. (*Documentary History of the Church,* 6:408–9)

It is not my intention to judge Joseph Smith on the basis of these comments, Elder. The Bible provides "tests" for those who would claim to be a "prophet" and I will simply apply the criteria given by God himself to the teachings and prophecies of Joseph Smith. I hope you will do the same thing.

The "tests" to which I refer are to be found in the book of Deuteronomy, chapters 13 and 18. The second is well known to most, and you are undoubtedly familiar with it:

> And if thou say in thine heart, How shall we know the word

which the LORD hath not spoken? When a prophet speaketh in the name of the LORD, if the thing follow not, nor come to pass, that is the thing which the LORD hath not spoken, but the prophet hath spoken it presumptuously; thou shalt not be afraid of him. (Deuteronomy 18:21-22)

If a person presumes to speak in the name of Jehovah, he must be *completely accurate* in what he says. As has been pointed out many times, just *one false prophecy* disqualifies one from being a prophet of God. We shall examine a few "prophecies" of Joseph Smith in this regard.

Many, however, are not as quick to apply the *first* test of a prophet given by Moses, that of Deuteronomy 13:1–5:

If there arise among you a prophet, or a dreamer of dreams, and giveth thee a sign or a wonder, and the sign or the wonder comes to pass, whereof he spoke unto thee, saying, Let us go after other gods, which thou hast not known, and let us serve them; Thou shalt not hearken unto the words of that prophet, or that dreamer of dreams: for the LORD your God proveth you, to know whether ye love the LORD your God with all your heart and with all your soul. Ye shall walk after the LORD your God, and fear him, and keep his commandments, and obey his voice, and ye shall serve him, and cleave unto him. And that prophet, or that dreamer of dreams, shall be put to death; because he hath spoken to turn you away from the LORD your God, which brought you out of the land of Egypt, and redeemed you out of the house of bondage, to thrust thee out of the way which the LORD thy God commanded thee to walk in. So shalt thou put the evil away from the midst of thee.

Note that in this instance, the "prophet" does not give a false prophecy—in fact, he prophecies correctly, and is able to show a wondrous sign. But, that alone does not make him a true prophet of God. The key here is the call of this "prophet" to go after another god, a god that the people of Israel had not "known." In other words, you can prophecy correctly, but if your teaching about God is incorrect, if your theology is wrong, you are still a false prophet. The prophets of God are accurate in *both* their theology of God and their prophetic utterances.

I believe that I have already laid a sufficient foundation for the "testing" of Joseph Smith as a prophet with regard to Deuteronomy 13:1–5. As we have seen, if one follows after the gods taught by Joseph

Smith, one is following after a *different* god than the God preached by Moses and all the other prophets of the Bible. You and I have already discussed how Mormons have to face the question of *which God they will worship,* and how following the advice of such LDS leaders as Bruce R. McConkie results in a direct violation of the very first commandment of God! The god of Joseph Smith is *not* the God of the Bible, Elder Hahn. Therefore, Smith fails the first test of a true prophet of God, for to follow him is to go after a god whom Israel, and the modern followers of Christ, "have not known."

Before looking at specific prophecies of Joseph Smith, and in connection with what I just said, I'd like to direct your attention toward the First Vision of Joseph Smith.

The First Vision

That glorious theophany which took place in the spring of 1820 and which marked the opening of the dispensation of the fulness of times is called the *First Vision.* It is rated as first both from the standpoint of time and of pre-eminent importance. In it Joseph Smith saw and conversed with the Father and the Son, both of which exalted personages were personally present before him and he lay enwrapped in the Spirit and overshadowed by the Holy Ghost.

This transcendent vision was the beginning of latter-day revelation; it marked the opening of the heavens after the long night of apostate darkness; with it was ushered in the great era of restoration, "the times of restitution of all things, which God hath spoken by the mouth of all his holy prophets since the world began" (Acts 3:21). Through it the creeds of Christendom were shattered to smithereens, and because of it the truth about those Beings whom it is life eternal to know began again to be taught among men. (*Mormon Doctrine*, pp. 284–85)

I am aware, of course, that you would know a good deal about the First Vision, Elder Hahn. I realize that you have probably related the story to many people during the course of your fifteen months on your mission. However, I am going to go back over all the details so that I can point out the *many* difficulties with the whole story. I hope a little basic "review" will not be out of order.

The *Pearl of Great Price*, part of your "inspired Scriptures," contains a section entitled "Joseph Smith—History." Here Smith relates the story of his early history, and included in this work is the story of the First Vision. This particular story was written by Smith in 1838, a full eighteen years *after* the supposed events he narrates concerning the First Vision. But, so that you can understand why I do not believe that this "vision" ever took place, both historically and theologically, let's go over Smith's story from the beginning to get a proper context.

Smith begins by noting that he was born on December 23, 1805, in Sharon, Windsor County, Vermont. He indicates that his father moved the family from Vermont to New York, and "in about four years after my father's arrival in Palmyra, he moved with his family into Manchester in the same county of Ontario." Interestingly enough, when he lists the family members that moved to Manchester, he includes his sister Lucy, who was born July 18, 1821, in Palmyra. He then immediately enters into the discussion of the revivals in the Manchester/Palmyra area, and his own resultant questions about religious truth. But note, Elder Hahn, that he writes that these revivals broke out "some time in the second year after our removal to Manchester." If Lucy was born in 1821, and this revival took place about two years later, then so far we would have Joseph Smith asserting that this revival in religion took place no earlier than 1823, possibly as late as 1824. As we shall see, Smith's story does not remain consistent on this point.

As Smith's description of these revivals is very, *very* important, I quote it here at length:

> Some time in the second year after our removal to Manchester, there was in the place where we lived an unusual excitement on the subject of religion. It commenced with the Methodists, but soon became general among all the sects in that region of country. Indeed, the whole district of country seemed affected by it, and great multitudes united themselves to the different religious parties, which created no small stir and division amongst the people, some crying, "Lo, here!" and others, "Lo, there!" Some were contending for the Methodist faith, some for the Presbyterian, and some for the Baptist.
>
> For, notwithstanding the great love which the converts to these different faiths expressed at the time of their conversion, and the great zeal manifested by the respective clergy, who were active in getting up and promoting this extraordinary scene of religious feeling, in order to have everybody converted, as they were pleased to

call it, let them join what sect they pleased; yet when the converts began to file off, some to one party and some to another, it was seen that the seemingly good feelings of both the priests and the converts were more pretended than real; for a scene of great confusion and bad feeling ensued—priest contending against priest, and convert against convert; so that all their good feelings one for another, if they ever had any, were entirely lost in a strife of words and a contest about opinions.

I was at this time in my fifteenth year. My father's family was proselyted to the Presbyterian faith, and four of them joined that church, namely, my mother, Lucy; my brothers Hyrum and Samuel Harrison; and my sister Sophronia.

Let's list the specifics as given by Smith: (1) this "revival" began some time in the *second year* after the Smiths' move to Manchester; (2) it took place "in the place where we lived" and spread to "the whole district of country"; (3) it began with the Methodists, and spread to the Presbyterians and the Baptists; (4) "great multitudes united themselves to the different religious parties"; (5) there was strife and conflict between the various denominations regarding the converts and to what group they would join themselves; (6) Smith was at this time in his "fifteenth year" which could be taken either to mean he was 14 or 15 years of age (resulting in the years 1820–1821, depending); (7) as a result of this religious excitement, members of Smith's family joined the Presbyterian faith. We will need to keep all these facts in mind a little later on. Don't you feel like you are in school again?

As a result of this excitement, young Joseph's mind was "called up to serious reflection and great uneasiness." He indicates that he "attended their several meetings as often as occasion would permit" but he made no commitment to any particular group, though he indicates that he was "somewhat partial to the Methodist sect" and felt some desire to join with them. But, he felt he could not decide who was right and who was wrong. The various sects spent a lot of energy proving the others wrong, and this resulted only in greater confusion for him. He continues,

> While I was laboring under the extreme difficulties caused by the contests of these parties of religionists, I was one day reading the Epistle of James, first chapter and fifth verse, which reads: *If any of you lack wisdom, let him ask of God, that giveth to all men liberally, and upbraideth not; and it shall be given him.*

Never did any passage of Scripture come with more power to the heart of man than this did at this time to mine. It seemed to enter with great force into every feeling of my heart. I reflected on it again and again, knowing that if any person needed wisdom from God, I did; for how to act I did not know, and unless I could get more wisdom than I then had, I would never know; for the teachers of religion of the different sects understood the same passages of scripture so differently as to destroy all confidence in settling the question by an appeal to the Bible.

It is truly a shame that Smith never learned that his questions could have been *resolved* by "an appeal to the Bible." If he had known the truth about God from Scripture, he would never have taught what he did. Note, Elder Hahn, that Smith went down the same path presented by nearly every religion of man—he did not believe that the Bible was *sufficient* to answer man's questions.

Smith decided to do what James 1:5 teaches and ask God in prayer who was right and who was wrong. As a result,

. . . I retired to the woods to make the attempt. It was on the morning of a beautiful, clear day, early in the spring of eighteen hundred and twenty. It was the first time in my life that I had made such an attempt, for amidst all my anxieties I had never as yet made the attempt to pray vocally.

After I had retired to the place where I had previously designed to go, having looked around me, and finding myself alone, I kneeled down and began to offer up the desires of my heart to God. I had scarcely done so, when immediately I was seized upon by some power which entirely overcame me, and had such an astonishing influence over me as to bind my tongue so that I could not speak. Thick darkness gathered around me, and it seemed to me for a time as if I were doomed to sudden destruction.

But, exerting all my powers to call upon God to deliver me out of the power of this enemy which had seized upon me, and at the very moment when I was ready to sink into despair and abandon myself to destruction—not to an imaginary ruin, but to the power of some actual being from the unseen world, who had such marvelous powers as I had never before felt in any being—just at this moment of great alarm, I saw a pillar of light exactly over my head, above the brightness of the sun, which descended gradually until it fell upon me.

Please note the specifics of Smith's account. First, he tells us that he went into the "sacred grove" (as modern LDS call it) on a beautiful spring day in 1820. Did he just make a little mistake in remembering when his sister Lucy was born in his previous listing? I shall wait to answer that till later. He went into the woods to pray to God and to ask Him who was right and who was wrong. As soon as he attempted to do so, however, he was seized upon by some kind of force, and was surrounded by thick darkness. Just at the point of despair he saw a pillar of light that descended toward him.

> It no sooner appeared than I found myself delivered from the enemy which held me bound. When the light rested upon me I saw two Personages, whose brightness and glory defy all description, standing above me in the air. One of them spake unto me, calling me by name and said, pointing to the other—*This is My Beloved Son. Hear Him!*

Smith claims to have seen two personages. One calls him by name and, pointing to the other, says, "This is My Beloved Son. Hear Him!" Of course, Mormons believe that these personages were God the Father, in a physical form, and Jesus Christ, also in a physical form. The Father spoke to Joseph, and pointed him to the Son. Smith's whole concept of a "plurality of gods" is seen in this vision. God the Father and Jesus Christ are separate and distinct "personages," just as D&C 130:22 teaches. This is why McConkie, in the citation above, said that this vision "smashed to smithereens" the "creeds of Christendom," for all those creeds are united in their confession that there is only one God, and that the Father and the Son share the one being that is God. But, this is not all. We must remember that when Smith wrote this account (1838) he was engaged in his own conflict against "religionists" on all fronts. So what does Smith allege these two Personages said to him?

> My object in going to inquire of the Lord was to know which of all the sects was right, that I might know which to join. No sooner, therefore, did I get possession of myself, so as to be able to speak, than I asked the Personages who stood above me in the light, which of all the sects was right (for at this time it had never entered into my heart that all were wrong)—and which I should join.
> I was answered that I must join none of them, for they were all wrong; and the Personage who addressed me said that all their

creeds were an abomination in his sight; that those professors were all corrupt; that: "they draw near to me with their lips, but their hearts are far from me, they teach for doctrines the commandments of men, having a form of godliness, but they deny the power thereof."

Smith asked the two Personages which church he should join. He was told he should join none of them: "They are all wrong—Methodists, Presbyterians, Baptists—the whole lot are in error." Their creeds, which present the basic elements of the Christian faith, were said to be "an abomination" in the sight of God. And what of church members, the "professors" of these faiths? "They are all corrupt." It is not that this was new for Joseph—he included this kind of rhetoric in the Book of Mormon as well when he said that one either is a part of the church of the Lamb or the church of the devil (1 Nephi 14:10). And I have indeed met many LDS who were consistent with Joseph's position— they condemned all Christian churches as being in error, their creeds an abomination, their "professors" corrupt. Bruce R. McConkie was certainly straightforward when he said that "there is no salvation outside The Church of Jesus Christ of Latter-day Saints" (*Mormon Doctrine*, p. 670). But, many LDS today are attempting to get away from the "harsh tone" of Joseph Smith. Such hardly seems a possibility without jettisoning *all* of Smith's story.

Smith goes on to allege that a few days after this vision he mentioned it to a Methodist minister who immediately told him it was of the devil. Following this he notes,

> I soon found . . . that my telling the story had excited a great deal of prejudice against me among professors of religion, and was the cause of great persecution, which continued to increase; and though I was an obscure boy, only between fourteen and fifteen years of age, and my circumstances in life such as to make a boy of no consequence in the world, yet men of high standing would take notice sufficient to excite the public mind against me, and create a bitter persecution; and this was common among all the sects—all united to persecute me.

As you are aware, Elder, according to LDS teaching the angel Moroni visited Joseph Smith beginning on September 21, 1823, and, four years later, Smith received the "golden plates" upon which the Book of Mormon was supposedly written. This "second vision" takes place, then, according to Mormon Scripture in "Joseph Smith—History," three and a half years *after* Smith's vision of the Father and the Son.

And so the story is told. I can barely begin to scratch the surface of all the problems that exist with reference to the First Vision, Elder Hahn. I go into them simply because the First Vision is (1) central to LDS theology about God, and (2) said to be a *true,* historical occurrence that took place at a specific place and time. Therefore, we can study it and determine if indeed this took place or not.

Let's summarize Smith's story: On a spring day in 1820 he went into the woods to ask God which church he should join. He did so because of a revival in "the place where we lived" that resulted in "multitudes" joining the various sects, specifically the Methodists, the Baptists, and the Presbyterians. God the Father and Jesus Christ, as two separate and distinct personages, appeared to him, and Christ told him not to join any of the churches, for they were all wrong. Nearly every single LDS person with whom I have spoken has, when asked, answered affirmatively the question, "Do you have a testimony that Joseph Smith saw God the Father and Jesus Christ as separate and distinct beings in the spring of 1820?" The Mormon Scriptures contain this story. So, if upon study we discover that this did *not* take place, what would be the honest action of any LDS person? Only you can answer that, Elder Hahn.

So did Joseph Smith see God the Father and Jesus Christ in the spring of 1820? For those who have access to the relevant historical information, the only possible answer is: *No, he did not!* Why do I say this? Let's look at *some* of the evidence.

Up until the 1960s, it was common for LDS apologists to say things similar to Preston Nibley's statement from 1944: "Joseph Smith lived a little more than twenty-four years after this first vision. During this time he told but one story . . ." (*Joseph Smith the Prophet*, p. 30). But, honest historians today do not make such claims, for it is obvious that Joseph *did* tell many different stories, most of which, Elder, contradict the others on important points. For example, in the mid–1960s a hand-written account of the First Vision became available to the public at large for the first time. It turned out that it was, in part, in Joseph Smith's own handwriting, most probably written in the year 1832. And what does it say about the First Vision? Here is how it reads (misspellings and original punctuation left intact):

. . . and while in the attitude of calling upon the Lord in the 16th year of my age a pillar of light above the brightness of the sun at noon day come down from above and rested upon me and I was filld with the spirit of God and the Lord opened the heavens upon me and I saw the Lord and he spake unto me saying Joseph my Son thy Sins are forgiven thee. go thy way and walk in my statutes and keep my commandments behold I am the Lord of glory I was crucifyed for the world that all those who believe on my name may have Eternal life behold the world lieth in sin at this time and none doeth good no not one they have turned aside from the Gospel and keep not my commandments they draw near to me with their lips while their hearts are far from me and mine anger is kindling against the inhabitants of the earth to visit them acording to this ungodliness and to bring to pass that which hath been spoken by the mouth of the prophets and Apstles behold and lo I come quickly as it written of me in the cloud clothed in the glory of my Father and my soul was filled with love and for many days I could rejoice with great joy and the Lord was with me but could fine none that would believe the hevenly vision. . . .

If you would like to read this account for yourself, it is available today in many LDS sources—you might find tracking down the December, 1984 *Ensign* magazine to be convenient—it is on pages 25–26 in an article by Mormon scholar Dean C. Jessee. Or, you might want to look at Jessee's 1989 work, *The Papers of Joseph Smith*, Volume I, pp. 6–7. Please note that in the earliest rendition known, and the only one we know of written in Smith's own handwriting, only one personage is seen, not two. Clearly, the Lord Jesus is portrayed speaking to Smith, but God the Father is conspicuous by His absence! Why would Smith neglect to mention seeing God the Father? I have an answer for that, but I'd like to look at a few more pieces of information before I mention it.

Smith's "diary" for November 9, 1835, contains yet another account of this vision. This one differs from *both* the 1832 account as well as the "official" 1838 account in that while it does mention two personages, these personages testify that "Jesus Christ is the Son of God." In this account angels are mentioned, but not God the Father or Jesus Christ. What makes this account even more interesting, Elder, is that in the *Documentary History of the Church,* under the date of November 14, 1835—only five days *after* the above account—we have another mention of this "vision." When the account was originally printed in serial form in the *Deseret News* on May 29, 1852, it recounted the story of Joseph Smith's telling a man by the name of Erastus Holmes of his experiences: ". . . from six years up to the time I received *the first visitation of angels,* which was when I was about fourteen years old. . . . " (emphasis mine). However, recent editions of the *Documentary History of the Church* have changed the wording, so that it now reads, ". . . from six years old up to the time I received *my first vision,* which was when I was about fourteen years old. . . . " (DHC 2:312) Given the close proximity in time of the diary account on November 9 and the clear editing of the DHC with reference to November 14, it seems clear that at this time Joseph Smith was *not* claiming to have seen God the Father! In fact, Elder, I would challenge you to produce any shred of evidence that Smith claimed to have seen God the Father prior to the year 1834, a full fourteen years after the event supposedly took place!

I realize this information might shock you, as you have told many, many people that Smith was immediately "persecuted" for telling people about his "vision." Yet, there simply is no evidence that this is true. Not only is there a massive *lack* of positive evidence, but there are many things that point to the conclusion that Smith did not begin to claim to have seen God the Father until the mid–1830s. Let me point out one of the most obvious proofs of this, taken from your own *Doctrine and Covenants,* 84:21–22. We read,

> ²¹And without the ordinances thereof, and the authority of the priesthood, the power of godliness is not manifest unto men in the flesh;
> ²²For without this no man can see the face of God, even the Father, and live.

This section in the D&C is dated September 22 and 23, 1832, the same time period as the handwritten account we examined above. Smith is speaking about the priesthood, a teaching that, as I shall show later, had begun to evolve in his mind only *after* the founding of the LDS Church on April 6, 1830. He asserts that it is impossible for a man who does not have the priesthood to see the face of God, that is, the Father, and live to tell about it. Now, hasn't this passage ever struck you as being a little strange? According to LDS teaching, Joseph Smith "received the priesthood" in 1829, yet, he supposedly saw God the Father in 1820, *nine years earlier!* Mormon leaders have come up with some ingenious ways around this obvious contradiction in Smith's teaching—most of the time it is said that D&C 84:21–22 is only valid when the Church is in existence upon the earth, though the passage in no way says this. Be that as it may, I would like to suggest to you that the reason Smith could say what he did in D&C 84:21–22 without even noticing that he was creating a contradiction is simply that at this point in time (1832) he had never claimed to have seen God the Father! Therefore, he could teach that men cannot see the Father without the priesthood and live without causing any problems at all—it was not till years later when he developed the concept of many gods that he had a problem. Smith's beliefs obviously evolved over time, and this is just another evidence that this is so. You must accept that either (1) D&C 84:21–22 is *wrong* (and therefore Smith is not a true prophet), or (2) Smith did not see God the Father in 1820 (and therefore Smith is not a true prophet), or (3) Smith did not claim to have seen God the Father until later, and the result is still the same—making up stories as you go along does not qualify one as a prophet, either.

I'm afraid that there is more, Elder Hahn. In 1834 a man by the name of E. D. Howe wrote and published what might be called the first "anti-Mormon" book. It was called *Mormonism Unveiled*. Howe gathered sworn affidavits from many of Smith's neighbors and acquaintances and spoke much of his early life—his involvement in an activity known as "money digging" and other activities that do not reflect well upon Smith. He attacks the Book of Mormon, and various other aspects of Mormonism. But he never mentions the First Vision. He never mentions that Smith claims to have seen God the Father. Why not? I believe the answer is simple—Smith had not yet claimed to have seen God the Father. *There simply is no reference in any writing—Mormon or otherwise—prior to the mid–1830s that clearly, unambiguously refers to the First Vision event and the supposed sighting of God the Father and Jesus Christ as two separate and distinct individuals.* Smith was still a monotheist at this point—he had not developed the ideas that come out so clearly in the King Follet discourse.

Rather than the modern concept of the First Vision, the early Mormon leaders spoke of *angels* visiting Joseph Smith—not just the angel Moroni, but angels appearing and telling Joseph that all the other churches were wrong. Look at just a few of these quotations from the *Journal of Discourses*:

But as it was in the days of our Savior, so was it in the advent of this new dispensation. It was not in accordance with the notions, traditions, and pre-conceived ideas of the American people. The messenger did not come to an eminent divine of any of the so-called *orthodoxy,* he did not adopt their interpretation of the Holy Scriptures. The Lord did not come with the armies of heaven, in power and great glory, nor send His messengers panoplied with aught else than the truth of heaven, to communicate to the meek, the lowly, the youth of humble origin, the sincere enquirer after the knowledge of God. But He did send His angel to this same obscure person, Joseph Smith jun., who afterwards became a Prophet, Seer, and Revelator, and informed him that he should not join any of the religious sects of the day, for they were all wrong; that they were following the precepts of men instead of the Lord Jesus; that He had a work for him to perform, inasmuch as he should prove faithful before Him. (Brigham Young, 2/18/1855, 2:171)

Joseph Smith had attended these meetings, and when this result was reached he saw clearly that something was wrong. He had read in the Bible and had found that passage in James which says, "If any of you lack wisdom let him ask of God that giveth to all men liberally and upbraideth not," and taking this literally, he went humbly before the Lord and inquired of Him, and the Lord answered his prayer, and revealed to Joseph, by the ministration of angels, the true condition of the religious world. When the holy angel appeared, Joseph inquired which of all these denominations was right and which he should join, and was told they were all wrong,—they had all gone astray, transgressed the laws, changed the ordinances and broken the everlasting covenant, and that the Lord was about to restore the priesthood and establish His Church, which would be the only true and living Church on the face of the whole earth. (President George A. Smith, 11/15/1863, 12:334)

. . . How did it commence? It commenced by an angel of God flying through the midst of heaven and visiting a young man named Joseph Smith, in the year 1827. That was the time of a great awakening among the sectarians of the day—a day of revivals and protracted meetings, when the people were called upon to join themselves to the sectarian churches. This young man looked around amid the confusion among the different sects, each proclaiming the plan of salvation differently, and each claiming it was right and that all others were wrong; in the midst of this contention he did not know which to join. While in this state of uncertainty he turned to the Bible, and there saw that passage in the epistle of James which directs him that lacks wisdom to ask of God. He went into his secret chamber and asked the Lord what he must do to be saved. The Lord heard his prayer and sent His angel to him, who informed him that all the sects were wrong, and that the God of heaven was about to establish His work upon the earth. This angel quoted many of the prophecies of Isaiah and Jeremiah, and told this young man that they were about to be fulfilled among the nations of the earth. . . . (Wilford Woodruff, 9/5/1869, 13:324)

Elder Hahn, do you think that if the First Vision story as you tell it today was being told over and over again back in 1869, that Wilford Woodruff, who eventually became the President of the Church, would not know about it? Clearly, in the citation immediately above, Woodruff connects today's "First Vision" with today's "second vision" and puts them all together. Really, if the early Mormon leaders believed so strongly that God the Father had appeared to Joseph Smith in 1820, would they be saying things like this? Yes, I know that Smith's "final edition" of the First Vision was published before he died. Why, then, would Woodruff and Young not know of it and preach it? First, remember that the *Pearl of Great Price* was not added to the canon of Mormon Scripture until 1880—and Joseph Smith's "History" is in the *Pearl of Great Price*. Secondly, I believe that statements like the ones made by Young and Woodruff further substantiate my contention that Smith's story "evolved" over time. At first he speaks of Jesus, then angels, and finally God the Father and Jesus Christ with a second visitation of the angel Moroni (though many early versions of the *Pearl of Great Price* even here were confused, calling this angel "Nephi"). The confusion of the early leaders after Smith's death is natural—Smith had *not* told one story all along, but had told many *different* stories between 1830 and his death in 1844.

So, as you can see, there is a great deal of evidence against the accuracy of the modern version of the First Vision. But, Elder Hahn, I have not yet commenced to begin! There is more . . . much more.

In 1967 the whole scene of Mormon historical research was radically altered by a Presbyterian minister by the name of Wesley Walters. His research into the early years of Joseph Smith's life—primarily in the period prior to the founding of the Church, including the writing of the Book of Mormon—was extensive. In 1967 he published an article entitled "New Light on Mormon Origins from the Palmyra (N.Y.) Revival.'' In this article Reverend Walters revealed the results of his study of a question that had not yet been addressed fully—was there really a revival in Manchester/Palmyra in 1820? Up to this point most everyone had just assumed that there had been. But Reverend Walters' research discovered that this was not so and laid the groundwork for later discoveries, *also* made by Wesley Walters, that would further demonstrate that Smith's story was the result of an evolutionary process of change over the years, and that it was not founded in historical reality.

The main thesis suggested by Walters in his 1967 article is this: The revivals described by Joseph Smith, as well as other early Mormon writers such as Oliver Cowdery and William Smith (Joseph's brother), did not take place in 1819/20, as Smith's account in the *Pearl of Great Price* asserts, but in fact they took place in 1824/25. Here is just *some* of the evidence he presented:

1) Both Oliver Cowdery (in his history of the church published 1834/35) and William Smith mention that a Reverend Lane, a Methodist minister, was a prime mover in the revivals. Cowdery dates the revival as taking place in 1823. Reverend Lane, Walters discovered, was not assigned to the Palmyra area until July of 1824.

2) William Smith also mentions a Presbyterian minister who took part in the revivals as well—Reverend Stockton. William Smith's account is most important, as it also relates the fact that Joseph Smith, Sr., did not like Reverend Stockton, and resisted his pleas that he and his family join the Presbyterian Church. It seems that Stockton had preached Alvin Smith's funeral, and had suggested (at least to Joseph Smith, Sr.'s mind) that Alvin had gone to hell because he did not belong to any church. Why is this important? Because Alvin Smith died November 19, 1823—again showing that the revivals had to take place *after* this point in time. Since both Stockton and Lane are mentioned, and Lane was only in Palmyra from July 1824 to January 1825, and Stockton was serving as pastor of the church at Skaneateles, New York, until June of 1822, and then was officially installed at the church in the Palmyra area in February of 1824, any revival in which *both* ministers were involved would have to have taken place in the fall of 1824 and would have continued on into the spring of 1825.

3) Walters discovered the actual account of the revivals in Palmyra written by Reverend Lane himself. According to this contemporary, eye-witness report, the revival broke out in September of 1824 among the Methodists. It spread quickly to the Presbyterians, and then to the

Baptists. By December it reached beyond the bounds of the town and into surrounding areas. It continued into the spring of 1825, and basically ended during the summer of that year. Numerous newspaper reports of the revivals in Palmyra/Manchester are to be found as well. Lane's description matches Joseph Smith's recounting of the revivals to a tee.

4) The records of the churches in the area also show that the revival spoken of by Smith took place in 1824/25. The Presbyterians reported 99 additions; the Baptists received 94, and the Methodists had an increase of 208. For towns the size of Palmyra and Manchester, numbers like these are truly "multitudes."

5) The records of the churches in the area also show that *no revival of this kind took place in 1819/20 in Palmyra/Manchester.* In fact, the records of the Methodist circuit in that area show that in 1819 they lost a net of 23 members; in 1820, they lost a net of 6 members, and in 1821 they lost even more—40 members. Hardly a big revival! The Baptist church in Palmyra did gain members—all of 6 in 1820, compared to *94 in 1825.* The other local Baptist churches reported losses in 1820, while the Palmyra Presbyterian Church reported no significant increase.

6) The denominational publications of the day carried the reports of an earlier revival in the Palmyra area in 1816/17, as well as the story of the great revival of 1824/25, but is *silent* about any such revival in 1819/20. Are we really to assume that such a revival as Smith describes was just passed over in silence by the religious publications?

Much more could be added with reference to the lack of revivals in 1820, but allow me quickly to move on to even more modern information. The source of this information is again Reverend Walters, whose activities of digging into all sorts of old historical records has resulted in rich rewards—well, depending on your viewpoint, I guess. Anyway, I won't go into a whole lot of detail on these particular findings as I've probably already given you enough information to be examining for the rest of the summer! But, as these new findings correlate *perfectly* with the previous research on the 1824 revival, I present these facts to you to show how *consistent* is the testimony to the 1824 revivals (in *opposition* to 1820 revivals).

The new information from Wesley Walters put together records photocopied by BYU in 1970, newly discovered land assessment records from Manchester township, and the records of "warning out" from Norwich, Vermont. What do these new historical records tell us?

First, as I pointed out when we reviewed Joseph Smith's 1838 version of things, the LDS story has been that the Smith family moved to Palmyra around 1816. They lived there for about two years, moving to Manchester in 1818. Then, as Smith says, "in the second year after our removal to Manchester" there were revivals, that being in 1820.

Recently the record of the Smiths being "warned out" of Norwich, Vermont, has been discovered. This "warning out" occurred March 15, 1816. "Warning out" was a common practice of the day. Nearly all newcomers, unless they were people of obvious means, were "warned out" within a year of their arrival. Why? Because the town had the responsibility of caring for the poor, and, if too many such individuals settled in an area, it would become a burden on the whole populace. So, if a family was "warned out" they would not be able to lay claim upon the town for long-term support. This "warning out" had to take place within a year of the family's arrival, or the town would become liable for providing support. Most towns performed this ritual soon after a poorer family would arrive, and therefore the Smiths most probably moved to Norwich in 1816 and lived there two years, until 1818. Walters also correlated Lucy Mack Smith's recollections of this time period with the weather records of the time and confirmed the conclusion that the Smiths did not leave Vermont until 1818, the date at which Mormon writers have the family moving to Manchester.

The next piece of information comes from the road-tax records of Palmyra. Here we find that the name of Joseph Smith, Sr., appears from 1817 *through* 1822. As all men 21 years of age and older as of April were required to be listed, Alvin Smith's name also appears in 1820. What does this tell us? It is evident that Joseph Smith, Sr., moved to Palmyra *before* the rest of his family, who joined him there at a later date. We know this from the fact that Alvin would have been listed in the 1819 road-tax records, had he been present in Palmyra (he turned 21 on February 11, 1819). Obviously, Lucy and the children did not arrive in time for Alvin's name to be found on the 1819 lists. It is important to note that Smith is listed as living in Palmyra until 1822—despite LDS scholars' contention that he moved from there *four years earlier* in 1818. Don't let all the dates become confusing—if the Smiths moved from Palmyra to Manchester in 1822, as this evidence suggests, then two years after this would be 1824, and this coincides perfectly with the information already presented on the revivals in the area.

Further information has come to light in the land assessment records for Manchester township. These records make it clear that the Smiths did not contract to buy the 100 acres of land for their farm in Manchester township until *after* June of 1820, for the tax rolls at that time show that all of the land was taxed to the original owners, the heirs of "Nicholas Evertson." However, in the tax rolls of 1821 we see that Joseph Smith, Sr., is taxed for the first time for 100 acres at $7.00 an acre—the price of raw, unimproved land at the time. The land is given the same value in the 1822 assessment, but in 1823 the value rises to $1,000, a jump of 40 percent, even though the other land values in the area only went up 4 percent in the same time period. This indicates that, for the first time, improvements were made to the land, including the construction of a home. What does this tell us? It suggests that the Smiths moved onto the land and lived there *after* the summer of 1822 and *before* the summer of 1823, which again perfectly matches with the data provided from all sources, especially the road-tax records mentioned above.

Land assessment records, road-tax records, records of "warning out," weather information, Lucy Mack Smith's own writings, church records, newspaper accounts, eyewitness accounts from the leading minister involved in the revivals—all pointing to the same conclusion. Joseph Smith fabricated the story years later, and, to make "room" for the First Vision without getting rid of Moroni and the golden plates, he "changes history" and pushes events back by four years. But, history has caught up with Joseph Smith.

When we put it all together, it is clear that the Smith family lived in Norwich, Vermont, in 1816. Joseph Smith, Sr., headed to New York prior to the rest of the family, arriving in 1817. In late 1819 or early 1820 the rest of the family arrived as well. They lived in Palmyra until 1822, when they moved to Manchester. Two years later there was a revival in the area, which extended into the spring of 1825. This is the revival spoken of by William Smith, Oliver Cowdery, and, aside from simply the error in the date, Joseph Smith himself.

You can see, immediately, some of the major problems this creates with LDS history. First, the 1820 date is a part of the canonized Scripture of the LDS Church—if the date is wrong, so is LDS "revelation." Secondly, if the revivals do not take place until 1824, and the first "spring day" that Smith can go into the woods to pray is in the spring of 1825, what happens to the "second vision" that supposedly takes place on September 21, 1823? Further, Smith says that he is undergoing this terrible persecution in 1820, yet, if no revivals have taken place, is he not *lying* about this "persecution"? It would seem so. If the "beginning of latter-day revelation" (as McConkie said above) is found to be incorrect, how can one trust the rest of it?

If you dig into these things, Elder Hahn, you will find that various Mormon scholars have been rather creative in their work of rescuing Joseph's story from hopeless contradiction. By centering *only* on one particular piece of information, it is possible to come up with some kind of alternative to the scenario presented above. Many of the attempted defenses have centered upon the Smiths' log cabin and its proximity to the border between Palmyra and Manchester. I honestly believe, however, that it is not possible to deal with *all* of the information and come up with a *consistent* historical story that allows Smith to have the First Vision in 1820. It just doesn't work.

Milton Backman, Jr., wrote a work entitled *Joseph Smith's First Vision*. Clearly, Backman attempts to deflect the impact of some of this information in his writing. Backman provides a number of appendices, some of which attempt to provide answers to the criticisms arising from Wesley Walters' 1967 article on the revivals. For example, "Appendix P" is entitled "Reports of Revivals Appearing in the Palmyra Register in 1820." The revivals reported, however, are not in Palmyra, but elsewhere, and none of them, of course, were connected with Reverends Lane or Stockton. None resulted in "multitudes" joining the churches in Palmyra. It seems that many modern LDS scholars would like to extend the meaning of "in the place where we lived" to an area covering hundreds of square miles, so desperate are they to find *some kind of revival* in 1820. The fact that the revival of 1824 is so *obviously* the same revival spoken of by Cowdery and William Smith is seemingly overlooked.

In the next appendix we find "A Reply to the Critics." In an obvious attempt to *stretch* the time periods given by Smith in his history, Backman asserts that the revivals might have taken place *prior to* 1819, and that Smith's "confusion" over what church he should join may have started much earlier in his life. Aside from the fact that this results in an obviously *strained* reading of Smith's history, it again only deals with one issue, not all together. Cowdery and William Smith are clear on which revivals resulted in Smith's going into the woods to pray—in fact, William Smith's account indicated that it was Reverend Lane who suggested the passage from James 1:5 to Joseph in the first place! As we know, Lane was nowhere near Joseph Smith until 1824; Backman's suggestion is shown to be mere wishful thinking.

The next issue presented is the idea that revivals did not always result in increases in church membership. While this is hardly ever true, the fact is that the revival of 1824/25 *did* result in an increase in church membership, and Joseph plainly indicated that the converts "united themselves to the different religious parties" to the point where some of his own family joined the Presbyterian Church! Simply pointing out that *some* revivals did not produce great increases in church membership does *not* prove that the revival mentioned by Smith did not. Smith's own words indicate otherwise.

Later in the same appendix Backman addresses the issue of the supposed "early persecution" of Smith. A quick perusal of the comments given shows that absolutely no positive evidence is brought forward that Smith ever even *claimed* to have seen God the Father in the 1820s. Rather, the main defense given is that "circumstantial evidence confirms Joseph Smith's testimony that in the early 1820s he was persecuted." But what does this mean? I will discuss in another letter how Smith was arrested and tried in 1826 for the crime of "glass looking," but that is a far cry from "persecution" for claiming to have seen God the Father and Jesus Christ! What "circumstantial evidence" does Backman produce? The only such evidence produced is the fact that various other individuals experienced religious bigotry or persecution during that time period. That's it. Nothing more. And while that in and of itself might be true, what does it have to do with Joseph Smith? Obviously, there is no answer to the simple fact that there is no evidence whatsoever that Smith claimed to have seen God the Father prior to the mid–1830s. In fact, this seems to be tacitly admitted by Backman when he writes,

> While tangible and circumstantial evidence confirms Joseph Smith's historical descriptions of events that occurred about the time of the First Vision, this evidence does not prove that he was visited by the Father and the Son in a peaceful grove in upper New York in the spring of 1820. The only route by which earnest seekers after truth will learn of the reality of the Restoration is through the guidance and power of the Holy Ghost. Faith is a gift of God, and a conviction that one of the greatest visions in the history of the world occurred in 1820 is one important element of that gift.

While I agree that faith is a gift of God, faith always has as its object the truth of God. True, Christian faith is placed in the Lord Jesus Christ, not Joseph Smith or his claims and visions. The Holy Spirit is the Spirit of truth, and He does not lead people to believe in that which is in reality untrue. Smith's story must be examined in the light of the fact that it claims to have *really happened* at a point in history. The facts of history, however, tell a different story. All the religious feelings in the world cannot change that fact.

I have decided to wait until my next letter to address the specific prophecies of Joseph Smith. I spent more time on the First Vision than I planned. I will start work on that letter at my earliest opportunity. If you don't mind, I will send that material to you as soon as I complete it, whether you reply to this letter first or not. If you have specific questions, or would like to talk, please remember that you have my number. I truly hope you will look into these things, Elder Hahn. If you continue to tell people that you *know* that Joseph Smith was a prophet of God, you *must* have the integrity to wrestle with these issues—not to find "some way out" but to *really know the truth*. If that means abandoning your faith in Joseph Smith, then please be willing to do so. May God bless you as you seek His will.

Sincerely,

James White

LETTER 7

Further Tests of Joseph Smith, "the Prophet"

Friday, June 29

Dear Elder Hahn,

As promised in my last letter, I am going to continue with my examination of Joseph Smith as a prophet of God, based upon the biblical guidelines of who is, and who is not, a "true prophet of God." I have not yet heard from you regarding my last letter (if something of that size can be called a "letter"!), but I would imagine it will take you a while to read it, digest the information, and do any research on your own before you would make any comments upon it. I hope you have had an opportunity to pick up the Tanners' books at the Christian bookstore, because what I will be discussing in the next two letters is covered in-depth in those works. I realize that you are *very* busy, but, as what we are discussing is directly relevant to the propriety of your missionary activities, I hope you will make time for study.

I have shared with you some of the reasons why I reject Smith's First Vision as being historically accurate and theologically correct. Now I would like to discuss the specific prophecies of Joseph Smith and ask the common question, "Did Joseph Smith give forth false or erroneous prophecies?" Obviously I believe that he did. I will gladly substantiate that position. However, I'd like to point something out first. In reality, the burden is upon you, Elder, and anyone else who would take the LDS position, to demonstrate *positively* that Smith was a prophet. *You* are claiming he was—it is not really my place to have to disprove an unsubstantiated claim. I will do so because I believe that your acceptance of Smith as a prophet is primarily "religious" in nature—what I mean by that is that you accept Smith as a prophet *not* because you have studied his prophecies or simply come to the conclusion on the basis of historical evidence that he was a prophet, but because you have been *told* that Smith was a prophet, and you have "faith" that he was.

I have attended a number of "fasting and testimony meetings" at LDS churches. I remember the first time I did so at the Glendale 6th Ward about ten years ago. I watched as individuals would get up behind the podium and give their testimonies. Many of the older folks would talk about various topics, but just about every single younger person said the same thing, and it ran something like this: "I testify that Jesus is the Christ, that Joseph Smith was a prophet of God, that (at that time) Spencer Kimball is a prophet of God, and that the Church is true. In the name of Jesus Christ, amen." The youngest folks frequently added "and I love my mommy and my daddy" as well. Now, Elder, if you were to say that over and over again from the time you were knee-high to a grasshopper until you were eighteen years of age, chances are pretty good that you would *really believe it* whether or not you had ever actually examined the evidence that could tell you whether Smith was, or was not, a prophet. Yes, I know, many Christians believe what they believe in the same way—I'm not picking on the Mormons for training their kids. What I *am* saying is that you cannot *assume* that Smith is a prophet, and then do whatever it takes to *keep* him as a prophet once the factual and historical data is examined. I am not saying that we should be unfair to Joseph Smith in examining his story—believe it or not, I really do try to be fair in weighing his claims. But, in my experience, most LDS are willing to close their eyes to the mountain of evidence that contradicts Smith's claims. I hope you will keep your eyes open and really consider the evidence about Joseph Smith.

You've probably seen some pretty long lists of "false prophecies" of Joseph Smith. I do believe that he made *many* prophetic errors during his lifetime—I fully believe that he expected Christ to return before the year 1890 or 1891. But, I don't expect you to put a whole lot of stock in my personal opinion. Also, I don't expect you to allow me to operate on a double standard either—in other words, I will not apply criteria to Joseph Smith that I would not allow to be applied to a biblical prophet such as Isaiah or Jeremiah or, yes, Jonah, too. So my list of false prophecies is considerably shorter than other versions you might have seen. It is not that I don't agree with some of those lists, or feel that they are inaccurate in what they say. I just don't feel it is best to attempt to multiply examples at the cost of the *effectiveness* of each individual example. For instance, it is common to hear someone allege that Joseph Smith "blew it" when, in Alma 7:10, the Book of Mormon says,

> And behold, he shall be born of Mary, at Jerusalem which is the land of our forefathers, she being a virgin, a precious and chosen vessel, who shall be overshadowed and conceive by the power of the Holy Ghost, and bring forth a son, yea, even the Son of God.

The allegation is that since Jesus was born in Bethlehem, not Jerusalem, Smith must have just been "mixed up" when he dictated this section and made a mistake. That may well be, but I do *not* believe that an airtight case can be made on the basis of this passage. It is *possible* that Bethlehem, being a small city, could be part of a larger area ("the land of our forefathers") called by the name of the major city of the area, Jerusalem. Since this is a logical possibility, I see no sense in pressing the issue. I'm willing to grant the benefit of the doubt in an instance such as this.

The same is to be said for a number of other prophecies of Joseph Smith. I don't feel that giving the benefit of the doubt in any way changes the simple fact that there are clear, unambiguous false prophecies in Smith's writings—in fact, by limiting the list of these prophecies to only those that are clearly errors on Smith's part I *strengthen* the case. So, in line with this, I shall offer you only two examples of false prophecies by Joseph Smith. They will not be taken from some obscure source, but both come directly from Mormon Scripture—specifically, the *Doctrine and Covenants*. And, to avoid the whole debate about whether a prophet has to say "thus saith the Lord" to be held accountable for the prophecy, both of these examples contain these important words. I begin with the 84th Section of the D&C, verses 1–5:

> [1]A revelation of Jesus Christ unto his servant Joseph Smith, Jun., and six elders, as they united their hearts and lifted their voices on high.
>
> [2]Yea, the word of the Lord concerning his church, established in the last days for the restoration of his people, as he has spoken by the mouth of his prophets, and for the gathering of his saints to stand upon Mount Zion, which shall be the city of New Jerusalem.

³Which city shall be built, beginning at the temple lot, which is appointed by the finger of the Lord, in the western boundaries of the State of Missouri, and dedicated by the hand of Joseph Smith, Jun., and others with whom the Lord was well pleased.

⁴Verily this is the word of the Lord, that the city New Jerusalem shall be built by the gathering of the saints, beginning at this place, even the place of the temple, which temple shall be reared in this generation.

⁵For verily this generation shall not all pass away until an house shall be built unto the Lord, and a cloud shall rest upon it, which cloud shall be even the glory of the Lord, which shall fill the house.

Let's outline the major elements of this passage: (1) it is "the word of the Lord" (verses 2 and 4); (2) "New Jerusalem" shall be built at this place (which according to verse 3 is in Missouri); (3) the temple would be built "in this generation"; (4) "this generation" would not pass away until the temple is built and the glory of the Lord rests upon it.

As I noted previously when referring to the major problems with D&C 84:21–22, this revelation was given September 22 and 23, 1832. The prophecy is that the temple would be built on the "temple lot" *within the time span of the current generation.* As we both know, Elder, no temple has been built on that site—in fact, the property is owned by another religious group that claims Joseph Smith as its founder, just as you. What then shall we say about this prophecy? I would like to note how the *friendly contemporaries* of Joseph Smith understood his words:

. . . Here we learn the arts of cultivation and of building; we learn to irrigate the land; we also, in many respects, prepare ourselves for a day when we shall go to the place that has been appointed for the building up of the city of Zion and for the building of the house which shall be a great and glorious temple, on which the glory of the Lord shall rest—a temple that will excel all others in magnificence that have ever been built upon the earth. Who is there that is prepared for this movement back to the centre stake of Zion, and where the architects amongst us that are qualified to erect this temple and the city that will surround it? We have to learn a great many things, in my opinion, before we are prepared to return to that holy land; we have to learn to practice the principles that we have been taught; we have to study to fill up every hour of our time in industrial pursuits and the acquisition of knowledge, and by economy and patience prepare ourselves as good and skilful workmen, as builders in the great building which our Father has prepared. And let me remind you that it is predicted that this generation will not pass away till a temple shall be built, and the glory of the Lord rest upon it, according to the promises. (Elder George A. Smith, *Journal of Discourses*, 3/10/1861, 9:71)

. . . From the day that God established this Church to the present the stream of revelation has continued to flow uninterruptedly. It flows pure for us to drink at until we are filled to repletion; and if we do not drink, it is our own fault. The servants of God are not to blame, for they have been laboring by day and by night, from the beginning, with us, as a people, to prepare us for the great things that are at our very doors, and that God intends to perform in this generation. I feel the importance of this, probably not as much as I ought, and wish to do; nevertheless, when I see the great events that are taking place at this time among the nations—when I view the destiny that awaits us as a people, and the great things God has in store for us, I almost feel as though I was a laggard on the path, and too slow entirely for the great events that are coming upon the earth. The day is near when a Temple shall be reared in the Center Stake of Zion, and the Lord has said his glory shall rest on that House in this generation, that is in the generation in which the revelation was given, which is upwards of thirty years ago. How much are we prepared for this? We talk about it, sing about it, and delight to dwell upon it; but are we prepared for this great manifestation of glory in our midst? (Elder George Q. Cannon, *Journal of Discourses*, 10/23/1864, 10:344)

. . . that is, that they should continue to gather, but not let their flight be in haste, and let all things be prepared before them. God led forth the Prophet that He had raised up to the western part of Missouri, and pointed out, by His own finger, where the great city of Zion should stand in the latter days, the great city of the New Jerusalem that should be built up on the American continent. I say He pointed out these things and gave direction to His people to gather to that land, and commanded them to lay the corner stone of a great and magnificent temple that was to be built during the generation in which the people then lived. The corner stone was laid in the summer of 1831, in Jackson County, State of Missouri. All these things were done by commandment and revelation, and in this way they still further showed, one to another and to all people as well as to the heavens, that they did love the Lord their God.

. . . God has been with us from the time that we came to this land, and I hope that the days of our tribulations are past. I hope this, because God promised in the year 1832 that we should, before the generation then living had passed away, return and build up the City of Zion in Jackson County; that we should return and build up the temple of the Most High where we formerly laid the corner stone. He promised us that He would manifest Himself on that temple, that the glory of God should be upon it; and not only upon the temple, but within it, even a cloud by day and a flaming fire by night.

We believe in these promises as much as we believe in any promise ever uttered by the mouth of Jehovah. The Latter-day Saints just as much expect to receive a fulfilment of that promise during the generation that was in existence in 1832 as they expect that the sun will rise and set to-morrow. Why? Because God cannot lie. He will fulfill all His promises. He has spoken, it must come to pass. This is our faith. (Elder Orson Pratt, *Journal of Discourses*, 5/5/1870, 13:360, 362)

It seems to me, Elder Hahn, that these men who were called "apostles of Christ" and who took active roles of leadership in the LDS Church understood D&C 84:4–5 in such as way as to preach that the temple would be built in Jackson County, Missouri, *within the generation that was alive in 1832*. There can be no mistaking that. And with reference to the meaning of "generation" in this passage, I note as well the definition given by Bruce R. McConkie when, in *Mormon Doctrine*, page 310, he addresses the term and says, "A generation may be measured in terms of the life of the oldest persons who live in a particular period" (D&C 45:30–31; 84:4–5). Note he specifically references D&C 84:4–5 in his definition.

One common defense given by LDS people is to be found in D&C 124:49–51, a "revelation" that was given after the Mormons were driven from Missouri, resulting in an inability to build the temple as D&C 84:1–5 had commanded. It is clear that the early apostles, such as those cited above, did not think that this passage released them from the *imperative* action of building the temple; however, modern LDS refer to it as an "explanation" of Smith's prophecy. The passage reads,

[49]Verily, verily I say unto you, that when I give a commandment

to any of the sons of men to do a work unto my name, and those sons of men go with all their might and with all they have to perform that work, and cease not their diligence, and their enemies come upon them and hinder them from performing that work, behold, it behooveth me to require that work no more at the hands of those sons of men, but to accept of their offerings.

⁵⁰And the iniquity and transgression of my holy laws and commandments I will visit upon the heads of those who hindered my work, unto the third and fourth generation, so long as they repent not, and hate me, saith the Lord God.

⁵¹Therefore, for this cause have I accepted the offerings of those whom I commanded to build up a city and a house unto my name, in Jackson county, Missouri, and were hindered by their enemies, saith the Lord your God.

This is, of course, a very convenient "out" for Joseph and his prophecy. However, it is also just as obviously an excuse for a false prophecy. Is God incapable of controlling the actions of men? In the Old Testament the enemies of Israel came against them and defeated them *as a part of God's will and purpose* (Isaiah 10:5–19). Nothing is mentioned about this by Smith—in fact, the blame is put squarely on the enemies of the LDS Church, not upon any sinfulness of the people. Are God's decrees really dependent upon the actions of evil men, Elder Hahn? The tests of a prophet given by the Holy Spirit in Deuteronomy 13 and 18 do not make a place for "failures due to enemies that are too strong to be resisted." Smith, upon failing to rear the temple in Missouri, came up with an excuse for the failure—but his excuse does not keep him from falling under the condemnation of God's Word as a false prophet.

No matter how you stretch it, Elder, this prophecy fails the test. Even if you were very liberal and gave to the word "generation" a meaning of a full hundred years, you still ran out of time over fifty years ago. Smith said it was the word of the Lord; he defined the exact event that would take place—the temple would be built at a specific location that is known to this day; he defined the time parameters in which it would take place—*prior* to the death of *that* generation. It is a classic prophecy that can be tested—and it fails.

I will address one more false prophecy and leave the subject at that, for as I noted in my last letter, it only takes *one* false prophecy to disqualify a person as a true prophet of God. The next prophecy is found in D&C, Section 114:

Verily thus saith the Lord: It is wisdom in my servant David W. Patten, that he settle up all his business as soon as he possibly can, and make a disposition of his merchandise, that he may perform a mission unto me next spring, in company with others, even twelve including himself, to testify of my name and bear glad tidings unto all the world.

²For verily thus saith the Lord, that inasmuch as there are those among you who deny my name, others shall be planted in their stead and receive their bishopric. Amen.

The revelation is dated April 17, 1838, and was given to Joseph Smith at Far West, Missouri. Daniel Ludlow, in his book *A Companion to Your Study of the Doctrine and Covenants* cites Joseph Fielding Smith's words from *Church History and Modern Revelation*, 2:85:

On April 17, 1838, the Prophet received a revelation for David W. Patten who had for some time been located in Missouri and with Elder Thomas B. Marsh was maintaining a steady influence amidst the opposition of disaffected brethren, including the three who had been appointed to preside, David Whitmer, William W. Phelps and John Whitmer. The Lord called upon Elder Patten to settle up his business as soon as possible, make a disposition of his merchandise, and prepare to take a mission the following spring, in company with others to preach the Gospel to all the world. . . . Elder Patten obedient to this revelation took steps to meet this call which had come to him. Events were to develop, however, which would change the nature of his mission before the following spring could arrive.

And what was the nature of these "events" spoken of by Joseph Fielding Smith? David W. Patten died October 25, 1838, in the "battle of Crooked River." He never lived to see the "next spring" as the revelation predicted. He went on no mission with eleven other men.

Why would the Lord command that Patten should prepare for a mission the next spring, which would take place in the company of eleven other men, if the Lord knew that he would not live to see that day? Is it not clear that here we have Joseph Smith, in the name of the Lord, giving instructions to a man to prepare for a mission, when in fact Smith did not know that Patten was going to die? How could he? This shows the *human* origin of Smith's "revelation." He did not know the future, and could not foresee what was going to happen to Patten.

But the true God knew what was going to happen. That is why, in fact, the true God of the Bible is able to *mock* the idols of the peoples in Isaiah 40 through 48—more than once he challenges these false gods to predict the future, but they cannot. Any predictions they make, any commands they may give, can be overthrown by something as simple as a musketball fired by a fleeing man near the Crooked River.

I have encountered three common responses from LDS people to this prophecy and its failure. The first runs like this: "All blessings are based upon obedience and faithfulness. Patten must not have remained faithful to his calling, and as a result lost his blessing. See, even the second verse talks about people denying God's name, and others being planted in their stead." Folks who respond in this way obviously know little of the historical situation in which Patten died. Note the story from the *Documentary History of the Church,* pages 170–175: According to the DHC, a "mob" takes some Mormon brethren captive. "Captain" David W. Patten (who was also an apostle, by the way) is dispatched with about seventy-five men to catch the mob and rescue the prisoners. Early on the morning of Thursday, October 25, they approach the mob's camp:

> Fifteen of the company were detached from the main body while sixty continued their march till they arrived near the ford of Crooked river, (or creek) where they dismounted, tied their horses, and leaving four or five men to guard them, proceeded towards the ford, not knowing the location of the encampment. It was just as the dawning of light in the east, when they were marching quietly along the road, and near the top of the hill which descends to the river that the report of a gun was heard, and young Patrick O'Banion reeled out of the ranks and fell mortally wounded. Thus the work of death commenced, when Captain Patten ordered a charge and rushed down the hill on a fast trot, and when within about fifty yards of the camp formed a line. The mob formed a line under the bank of the river, below their tents. It was yet so dark that little could be seen by looking to the west, while the mob looking towards the dawning light, could see Patten and his men, when they fired a broadside, and three or four of the brethren fell. Captain Patten ordered the fire returned, which was instantly obeyed, to great disadvantage in the darkness which yet continued. The fire was repeated by the mob, and returned by Captain Patten's company, who gave the watchword "God and Liberty." Captain Patten then

ordered a charge, which was instantly obeyed. The parties immediately came in contact, with their swords, and the mob was soon
put to flight, crossing the river at the ford and such places as they
could get a chance. In the pursuit, one of the mob fled from behind
a tree, wheeled, and shot Captain Patten, who instantly fell, mor-
tally wounded, having received a large ball in his bowels. . . .

I went with my brother Hyrum and Lyman Wight to meet the
brethren on their return, near Log creek, where I saw Captain Patten
in a most distressing condition. His wound was incurable.

Brother David Patten was a very worthy man, beloved by all
good men who knew him. He was one of the Twelve Apostles, and
died as he had lived, a man of God, and strong in the faith of a
glorious resurrection, in a world where mobs will have no power
or place. One of his last expressions to his wife was—"Whatever
you do else, O! do not deny the faith". . . .

Saturday, 27.—Brother Patten was buried this day at Far West,
and before the funeral, I called at Brother Patten's house, and while
meditating on the scene before me in presence of his friends, I
could not help pointing to his lifeless body and testifying, "There
lies a man that has done just as he said he would—he has laid down
his life for his friends."

As can be seen, Patten died "strong in the faith" according to Joseph
Smith himself. The mention of men denying God's name and being
removed from their bishoprics in verse 2 of Section 114 is not in any
way in reference to Patten—rather, it is in reference to a situation that
existed at the time in Far West where David Whitmer, John Whitmer,
and William W. Phelps were "causing trouble" and had been removed
from the local presidency. See Elder George Q. Cannon's narration of
these events in his *Life of Joseph Smith the Prophet*, pp. 221–224.

The most common defense raised is that Patten did indeed serve a
mission—but his mission was in the "spirit world" where he went after
he died. But surely you can see that this is not what the "revelation"
says at all. There are far too many objections to this understanding.
First, did the eleven other men also die and go to the "spirit world"
with Patten? Second, what is "spring" in the spirit world? Are there
seasons there? Third, the revelation says that he would "testify of my
name and bear glad tidings unto all *the world,*" not to the spirit world.
This revelation clearly speaks of an *earthly* mission to take place in the
spring of 1839, not a spiritual mission to take place in the fall of 1838.

Finally, a not very common, but plausible defense is this: This is not really a prophecy of a future event, but simply a command to David Patten to be *prepared* to go on a mission. It is not *explicitly* stated that he was going to *go* on the mission at all, rather he was simply to be *prepared* to do so. You can probably see immediately, Elder Hahn, how this perspective can create a route of escape for Joseph Smith by stretching the revelation to the breaking point so as to avoid his obvious error. It is true that the spring mission itself is not *specifically* prophesied; however, the spring mission is given as the reason why Patten was to settle up his business and make a disposition of his merchandise. There is not even a hint that this was just a "theoretical" mission, or simply a "testing" of Patten's obedience. None of this comes from the text itself. It is interesting to note with reference to this the fact that according to the DHC 3:23, another revelation was received by Smith on the same day as Section 114, though this revelation is not a part of the D&C. It reads:

> Verily thus saith the Lord, let my servant Brigham Young go unto the place which he has bought, on Mill Creek, and there provide for his family until an effectual door is opened for the support of his family, until I shall command him to go hence, and not to leave his family until they are amply provided for. Amen.

Note that both of these "revelations" were giving specific directions for specific men to do specific things. There is nothing in the "revelation" for Brigham Young that would lead us to believe that he was "testing" him, nor is there anything in D&C 114 that would suggest that this was anything but a straightforward command to prepare for a mission that was *supposed* to take place the next spring, that being the spring of 1839. Smith had no way of knowing Patten would not live that long—Patten was only about thirty-eight years of age. Also, the fact that he says that this mission would be conducted "in the company with others, even twelve including himself" indicates that Smith was laying out the specifics of *how* the mission would be run. *If* this is really the "word of the Lord" as Smith claims, why would God speak in this way? Why would God describe the *specifics* of a mission that would never take place?

So here you have two prophecies, Elder Hahn. Remember at the outset that I said that it is not really my duty to have to prove them wrong, but, since you claim Smith was a prophet, it is really your duty to prove them right! Can you do so? Can you show me how D&C 84:1–

5 has come to pass within the time frames contained within the revelation itself? Can you show me how D&C 114 came to pass within the time frame provided again within the text itself? If not in *either* case, you have to admit that you cannot call Joseph Smith a true prophet in the biblical sense of the word.

Now before I move on to a few other issues, I want to make some brief comments in reply to a common objection that is raised to the criticism of Joseph Smith on the basis of prophecies such as those given above and others. It normally follows along this line: We allege that Smith gave false prophecies because what he said didn't come to pass, but biblical prophets did the same thing. The classic example? Jonah. According to the Bible, Jonah was commanded to "go to Ninevah, that great city, and cry against it; for their wickedness is come up before me" (Jonah 1:2). Of course, Jonah ran the other way. After his run-in with a rather large-size fish, God repeated His command: "Arise, go unto Ninevah, that great city, and preach unto it the preaching that I bid thee" (Jonah 3:2). Unfortunately, we are not given an exact recitation of what the LORD told Jonah to say—all we get is a very brief quotation from Jonah 3:4: "Yet forty days, and Ninevah shall be overthrown." Not a very moving message, it would seem. But, according to the Bible, the people of Ninevah were convicted—so much so that it is said that they "believed God, and proclaimed a fast, and put on sackcloth, from the greatest of them even to the least of them." The king gave forth a decree and said, "Who can tell if God will turn and repent, and turn away from his fierce anger, that we perish not?" Obviously, somehow, the people knew that God was angry at them for their sin, though we don't find any mention of sin in Jonah's one-line message (which seems to indicate that there was more to what he said than just the proclamation of the destruction of Ninevah).

So, though Jonah had said that Ninevah was going to be destroyed in forty days, it wasn't. The people repented of their sins (though we know historically that this repentance didn't last long—they went back to their evil ways and were destroyed as a result), and God spared the city, at least temporarily. So poor Jonah is found in chapter 4 sitting on the hillside waiting to see God destroy the wicked capital of the enemy of his people, the Assyrians. When it doesn't happen he is all upset, and says, in the modern vernacular, "I knew it, I knew it, I knew it! It's just like I said back in Tarshish—I knew you were a God of mercy and kindness, that you are slow to anger, and that you are willing to hold back your punishment of man. I knew it all along" (Jonah 4:2). In fact, he is so upset, he wants to die (4:3). So God shows him a great object lesson with the gourd in chapter 4, and closes with a strong rebuke of Jonah's self-centeredness and Israel's lack of concern for other nations. But, all of that aside, is not Jonah *technically* a false prophet? He *said* Ninevah would be overthrown in forty days, *and it wasn't*. Christians accept Jonah's book as part of the Bible, so why accuse Joseph Smith as being a "false prophet" when we don't do the same thing for Jonah?

A principle of God's dealing with men is brought out by the prophet Jeremiah in the eighteenth chapter of his prophecy, verses 7–10:

> At what instant I shall speak concerning a nation, and concerning a kingdom, to pluck up, and to pull down, and to destroy it, if that nation, against whom I have pronounced, turn from their evil, I will repent of the evil that I thought to do unto them. And at what instant I shall speak concerning a nation, and concerning a kingdom, to build and to plant it, if it do evil in my sight, that it obey not my voice, then I will repent of the good with which I said I would benefit them.

As creatures, we are locked in time, and only see things as they come to pass. The eternal God of the Bible, not being limited by time, is working out His purpose and decree in the world. From our viewpoint, we hear God proclaiming destruction upon a nation for its wickedness. The people repent of their sin and cry to God for mercy. The only way they could possibly think this would do any good is if God is able to be merciful, to withdraw the sentence of death. Now, we know that from God's perspective, that was His will all along—the decree of judgment was designed specifically to bring about repentance—but the people didn't know that. In the same way, God decreed judgment on Judah, and, though she had so many times cried to God for deliverance in the past and had received mercy, this time she did not, and was destroyed in 586 B.C. To us it looks just like it is found in Jeremiah— if people will repent, mercy will be found. If people will be disobedient, judgment will be found.

Jonah's message to the city of Ninevah was directly connected with their sin. It was a message of judgment upon sin. The specific event proclaimed by Jonah was a destruction that was *due to sin*. The men repented of their sin. God was merciful and did not destroy them. Does this make Jonah a false prophet?

No, it doesn't. Remember that a false prophet is one who speaks a word in the name of the LORD that God did not command him to speak. God commanded Jonah to say what he did for a specific purpose (Deuteronomy 18:20). Jonah's message was one relevant to sin and judgment, and the true God of Israel is a God of mercy and compassion. If we were to say that a message of judgment cannot possibly in any way be rescinded, then we would have no hope, for the Bible teaches that "the soul who sins shall die" (Ezekiel 18:4). If any sinner receives eternal life, then God has lied. We both realize that this is not the case and are thankful that God can have mercy, too. Jonah *knew* that God was a merciful God, and became furious when God proved himself as merciful to Gentiles as He had been so often to the Jews.

But when we turn to the prophecies of Joseph Smith, particularly the two we examined above, do we find the same situation? Is Smith speaking of sin and judgment? No, he is not. The events he prophesied are not acts of judgment upon sinful men. They are specific occurrences—in the case of D&C 84:1–5, the building of a temple, in D&C 114, the performance of a mission. There is no relationship between Smith's prophecies of events and Jonah's proclamation of the destruction of Ninevah.

Joseph Smith and the Occult

Aside from the clear false prophecies in direct statements such as the above, and aside from the false teachings about God found in Smith's sermons as seen previously, there is yet another set of historical facts that demonstrates that Joseph Smith was not led by the Holy Spirit of God as a prophet. This set of facts has to do with Smith's lifelong involvement with the occult—magic, superstition, and the like. Let me refer to three points of information that will lay a foundation for my position.

Frazer's Magazine of February 1873, (pp. 229–230), carried an account of a court action that took place in March of 1826. The defendant was Joseph Smith, Jr., The charge was "glass looking." Here is what is found in *Frazer's Magazine* on that date:

STATE OF NEW YORK *v.* JOSEPH SMITH.

Warrant issued upon written complaint upon oath of Peter G. Bridgeman, who informed that one Joseph Smith of Bainbridge was a disorderly person and an imposter.

Prisoner brought before Court March 20, 1826. Prisoner examined: says that he came from the town of Palmyra, and had been at the house of Josiah Stowel in Bainbridge most of time since; had small part of time been employed by Stowel on his farm, and going to school. That he had a certain stone which he had occasionally looked at to determine where hidden treasure in the bowels of the earth were; that he professed to tell in this manner where gold mines were a distance under ground, and had looked for Mr. Stowel several times, and had informed him where he could find these treasures, and Mr. Stowel had been engaged in digging for them. That at Palmyra he pretended to tell by looking at this stone where coined money was buried in Pennsylvania, and while at Palmyra had frequently ascertained in that way where lost property was of various kinds; that he had occasionally been in the habit of looking through this stone to find lost property for three years, but of late had pretty much given it up on account of its injuring his health, especially his eyes making them sore; that he did not solicit business of this kind, and had always rather declined having anything to do with this business.

Josiah Stowel sworn: says that prisoner had been at his house something like five months; had been employed by him to work on farm part of time; that he pretended to have skill of telling where hidden treasures in the earth were by means of looking through a certain stone; that prisoner had looked for him sometimes; once to tell him about money buried in Bend Mountain in Pennsylvania, once for gold on Monument Hill, and once for a salt spring; and that he positively knew that the prisoner could tell, and did possess the art of seeing those valuable treasures through the medium of said stone; that he found the (word illegible) at Bend and Monument Hill as prisoner represented it; that prisoner had looked through said stone for Deacon Attleton for a mine, did not exactly find it, but got a p— (word unfinished) of ore which resembled gold, he thinks; that prisoner had told by means of this stone where a Mr. Bacon had buried money; that he and prisoner had been in search of it; that prisoner had said it was in a certain root of a stump five feet from surface of the earth, and with it would find a tail feather; that said Stowel and prisoner thereupon commenced digging, found a tail feather, but money was gone; that he supposed the money moved down. That prisoner did offer his services; that he never deceived him; that prisoner looked through stone and described Josiah Stowel's house and outhouses, while at Palmyra at Simpson

Stowel's, correctly; that he had told about a painted tree, with a man's head painted upon it, but means of said stone. That he had been in company with prisoner digging for gold, and had the most implicit faith in prisoner's skill.

Arad Stowel sworn: says that he went to see whether prisoner could convince him that he possessed the skill he professed to have, upon which prisoner laid a book upon a white cloth, and proposed looking through another stone which was white and transparent, hold the stone to a candle, turn his head to book, and read. The deception appeared so palpable that witness went off disgusted.

McMaster sworn: says he went with Arad Stowel, and likewise came away disgusted. Prisoner pretended to him that he could discover objects at a distance by holding his white stone to the sun or candle; that prisoner rather declined looking into a hat at his dark coloured stone, as he said it hurt his eyes.

Jonathan Thompson says that prisoner was requested to look for chest of money; did look, and pretended to know where it was; and prisoner, Thompson, and Yeomans went in search of it; that Smith arrived at spot first; was at night; that Smith looked in hat while there, and when very dark, and told how the chest was situated. After digging several feet, struck upon something sounding like a board or plank. Prisoner would not look again, pretending that he was alarmed on account of the circumstances relating to the trunk being buried, [which], came all fresh to his mind. That the last time he looked he discovered distinctly the two Indians who buried the trunk, that a quarrel ensued between them, and that one of said Indians was killed by the other, and thrown into the hole beside the trunk, to guard it, as he supposed. Thompson says that he believes in the prisoner's professed skill; that the board which he struck his spade upon was probably the chest, but on account of an enchantment the trunk kept settling away from under them when digging; that notwithstanding they continued constantly removing the dirt, yet the trunk kept about the same distance from them. Says prisoner said that it appeared to him that salt might be found at Bainbridge, and that he is certain that prisoner can divine things by means of said stone. That as evidence of the fact prisoner looked into his hat to tell him about some money witness lost sixteen years ago, and that he described the man that witness supposed had taken it, and the disposition of the money:

And therefore the Court find[s] the Defendant guilty. Costs: Warrants, 19c. Complaint upon oath, 25½ c. Seven witnesses, 87½ c. Recongnisances, 25 c. Mittimus, 10 c. Recongnisances of witnesses, 75 c. Suboena, 18 c.—$2.68

This account was referred to in Fawn Brodie's famous work *No Man Knows My History*. Mormon leaders, up until the early 1970s, were quick to deny the authenticity of the *Frazer's* account. Mormon Apostle John Widtsoe said, "There is no existing proof that such a trial was ever held" (*Joseph Smith—Seeker after Truth*, p. 78) and Dr. Hugh Nibley wrote in his book *The Myth Makers* that ". . . if this court record is authentic it is the most damning evidence in existence against Joseph Smith" and that if the record were indeed authentic it would be "the most devastating blow to Smith ever delivered" (p. 142). And Mormon scholar Francis Kirkham wrote, "If any evidence had been in existence that Joseph Smith had used a seer stone for fraud and deception, and especially had he made this confession in a court of law as early as 1826, four years before the Book of Mormon was printed, and this confession was in a court record, it would have been *impossible* for him to have organized the restored Church" (*A New Witness for Christ in America*, Vol. 1, p. 387).

But guess who discovered the 1826 trial bill in the basement of the county jail in Norwich, New York, in 1971? Yes, Reverend Wesley Walters. The trial bill was found among many other such bills from 1826. Here is what it looks like:

Note that it says,

<table>
<tr><td></td><td>Same</td><td></td></tr>
<tr><td></td><td>vs.</td><td>Misdemeanor</td></tr>
<tr><td></td><td>Joseph Smith</td><td></td></tr>
<tr><td></td><td>The Glass Looker</td><td>To my fees in examination</td></tr>
<tr><td></td><td>March 20, 1826</td><td>of the above cause   2.68</td></tr>
</table>

Further documents have been found since that time that substantiate this historical event—Smith was examined with reference to "glass looking" in March of 1826. Later study caused Wesley Walters to view this incident not as a full-blown trial, but as what we might call a "pre-trial hearing" that would have resulted in a later full trial had Joseph Smith not taken what Joel K. Noble called "leg bail" (i.e., he fled the area). Walters pointed out that even Joseph Smith called a pre-trial hearing a "trial" in his 1843 journal (*An American Prophet's Record: The Diaries and Journals of Joseph Smith*, ed. Scott H. Faulring, pp. 432–33), so there is no need to quibble over terminology. The point is that Smith was actively involved in abominable practices and ran afoul of the law in the process. Think about what this means, Elder Hahn. According to Joseph Smith's story in the *Pearl of Great Price*, this examination took place six years *after* Joseph's supposed vision of God the Father and Jesus Christ; and it takes place right in the middle of the period of time when Smith is supposedly meeting with the angel Moroni each September twenty-first. What is he doing "glass looking" and digging for buried treasure when God is supposedly preparing him to be a prophet? "Glass looking" is very similar to modern occultic practices such as using a crystal ball—"New Agers" would love it! Is this a proper activity for a "prophet"?

"Well," someone might say, "Smith could have repented of this kind of activity later on. It does not automatically disqualify him as a prophet." But do we have evidence that he repented of his involvement in the occult? No, but we *do* have evidence that he *continued* his involvement. One such piece of evidence is to be found in comparing the above trial account, our knowledge of the common magical folklore of the day, and the Book of Mormon. Remember that Josiah Stowell and Jonathan Thompson, in their sworn testimony to the court, had spoken of the buried treasure "slipping away" or "going down" when they got close to it. This was a common belief of the day—that buried treasure that was protected by a curse or a spell would slip down into the earth so that it could not be recovered except by those who knew how to get around the magic spell. It is fascinating to note that this same kind of magic belief is to be found in the Book of Mormon! Note the following passages:

> And these Gadianton robbers, who were among the Lamanites, did infest the land, insomuch that the inhabitants thereof began to hide up their treasures in the earth; and they became slippery, because the Lord had cursed the land, that they could not hold them, nor retain them again. (Mormon 1:18)

And behold, if a man hide up a treasure in the earth, and the Lord shall say—Let it be accursed, because of the iniquity of him who hath hid it up—behold, it shall be accursed. And if the Lord shall say—Be thou accursed, that no man shall find thee from this time henceforth and forever—behold, no man getteth it henceforth and forever. (Helaman 12:18–19)

Behold, we lay a tool here and on the morrow it is gone; and behold, our swords are taken from us in the day we have sought them for battle. Yea, we have hid up our treasures and they have slipped away from us, because of the curse of the land. O that we had repented in the day that the word of the Lord came unto us: for behold the land is cursed, and we cannot hold them. (Helaman 13:34–36)

So we have Joseph Smith examined for "glass looking" in March of 1826; in the Book of Mormon we find more evidence of his belief in the same magical practices found in the testimony given at his trial. Then, by comparing changes made in the revelations contained in the 1833 *Book of Commandments* and the same revelations in the 1835 *Doctrine and Covenants*, we can find *further evidence* of Smith's continuing fascination with the occult. Note first verse 3 of Section 76 of the 1833 *Book of Commandments* (emphasis made to point out changes):

O remember, these words and keep my commandments. Remember this is your gift. Now this is not all, for you have another gift, which is the gift of *working with the rod:* behold it has told you things: behold there is no other power save God, that can cause this *rod of nature,* to work in your hands, for it is the work of God; and therefore whatsoever you shall ask me to tell you by that means, that will I grant unto you, that you shall know.

The modern D&C contains this revelation as Section 8, verses 5–9. The date of this revelation is given as April, 1829, in the 1833 *Book of Commandments,* in the 1835 D&C, and in the modern edition. The 1835 D&C contained this revelation as Section 34, but *changed* the wording:

O remember these words, and keep my commandments.—Remember this is your gift. Now this is not all thy gift; for you have another gift, *which is the gift of Aaron:* behold it has told you many things: behold there is no other power save the power of God that can cause this *gift of Aaron* to be with you; therefore, doubt not, for it is the gift of God, and you shall hold it in your hands, and do marvelous works; and no power shall be able to take it away out of your hands; for it is the work of God. And therefore, whatsoever you shall ask me to tell you by that means, that will I grant unto you and you shall have knowledge concerning it.

Originally in this revelation to Oliver Cowdery, Smith spoke of the "rod of nature." Supposedly, Cowdery's ability to "work the rod" (as in a dowsing rod, a common magical practice of the day) was from God and was an avenue of revelation ("whatsoever you shall ask me to tell you by that means, that will I grant unto you, and you shall know"). However, sometime between the original publication of this revelation and the printing of the 1835 D&C, Smith decided it would be best to "edit" this revelation, and in so doing he not only expanded it a good deal (as you can see above), but he changed the obvious "working with the rod" to the *less* obvious "gift of Aaron." Now, he is still referring to the "witching rod" of common occultic practice—the dowsing rod was also called the "rod of Aaron" by some practitioners. Modern Mormons might be tempted to think that he is here referring to the Aaronic priesthood; however, it must be remembered that this revelation is dated April 1829, and Joseph Smith did not allegedly receive the priesthood until May 15, 1829. *If* Smith were trying to "smuggle" the priesthood into an earlier revelation, he got his dates mixed up in the process. More likely, he is using a less blatant (and more religious) name for the practice of using the dowsing rod.

In passing I would like to point out that the idea that Joseph "edited" his revelations to fit his evolving theology is founded on numerous examples of his doing just that. As David Whitmer pointed out clearly in his book *An Address to All Believers in Christ*, Smith had developed the concept of the "priesthood" *after* the founding of the Church in 1830. The modern Section 27 of the D&C has had over 400 words added or deleted, nearly *all* of which were relevant to the priesthood. *No indication is made in the introduction that this has taken place.* It is still indicated that this revelation was given in August of 1830, when, in fact, barely six verses of the eighteen are to be found in the original version.

Aside from all of this, we see that *after* the founding of the LDS Church, even as late as 1833, Joseph sees no problem with a revelation that speaks of a "rod of nature" and in 1835 only changes the name to the "gift of Aaron" while still, in all probability, retaining the same concept of the dowsing rod. Joseph and his close companions (such as Oliver Cowdery) are still deeply influenced by magic beliefs, and there is no sign of repentance from this practice.

But what about Joseph's later life? Is there any indication that Joseph continued in these kinds of activities? There certainly is. Below I am providing you with another photocopy, this time of a small item that Joseph Smith owned. The copy gives you the front (left) and back (right) of the piece:

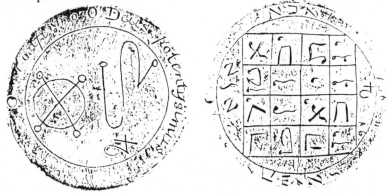

Mormon scholar LaMar C. Berret stated that the piece was in Joseph Smith's pocket the day he died (*The Wilford Wood Collection,* 1972, Vol. 1, p. 173). Charles Bidamon stated that Emma Smith "prized this piece (the one shown above) very highly on account of its being one of the prophet's intimate possessions" (Charles E. Bidamon Affidavit, *Wood Collection,* #7-J-b–21). The same affidavit also stated, "I certify that I have many times heard her say, when being interviewed, and showing the piece. That it was in the Prophet's pocket when he was martyred at Carthage, Ill."

For many years people were not aware of its true nature, nor its significance. Then in 1974 Dr. Reed Durham of the Mormon Historical Association discovered the actual identity of the item. He discovered that it is actually a "Jupiter talisman," an occultic item that when properly invoked was supposed to gain its possessor "riches, and favor, and power, and love and peace," and further that the bearer of this object would "obtain the power of stimulating anyone to offer his love to the possessor . . . whether from a friend, brother, relative, or even any female" (speech before the Mormon History Association on April 20, 1974, from *Mormon Miscellaneous,* published by David C. Martin,

Vol. 1, no. 1, October 1975, p. 15). Talismanic magic is a very common aspect of the occult, and was very popular in the folklore and superstition of upstate New York at the beginning of the nineteenth century.

If you would like confirmation of Dr. Durham's identification, then drop by just about any secular bookstore, find the "occult" section, and look for a book entitled *The Magus: A Complete System of Occult Philosophy* by Francis Barrett, published by Citadel Press, and look on pages 175 and 142. I have the book in my library, if you'd like to stop by and take a look at it.

The 1826 examination for "glass looking"; the Book of Mormon talking about treasures becoming "slippery"; sections of the *Book of Commandments* and *Doctrine and Covenants* either containing magic practices or changed to hide them; and, at the very end of his life, Smith is still owner of a "magic talisman." What does the Bible say about all of this? God is very clear:

> When thou art come into the land which the LORD thy God giveth thee, thou shalt not learn to do after the abominations of those nations. There shall not be found among you anyone who maketh his son or his daughter pass through the fire, or that useth divination, or an observer of times, or an enchanter, or a witch, or a charmer, or a consulter with familiar spirits, or a wizard, or a necromancer. For all that do these things are an abomination unto the LORD: and because of these abominations the LORD thy God doth drive them out from before thee. (Deuteronomy 18:9–12)

Joseph Smith's magic practices were an abomination to God, and no true prophet of God would ever be involved in them. In Acts 19:19 we see that those who truly accepted Christ as their Savior repudiated their connections with the occult, and destroyed all the paraphenalia they owned that had anything to do with it. Yet Joseph Smith, even *after* supposedly meeting God the Father and Jesus Christ in 1820, *continued* to practice magic and sorcery.

Elder Hahn, we are told to examine those who claim to be prophets. If he gives a false prophecy, or if he prophesies in the name of another God, he is a false prophet. Joseph Smith not only gave false prophecies, and prophesied in the name of a false god, as we saw above, but he willfully rejected the Lord's command to abstain from any sort of sorcery or magic or occultism. The Holy Spirit of God would *never* give someone a testimony that Joseph Smith was a true prophet—*only one of the spirits Joseph Smith called on and used in his occultic practices would do that.*

With your permission, I will send this letter out and follow it up with another letter on the Book of Mormon and the results of my research into that document. I will also add a few comments on the Book of Abraham as well, though that is quite a topic in and of itself! I believe that you have my number, and I'd like to mention that the vast majority of the sources I've cited are in my library, or I know how to track them down. Again, I challenge you to look into these things for yourself. My door is open to you.

Truly yours,

James White

The Book of Mormon and the Book of Abraham

Thursday, July 5

Dear Elder Hahn,

I received your note yesterday morning. I have considered just how to respond, and feel that I should indeed continue on and address the topic of the Book of Mormon. But I will do so in such a way as to answer your request. You wrote,

> Mr. White, I appreciate all the study you have done on these issues, and I admit that I am not a Bible scholar, and cannot give you an answer for each topic you have presented. However, I ask you, I strongly urge you, to *pray about the Book of Mormon.* I have done this, and though I can't explain all of it to you, I *know* that it is true. Before you write to me and attack that book, please pray about it and ask God, in accordance with Moroni 10:4–5, if it is true.

I hope you understand, Elder Hahn, that I have heard the same plea from innumerable LDS individuals over the past number of years. It is probably the single most consistent comment made by those who would seek to defend your faith, and, of course, it is something that every single LDS missionary in the field urges prospective converts to do. And, on the surface, it seems quite innocent, quite simple. Who wouldn't be willing to pray to God and ask if something is true?

Me. Why? Many, many reasons. Let's start with a real obvious example and go from there. Would you pray and ask God if the *The*

Satanic Bible by Anton LaVey is true? No, I am not making a direct comparison of the two, I am just asking you if you would pray about such a book. I know that I would not. Why? Because it is obviously not from God—it is blatantly false. So to come to God and say, "Lord, I know that you have already revealed that this is in error, but I'd like to ask again, just in case," is to *test God*. Now, if an angel came to you and told you to go murder someone, would you pray about this? I wouldn't, and for the same reason. God has said that murder is wrong, and I am not going to get "a second opinion" on the matter. I remember all too well what happened to the Israelites when they didn't believe what God said about entering into the promised land. That generation wandered in the wilderness for forty years until a new generation came along, *one that would take God at His word*. Testing God is not a wise procedure—He has revealed His truth, and expects to be believed on that basis. If someone came to me and said "pray about this new teaching that says that Jesus really didn't rise from the dead, but rather was re-created as a spirit-creature" I wouldn't so much as begin to bend my knees—such a teaching is directly opposed to scriptural truth, and I will not question God's truth by praying about it.

So, Elder, I believe that God has revealed His truth in the Word of God, the Bible, and I will not *question His truth* by praying about the truth of something that is opposed to biblical teaching. To do so would not only be an act of unbelief, but of *rebellion against God,* and could have dire results. Those who question God may just be left open to all sorts of falsehoods and errors.

Now in reference to your plea for me to pray about the Book of Mormon, my main reason for refusing to do so is simply because I have *read and studied* the Book of Mormon, and have found it to be in contradiction to clear biblical teaching. So, though it may not teach what *The Satanic Bible* teaches, it is *still* in opposition to God's truth. I will not disbelieve God to pray about it. I shall enumerate my reasons for feeling the Book of Mormon is in error below. I do want to make a comment on the passage you cited above, Moroni 10:4–5. It reads,

> And when ye shall receive these things, I would exhort you that ye would ask God, the Eternal Father, in the name of Christ, if these things are not true; and if ye shall ask with a sincere heart, with real intent, having faith in Christ, he will manifest the truth of it unto you, by the power of the Holy Ghost. And by the power of the Holy Ghost ye may know the truth of all things.

This passage is used more often by LDS people than any other passage of which I am aware. But if you examine it closely, you see that it is a "no win" proposition that is presented here. In other words, if a person does not feel that the Holy Spirit testifies that the Book of Mormon is true, then the Mormon has a ready answer, provided by the passage itself—such a person must not have a sincere heart, or have real intent, or have faith in Christ. *If* a person were sincere, honest, and believed in Christ, *then* that person would *have to know*, by the power of the Holy Spirit, that the Book of Mormon is true. That makes things quite easy, for everyone who doesn't believe in the Book of Mormon must be dishonest at heart, lack the proper intentions, and certainly does not have faith in Christ. I reject this kind of concept—any group (and many of them have done so in the past and continue to do so today) can construct such a "test" about the truthfulness of *their* teachings. They would look at you, if you do not believe them, and say "Well, you didn't ask in proper faith." What would you say to them, Elder? You'd have nothing to say, since you are doing the same thing every time you ask someone to follow the council of this passage.

I do not question the sincerity of your testimony to the Book of Mormon, Elder. I am sure that you *feel* that you have received a testimony. But as I mentioned in my very first letter, your *feelings* do not

---

A Brief Description of the Book of Mormon

For those not familiar with the contents of the Book of Mormon, I here provide a *very brief* summary: The main story of the Book of Mormon revolves around a migration undertaken by a pious Jew named Lehi. This man lived in Jerusalem prior to the destruction of that city by the Babylonians in 586 B.C. Around the year 600 B.C. (modern editions of the Book of Mormon provide dates at the bottom right of each page) Lehi is instructed to leave Jerusalem because of the impending destruction. He does so, taking his sons, including Nephi and Laman, who become the main characters in the story. Lehi takes his family south into the "wilderness." Eventually they come to "large waters" which some have assumed to be connected, somehow, with the Indian Ocean. They build a ship and come across the "large waters" (ostensibly the Pacific, though this is not directly stated) and arrive in the "promised land." Upon landing, two distinct groups quickly develop—the descendants of Nephi, known as Nephites, and the descendants of Laman, known as Lamanites. These two groups are frequently battling with one another. The Nephites are righteous people by and large, and the Lamanites are wicked people. We read with reference to the Lamanites in 2 Nephi 5:21:

And he caused the cursing to come upon them, yea, even a sore cursing,

make the Book of Mormon *true*. Your feelings could quite simply be wrong. I have feelings as well, and my feelings are that the Book of Mormon is wrong. So we obviously have to look to other sources for a determination of the truth or falsity of that book.

I said that I would not pray about the Book of Mormon, and I told you why—such would be *testing God*. What I would like to do is give you five reasons why I do not feel that *anyone* should pray about the Book of Mormon. Each of these items I bring up is discussed further in *Mormonism: Shadow or Reality?*, pages 50–125J.

Reason #1: The Book of Mormon is historically inaccurate. This can be seen in a number of ways, but I will limit my points to two areas: first, the concept of "Book of Mormon archaeology" and second, the close relationship between Ethan Smith's book *View of the Hebrews* and the plot of the Book of Mormon.

In the summer 1973 issue of *Dialogue: A Journal of Mormon Thought,* Dr. Michael Coe, Professor of Anthropology and Curator in the Peabody Museum of Natural History at Yale University, author of many books on Meso-American archaeology and history, such as *Mexico, The Maya, In the Land of the Olmec,* and *The Maya Scribe and His World,* made the following comments:

---

because of their iniquity. For behold, they had hardened their hearts against him, that they had become like unto flint; wherefore, as they were white, and exceedingly fair and delightsome, that they might not be enticing unto my people the Lord God did cause a skin of blackness to come upon them.

Numerous "prophets" are described during the period between the arrival of the people of Lehi on this continent and the coming of Jesus Christ after His death in Jerusalem. Many of these "prophets" parallel biblical stories, even to the point of quoting New Testament passages! Alma's story, for example, is so closely parallel to Paul's in the New Testament that few could possibly question Joseph Smith's borrowing from Paul's story. See, for example, Mosiah 27:11, 13. The Book of Mormon prophets know the exact name of Jesus Christ long before He comes. When Christ does come, He establishes a church with twelve apostles, just like He did in the Old World. He quotes the Sermon on the Mount (almost verbatim from the King James Version of the Bible), and also from the book of Acts (which had not been written yet) in 3 Nephi 20:23–26. He also offers to His apostles whatever they desire. Nine of them desire to "speedily" enter into the kingdom, and this is granted (3 Nephi 28:2–3). But the three other Nephite apostles request that which John, the beloved apostle of the New Testament, supposedly desired. We read,

⁶And he said unto them: Behold, I know your thoughts, and ye have

Mormon archaeologists over the years have almost unanimously accepted the Book of Mormon as an accurate, historical account of the New World peoples between about 2000 B.C. and A.D. 421. They believe that Smith could translate hieroglyphs, whether "Reformed Egyptian" or ancient American. . . . Let me now state uncategorically that as far as I know there is not one professionally trained archaeologist, who is not a Mormon, who sees any scientific justification for believing the foregoing to be true, and I would like to state that there are quite a few Mormon archaeologists who join this group. . . .

. . . The bare facts of the matter are that nothing, absolutely nothing, has ever shown up in any New World excavation which would suggest to a dispassionate observer that the Book of Mormon, as claimed by Joseph Smith, is a historical document relating to the history of the early migrants to our hemisphere. (pp. 41–42, 46)

You have, no doubt, heard otherwise. I can't tell you how many Mormons have an uncle who is friends with an archaeologist who has discovered what he thinks is the city of Zerahemla (or Bountiful, or Zeezrom, etc.). I remember talking with one of the tour guides at Temple Square in Salt Lake City. We had just watched a film on the subject of supposed archaeological evidence for the Book of Mormon, and I was

---

desired the thing which John, my beloved, who was with me in my ministry, before that I was lifted up by the Jews, desired of me.

7Therefore, more blessed are ye, for ye shall never taste of death; but ye shall live to behold all the doings of the Father unto the children of men, even until all things shall be fulfilled according to the will of the Father, when I shall come in my glory with the powers of heaven.

8And ye shall never endure the pains of death; but when I shall come in my glory ye shall be changed in the twinkling of an eye from mortality to immortality; and then shall ye be blessed in the kingdom of my Father.

So Mormons believe that not only is John, the apostle of the New Testament, still alive (John 21:20–22 being used as support), but there are also three Nephite apostles somewhere on this continent who are working on celebrating their 2,000th birthday. After Jesus is received up into heaven, the Nephites and Lamanites experience about 200 years of peace in Christian brotherhood. But after this the old wars start up again. Mormon (after whom the book is named) leads the Nephite armies beginning around A.D. 322 There are nearly continuous battles until in approximately A.D. 385 Mormon sends an "epistle" to the leader of the Lamanites, asking him to meet for one final battle "in the land of Cumorah" by a hill which was called Cumorah (which just happens to be quite near Joseph Smith's home in upstate New York). In the ensuing battle the Nephites are almost totally extermi-

asking questions and pointing out a number of inconsistencies in the film—like showing a structure that looks *just like* the famous Mayan temple at Tikal in the background of a picture of Jesus Christ as He visits the Nephites. With great honesty he assured me that he *knew* of specific archaeological evidence that *proves* the Book of Mormon to be true. He could not give me any specifics—few ever do—but I could tell he was *real* honest about it. I know of no reason why the statement made by Mormon anthropologist M. Wells Jakeman thirty years ago is not still valid today:

> It must be confessed that some members of the "Mormon" or Latter-day Saint Church are prone, in their enthusiasm for the Book of Mormon, to make claims for it that cannot be supported. So far as known to the writer, no non-Mormon archaeologist at the present time is using the Book of Mormon as a guide in archaeological research. Nor does he know of any non-Mormon archaeologist who holds that the American Indians are descendants of the Jews, or that Christianity was known in America in the first century of our era. (*The Changing World of Mormonism*, pp. 135–36)

About seven years later John L. Sorenson seemed to hold the same view as Jakeman:

> Various individuals unconnected with these institutionalized activities have also wrestled with the archaeological problem. Few of the writings they have produced are of genuine consequence in archaeological terms. Some are clearly on the oddball fringe; others have credible qualifications. Two of the most prolific are Professor Hugh Nibley and Milton R. Hunter; however, they are not qualified to handle the archaeological materials their works involve. . . .
> . . . As long as Mormons generally are willing to be fooled by (and pay for) the uninformed, uncritical drivel about archaeology

---

nated—by A.D. 401 only Moroni, Mormon's son, is alive (Mormon 8:6–8). Moroni "hides up" the record (the plates) in approximately A.D. 421. The Lamanites become the modern-day Indians, meaning that the Indians are actually Semitic in origin, Jews by bloodline.

Modern defenders of the Book of Mormon have departed somewhat from the story given above, asserting that the Book of Mormon story actually took place over a very small area (instead of the large area one would gather from reading the book itself), probably in the area of Guatemala. The Hill Cumorah, these defenders state, is somewhere in Central America, not in upstate New York, despite the fact that the LDS Church leadership continues to state otherwise.

and the scriptures which predominates, the few L.D.S. experts are reluctant even to be identified with the topic. (*Dialogue: A Journal of Mormon Thought*, Spring 1966, pp. 145, 149)

Eleven years after the statements by Dr. Coe quoted above, in August of 1984, a Sunstone symposium was held in Salt Lake City. The topic was "Book of Mormon Archaeology." One of the speakers was Dr. John Carlson from the University of Maryland; the other two speakers were from Brigham Young University—Ray Matheny and Bruce Warren, both professors of Anthropology. Taking my information from a typewritten copy of notes recorded at the seminar, I note that Dr. Carlson, who is not a Mormon, pointed out that basically there is no such thing as "Book of Mormon archaeology" in the true sense of the term. To have "Book of Mormon archaeology" one needs a base of data to examine, and there is none. He said,

"The Book of Mormon itself has not made a significant contribution to New World archaeology. Ask any New World archaeologist. . . . To the best of my knowledge there are no non-LDS archaeologists who are influenced by the Book of Mormon or who use it in their work. I don't know of a single soul."

His words are strangely reminiscent of Dr. Coe's words, are they not? Dr. Carlson also discussed what he called "picture books." I believe he was referring to the numerous publications available today that really make a mockery out of true archaeology by showing a pit and saying it is a baptismal font, or showing a painting of a Mayan temple and saying that the people who built it were Nephites or Lamanites, or by talking about a certain stele and saying it is Lehi and the Tree of Life. As he said himself,

They are a wealth of misinformation and a disservice. . . . I will just tell you in my reading of some of those older books that purport to deal with Book of Mormon archaeology, they are making errors on the level of someone saying, oh yeah, Salt Lake City, that's in Wyoming. Now if you read a book that said that, Salt Lake City, Wyoming, you'd say, "This guy doesn't know what he's talking about!" And believe me, . . . that is the level of scholarship. . . .

Even the Church leadership has made comments about the common claims made by Mormons regarding the Book of Mormon and archaeology. In the Church Section of the *Deseret News* of July 29, 1978, we read,

> The geography of the Book of Mormon has intrigued some readers of that volume since its publication. But why worry about it?
>
> Efforts to pinpoint certain places from what is written in the book are fruitless because the record does not give evidence of such locations in terms of modern geography.
>
> Attempts to designate certain areas as the Land Bountiful or the site of Zarahemla or the place where the Nephite city of Jerusalem sank into the sea "and waters have I caused to come up in the stead thereof" can bring no definitive results. So why speculate?
>
> To guess where Zarahemla stood can in no wise add to anyone's faith. But to raise doubts in people's minds about the location of the Hill Cumorah, and thus challenge the words of the prophets concerning the place where Moroni buried the records, is most certainly harmful. And who has the right to raise doubts in anyone's mind?
>
> Our position is to build faith, not to weaken it, and theories concerning the geography of the Book of Mormon can most certainly undermine faith if allowed to run rampant.
>
> Why not leave hidden the things that the Lord has hidden? If He wants the geography of the Book of Mormon revealed, He will do so through His prophet, and not through some writer who wishes to enlighten the world despite his utter lack of inspiration on the point.
>
> Some authors have felt "called upon" to inform the world about Book of Mormon geography and have published writings giving their views. These books, however, are strictly private works and represent only their personal speculations.

It is not exactly accurate to say that there is "no data" relevant to the Book of Mormon's representation of life on this continent between, say, 600 B.C. and A.D.421—such information exists. The problem is, on the matters of material culture, it is by and large *contradictory* to the Book of Mormon. Let me explain.

The main reason I feel the Book of Mormon is not what it is claimed to be is that there is such a *mountain* of evidence that it is *not* an "ancient record" but is rather a *modern production, produced in upstate New York around the year 1830*. The description of the material culture given by the Book of Mormon is an example of just this. The description of the Nephites and the Lamanites is, quite obviously, a depiction of an *Old World culture,* and it is contradictory in many important points to the *facts* that we know of the *New World cultures.*

Here are some examples: Relevant to the warfare presented in the Book of Mormon, we note that the Nephites and Lamanites supposedly had such items as bows and arrows with quivers, swords, javelins, daggers, metal armor and shields, and horse-drawn chariots. Historically speaking, this continent did not see a horse until the Spanish brought some over from the Old World; so, horse-drawn chariots would be a little difficult to build. The New World cultures lacked any kind of advanced metallurgy during the "Book of Mormon" period, so they lacked iron, steel and brass, and therefore did not have armor or swords. Alma chapter 11 describes a complex system of coinage, including such items as a "senine of gold, a seon of gold, a shum of gold, and a limnah of gold" (Alma 11:5) along with a "senum of silver, an amnor of silver, and ezrom of silver, and an onti of silver" (11:6). Needless to say, Elder, no such coins have ever been found. The people who lived on this continent did not use a system of coinage—gold, for example, was so common that it was not considered particularly precious with reference to barter and trade. Instead, we know from our historical studies that jade and cocoa beans were prized highly and used widely as a form of currency in trade. Both items are conspicuous by their absence from the Book of Mormon. The description of the culture of the Book of Mormon peoples with reference to metal objects and objects of warfare is *very similar* to the Old World cultures with which Joseph Smith would be familiar—yet, the actual fact of the New World cultures is found to be contradictory to the Book of Mormon story.

The Book of Mormon also betrays its modern origin in what it says about other aspects of the life of the culture of its time. The agricultural "scene" in the Book of Mormon is *remarkably* like that of 1830 in New York State—crops such as corn, barley, cows, oxen, asses, sheep, and swine are said to have been part of the food and animal scene of Nephite and Lamanite culture, yet the actual inhabitants of this hemisphere did not have these things during the "Book of Mormon period."

Most of those Mormons who hazard a guess at the basic area in which the Book of Mormon story took place point to Central America as the prime candidate. The large majority of Book of Mormon research has taken place in Central and northern South America, and the films shown in the Church's visitors' centers unashamedly show Mayan ruins as being the actual creations of the Nephites and Lamanites. If this is so, then we can be more specific about the culture that we know existed between B.C. 600 and A.D. 421.

Certain aspects of the real culture of Meso-America would not have been known to Joseph Smith, such as their usage of jade and cocoa beans mentioned above. Another aspect has to do with the impact of weather upon the native peoples. Drought and flood were the expected norm of the times. Entire cultures disappeared due to climatic changes. Yet, in the Book of Mormon only two droughts are mentioned.

The religions of the inhabitants of Central America bear no resemblance whatsoever to Christianity. Oh, yes, I know, I have read entire articles about supposed parallels between native religions and Christian belief—and each one was so obviously *strained to the limit of rational belief* that it made me wonder how such individuals, who are obviously well trained and learned, could produce such material. Have you ever wondered, Elder, why the only material that is produced seeks to find even the smallest point of contact rather than dealing with the *real* issue—that being the incredible *differences* between the religions of the native peoples of America and Christianity?

But I see I am going long—there is so much that could be said about this subject. Let me add one more thing concerning the obvious modern nature of the Book of Mormon. A book was published in 1823 and then reprinted in 1825 entitled *View of the Hebrews*. It was written by Ethan Smith. Mormon scholar and General Authority, B.H. Roberts, possibly the greatest scholar Mormonism has ever known, upon reading *View of the Hebrews*, recognized the many parallels between this book and the story of the Book of Mormon. The book suggests (five to seven years *before* the Book of Mormon) such things as the concept of the American Indians being the offspring of the Hebrews; it utilized the book of Isaiah in the Bible in seeking to establish the story's basis (over seventeen chapters of Isaiah's prophecy are to be found in the Book of Mormon). It even spoke of a book preserved by the Indians for a long period of time and then buried! Roberts found eighteen parallels between the Book of Mormon and *View of the Hebrews*. It is very likely that the subject matter of the book would be at the very least *familiar* to Joseph Smith, even if he himself did not read the book. What is certainly true is that the concept of the Indians being Hebrew in origin was known in upstate New York *prior to* the publication of the Book of Mormon.

Joseph Smith would have had access to plenty of sources of information and speculation upon which he could have based the story of the Book of Mormon.

In other studies done later in his life, B.H. Roberts continued to struggle with the Book of Mormon. Most Mormons today are not aware of the fact that Roberts came to some very interesting conclusions. For example, many LDS today argue that Joseph Smith could not possibly have written the Book of Mormon himself, due to his lack of schooling. Yet Roberts wrote,

> One other subject remains to be considered in this division of the "study" here conducted, viz.—was Joseph Smith possessed of a sufficiently vivid and creative imagination as to produce such a work as the Book of Mormon from such materials as have been indicated in the preceding chapters—from such common knowledge as was extant in the communities where he lived in his boyhood and young manhood; from the Bible, and more especially from the *View of the Hebrews*, by Ethan Smith? That such power of imagination would have to be of a high order is conceded; that Joseph Smith possessed such a gift of mind there can be no question. (B.H. Roberts, *Studies of the Book of Mormon*, University of Illinois Press, 1985, p. 243)

And how did Roberts conclude this section of his study?

> In the light of this evidence, there can be no doubt as to the possession of a vividly strong, creative imagination by Joseph Smith, the Prophet, an imagination, it could with reason be urged, which, given the suggestions that are to be found in the "common knowledge" of accepted American antiquities of the times, supplemented by such a work as Ethan Smith's *View of the Hebrews*, would make it possible for him to create a book such as the Book of Mormon is. (*Studies of the Book of Mormon*, p. 250)

Indeed, when reviewing a particular aspect of the Book of Mormon text, Roberts made these startling statements:

> There were other Anti-Christs among the Nephites, but they were more military leaders than religious innovators, yet much of the same kidney in spirit with these dissenters here passed in review; but I shall hold that what is here presented illustrates sufficiently the matter taken in hand by referring to them, namely that *they are*

all of one breed and brand; so nearly alike that one mind is the author of them, and that a young and undeveloped, but piously inclined mind. *The evidence I sorrowfully submit, points to Joseph Smith as their creator.* It is difficult to believe that they are the products of history, that they come upon the scene separated by long periods of time, and among a race which was the ancestral race of the red man of America. (*Studies in the Book of Mormon,* p. 271, emphasis added)

So when I suggest to you that Joseph Smith did indeed have the ability to write the Book of Mormon, and that he drew from contemporary sources to do so, I am only coming to the same conclusions that one of the greatest minds in LDS history presented many years ago.

Reason #2: The Book of Mormon contains false doctrine. The second reason that I will not disbelieve God by praying about the Book of Mormon is the fact that the book contains false doctrine—teachings that are directly opposed to biblical truth. The Book of Mormon does *not* teach the vast majority of the distinctive LDS doctrines such as the plurality of gods, exaltation to godhood, the priesthood concepts, temple endowments, ordinances, and so on. Why not? Joseph Smith did not believe in these things at the time he wrote the Book of Mormon. But, despite this, the work still contains teachings that are opposed to biblical truth. Let me list two examples:

For we labor diligently to write, to persuade our children, and also our brethren, to believe in Christ, and to be reconciled to God; for we know that it is by grace that we are saved, after all we can do. (2 Nephi 25:23)

The key phrase, Elder, is ". . . it is by grace that we are saved, after all we can do." While I wish to hold the whole discussion of salvation and God's grace for the proper time, I would like to point out that we are *not* saved by grace "after all we can do," but we are saved by grace *in spite of all we have done!* The concept put forth here by Joseph Smith is directly opposed to the teachings of Paul in the books of Romans and Galatians. Some have tried to soften the teaching presented here, but the task seems impossible in light of the comments made in the Bible dictionary in the back of the LDS version of the Bible under the topic of "grace":

. . . This grace is an enabling power that allows men and

women to lay hold on eternal life and exaltation after they have expended their own best efforts.

Divine grace is needed by every soul in consequence of the fall of Adam and also because of man's weaknesses and shortcomings. However, grace cannot suffice without total effort on the part of the recipient. Hence, the explanation, "It is by grace that we are saved, after all we can do." (2 Nephi. 25:23)

The same false concept of God's grace can be found in Moroni 10:32 as well. I hope to address this passage at a later time.

The next example of false doctrine in the Book of Mormon is found in Mosiah 15:1–4:

> [1]And now Abinadi said unto them: I would that ye should understand that God himself shall come down among the children of men, and shall redeem his people.
>
> [2]And because he dwelleth in flesh he shall be called the Son of God, and having subjected the flesh to the will of the Father, being the Father and the Son—
>
> [3]The Father, because he was conceived by the power of God; and the Son, because of the flesh; thus becoming the Father and Son—
>
> [4]And they are one God, yea, the very Eternal Father of heaven and of earth.
>
> [5]And thus the flesh becoming subject to the Spirit, or the Son to the Father, being one God, suffereth temptation, and yieldeth not to the temptation, but suffereth himself to be mocked, and scourged, and cast out, and disowned by his people.

It is evident that, at the time of the writing of the Book of Mormon, Joseph Smith did not believe in a plurality of gods at all. He was still, technically at least, a "monotheist." The presentation of the Father and the Son here in Mosiah 15 is a common *mis*conception among untaught people regarding the Trinity. If Joseph Smith had attended revival meetings with his parents, he would have come away, had he not had further specific instruction, with just the concept that is put forward in this passage—and it is a blatant misunderstanding of the doctrine of the Trinity, which he is here attempting to put forward. The Book of Mormon is filled with statements about there being "one God" (1 Nephi 13:41; 2 Nephi 31:21; Alma 11:28, 35, 14:5; Mormon 7:7; "The Testimony of the Three Witnesses"), and just how the Father and the Son are related, then, is what Smith addresses here in Mosiah 15. In the process he manages to present an ancient heresy of the Church known as *modalism* or *Sabellianism.* In any case, it is not the proper teaching that is found in the Bible concerning the nature of God, especially with reference to the Father and the Son. Instead, this shows that it is out of harmony with the Bible, and therefore does not find its origin with the Holy Spirit. Rather, it is clearly the production of Joseph Smith.

Reason #3: The Book of Mormon was given by a false prophet. I have already provided my reasons for believing this in our previous correspondence. Smith qualified as a false prophet under both of the tests set forth by the Bible, and therefore a book of "scripture" that he would introduce to the world would not come from God. And let me note in passing here as well the fact that Smith's belief in magic and occultic practices, since they appear in the Book of Mormon as well, would further disqualify the book as a revelation of God.

Reason #4: The Book of Mormon has grave textual problems. Again, here, one could write a book just about this topic—there are so *many* items that could be addressed. As I've said, the Book of Mormon betrays itself as a modern composition in a number of ways, and one of the most obvious is the presence of *anachronisms* in the text.

During the Middle Ages it was common for people to assume that things had always been the way they were then. If you've looked at paintings done in Europe during that time you may have noted that even biblical characters such as David or the apostles lived in castles and dressed just like the people of the twelfth or thirteenth centuries. The Renaissance dispelled this concept from people's minds, and they were able to see that things had indeed changed a good bit over time.

Sometimes, however, people are not aware just when a particular item was invented or came into use. In Joseph Smith's case, he inserted a number of items into the Book of Mormon in such a way as to make them *anachronistic;* either they were not to be found in the culture of that time, or they simply had not yet been invented. Though they might have been common to Joseph Smith, they would not have been known to the *real* ancient inhabitants of this hemisphere. I have already mentioned, with reference to archaeology and the Book of Mormon, some of these items. For example, a horse in the New World is an anachronism—there were no horses here prior to the arrival of the Spanish. If the Book of Mormon was actually written by a scribe living nearly two thousand years ago, he would not have been discussing horses, as he would never have seen one.

In 1 Nephi 11:33 (and elsewhere) the "cross" is mentioned. The cross upon which Jesus died would have had no meaning to the Nephites or Lamanites, as crucifixion was not a practice in and around Jerusalem when Lehi and his family supposedly left that place. It was Persian in origin, and became widely used under the Romans, five centuries after Lehi landed in the New World. The word would have meant nothing to someone who lived on this continent two millennia ago.

The "Bible" is mentioned in 2 Nephi 29:3. Again, this was a common term to Joseph Smith, but what would it have meant to an inhabitant of this hemisphere long ago? Nothing at all. The term was not applied to the Scriptures until long after Lehi left the Old World.

In 1 Nephi 18:12 we read of a "compass" being used by Nephi on the trip across the ocean to the "promised land." The compass was not invented till some time later. You might say that this was simply a "miracle," but why do we not find examples of compasses among the descendants of these people?

Joseph Smith claimed that there was "no Greek or Latin upon the plates from which I, through the grace of God, translated the Book of Mormon" (*Teachings of the Prophet Joseph Smith*, p. 299). Yet, we find numerous Greek terms in the Book of Mormon. For example, "synagogues" are mentioned in Alma 16:13. The term *synagogue* comes from the Greek term *sunagoge*. This is also an historical anachronism—that is, the concept of synagogues did not exist when Lehi left Jerusalem—it developed at a later point. So how did the term, and the concept, end up in the Book of Mormon? We also find Greek in 3 Nephi 9:18: "I am the Alpha and Omega, the beginning and the end." *Alpha* is the first letter of the Greek alphabet, *omega* is the last. But what would a Nephite have made of this? It would be like my saying, "I am the drummon and the lophar." Doesn't communicate much, does it? In fact, the final words of the Book of Jacob (7:27) must have struck the Nephites a little strangely, "Brethren, adieu." I doubt many of them knew French.

I mentioned above the fact that sections of the New Testament are quoted in the Book of Mormon—how could this be? How can Acts be quoted before it is written? Do you *really* think that Peter was actually quoting the Book of Mormon when he gave his speech in Acts 3:22–26 (in comparison with Deuteronomy 18:15, 18–19/3 Nephi 20:23–

26)? The Tanners have provided many, many examples of the obvious plagiarism of the King James Version of the Bible (also known as the "Authorized Version" or AV) in *Mormonism: Shadow or Reality?* on pages 74–79. Not only is the Old Testament copied, but the New Testament as well.

When Jesus comes to the New World in 3 Nephi, He quotes the "Sermon on the Mount" from the King James Version of the Bible (3 Nephi 12–14) with a few rather intriguing additions and changes. But, quite interestingly, He quotes a number of sections from the KJV that are not a part of the earliest and best texts of the New Testament (such as 3 Nephi 13:13), and he also cites Matthew 5:22 that uses the term *Raca*. If these people were using "reformed Egyptian" or "reformed Hebrew," what would the Aramaic term *Raca* mean to them?

This brings us to another question: Is the fact that Joseph Smith *obviously* used the King James Version of the Bible a problem? I have pointed out problems with the text that would be problems only if Joseph Smith had received the words of the Book of Mormon from God himself. In other words, if God just "gave the thoughts" to Joseph Smith and allowed him to express those thoughts in his own words, a number of the above problems would be circumvented (though certainly not *all* of them—this would not explain, for example, why Jesus would quote from Acts rather than from Deuteronomy). Many modern Latter-day Saints take just this view, and it is obvious why—anyone who has read the 1830 Book of Mormon knows that *if* the very words were given by God, then God is unable to speak decent English. So it is easier to say that God gave Joseph "inspired concepts" and left the expression of those concepts in English to Smith who then did the "best he could."

David Whitmer, one of the "Three Witnesses" to the Book of Mormon, described the manner in which the Book of Mormon was translated in his work *An Address to All Believers in Christ*:

> I shall now give to you a description of the manner in which the Book of Mormon was translated. Joseph Smith would put the seer stone into a hat, and put his face in the hat, drawing it closely around his face to exclude the light; and in the darkness the spiritual light would shine. A piece of something resembling parchment would appear, and on that appeared the writing. One character at a time would appear, and under it was the interpretation in English. Brother Joseph would read off the English to Oliver Cowdery, who was his principal scribe, and when it was written down and repeated

to Brother Joseph to see if it was correct, then it would disappear, and another character with the interpretation would appear. Thus the Book of Mormon was translated by the gift and power of God, and not by any power of man. (p. 12)

You will note as well that Cowdery uses the term *translate* with reference to the work, just as Smith did above on page 299 of *Teachings of the Prophet Joseph Smith*. Both the "Testimony of the Three Witnesses" as well as "The Testimony of Eight Witnesses" use the term *translate* as well. Translation is a process of rendering one language into another—it is not done by "inspiration" in the same way that Scripture is originally written down. Of course, it is said that Smith could not actually *translate* the characters on the plates, written, supposedly, in "reformed Egyptian" (Mormon 9:32), but had to depend upon God to show him how to do this. At the same time, when God "inspires" someone to *translate,* will they then *translate* or will they simply get "inspired thoughts or concepts" that they are then left to render into their own language?

In the *Documentary History of the Church*, Volume 1, page 55, we read of an encounter between Joseph Smith, David Whitmer, Oliver Cowdery, and an angel who is supposedly holding the golden plates. The angel speaks and says,

These plates have been revealed by the power of God, and they have been translated by the power of God. The translation of them which you have seen is correct, and I command you to bear record of what you now see and hear.

This "vision" took place in June of 1829. Even the angel uses the term *translation* with regard to the plates, and then says that the translation of them which they had seen was correct. We will return to this fact when we address the issue of the many *changes* that have been made in the Book of Mormon since that time. The point is that the angel said they were "translated" by the power of God. Nothing here suggests that only the *concepts* of the Book of Mormon are inspired, while the actual words are not. Certainly David Whitmer, who was one of those who saw the angel, did not understand the angel's words to refer to anything other than a *correct translation* of the Book of Mormon.

The "Journal of Oliver B. Huntington" also provides us with further insights into early Mormon belief about the "translation" of the Book of Mormon. Here, from 1881, Huntington describes the teachings of

Joseph F. Smith (who later became the president of the LDS Church) relevant to the translation of the Book of Mormon:

> Saturday Feb. 25, 1881, I went to Provo to a quarterly Stake Conference. Heard Joseph F. Smith describe the manner of translating the Book of Mormon. . . . Joseph did not render the writing on the gold plates into the English language in his own style of language as many people believe, but every word and every letter was given to him by the gift and power of God. . . . The Lord caused each word spelled as it is in the book to appear on the stones in short sentences or words, and when Joseph had uttered the sentence or word before him and the scribe had written it properly, that sentence would disappear and another appear. And if there was a word wrongly written or even a letter incorrect the writing on the stones would remain there . . . and when corrected the sentence would disappear as usual. (p.168 of typed copy at Utah State Historical Society, as cited in *The Changing World of Mormonism*, p. 132)

You will note that Joseph F. Smith's teaching is remarkably similar to the statements of David Whitmer on the same subject. Obviously, this concept of the method of "translation" was widely held at the time, and was promulgated by at least one of the "Three Witnesses" as well as by an apostle who became the president of the LDS Church. The modern concept that Joseph used his own language to express "inspired thoughts" certainly allows the Mormon to avoid a number of embarrassing problems with the text of the Book of Mormon, but it does great injustice to the term *translation* with reference to the "plates" (indeed, why would he need the plates at all?), and it certainly causes one to wonder when Smith claims that the "Book of Mormon was the most correct of any book on earth . . ." (*Documentary History of the Church*, 4:461).

But other Mormons take a slightly different track. Some say that Smith was indeed *translating* the text, but he utilized the King James Version when it was "close enough" to that which was found on the plates. This defense allows the Mormon to explain at least some of the obvious plagiarisms of the KJV, but it doesn't explain why the *plates themselves* would quote the New Testament (as seen above) or why items such as swords, horses, or Greek and French words end up in the Book of Mormon. Were these words on the plates as well?

So, as you can see Elder Hahn, there are many problems with the text of the Book of Mormon, the vast majority of which point to a modern date of composition for the work.

Reason #5: The text of the Book of Mormon has been purposefully changed (edited) in thousands of places. I'm sure you have heard this objection before, Elder Hahn, and perhaps I can anticipate a very common answer: "All the changes in the Book of Mormon are changes in spelling and punctuation *only."* Yes, a large number of changes have been made in the Book of Mormon relevant to spelling and punctuation—but the changes in that book go beyond this to matters of doctrine and history itself.

Now before I examine a few of the changes (edits) that have been made in the Book of Mormon, let me say right up front that the vast majority of the story of the Book of Mormon is not affected by the changes that have been made. In fact, in comparison with the major changes made in the D&C as well as in Joseph Smith's *History of the Church,* the changes in the Book of Mormon are rather minor. You won't find chapters of the Book of Mormon completely overhauled after publication so as to change the entire doctrinal slant of the work. But the changes are significant and are part of my reasons for rejecting the Book of Mormon as a divine revelation.

Mormon Apostle Joseph Fielding Smith (who became the president of the LDS Church) served for a long period of time as the Church Historian. With reference to the question of changes in the Book of Mormon he wrote:

> In the case of the Book of Mormon, your attention is called to the fact that the publisher of it was unfriendly to the Church. It required the utmost care on that account. Being unfriendly, it would have been a natural thing for him to permit some errors to appear. A careful check of the list of changes submitted by these critics shows there is not one change or addition that is not in harmony with the original text. Changes have been made in punctuation and a few other minor matters that needed correction, but never has any alteration or addition changed a single original thought. As it appears to us, the changes mentioned are such that make the text clearer and indicate that they were omitted. I am sure that the mistakes or omissions in the first edition were in large measure the fault of the compositor or the printer. . . .
>
> Some of the original manuscript of the Book of Mormon is still with the Church, and some of it was destroyed. Copies of the first

edition of the Book of Mormon are in the Historian's Office library, and it bears witness that no drastic changes have been made.

There have been thousands of changes in the Bible in recent years, but people do not seem to complain about that. (*Answers to Gospel Questions*, Volume 2, p. 200)

I have already pointed out to you the error of Joseph Fielding Smith's final comment about "changes" in the Bible. It is common for Mormons to attempt to deflect the criticism of the Book of Mormon by trying to point out differences in various translations of the Bible. Aside from the fact that such differences are normally simply a matter of translation, not a matter of the underlying text, the changes that have been made in the Book of Mormon are of a very specific kind—they are evidence of blatant *purposeful editing* of the text. Let's look at a few of these changes below. Emphasis is added to illustrate the changes.

The 1830 Book of Mormon, on page 25 says:

Knowest thou the condescension of God? And I said unto him, I know that he loveth his children; nevertheless, I do not know the meaning of all things. And he said unto me, Behold the virgin which thou seest, *is the mother of God,* after the manner of the flesh.

The modern editions read like this in 1 Nephi 11:16–18:

[16]And he said unto me: Knowest thou the condescension of God?

[17]And I said unto him: I know that he loveth his children; nevertheless, I do not know the meaning of all things.

[18]And he said unto me: Behold, the virgin whom thou seest is the *mother of the Son of God,* after the manner of the flesh.

The confusion as to just who Jesus is (God, Son of God, Father, Son of the Father, etc.,) is seen in more than one of the changes in the Book of Mormon that are doctrinal in nature. Note the two examples below:

1830 Book of Mormon, page 25:

And the angel said unto me, behold the Lamb of God, yea *even the Eternal Father*! Knowest thou the meaning of the tree which thy father saw?

Modern edition, 1 Nephi 11:21:

> [21]And the angel said unto me: Behold the Lamb of God, yea, even *the Son of the Eternal Father*! Knowest thou the meaning of the tree which thy father saw?

1830 Book of Mormon, page 26:

> And it came to pass that the angel spake unto me again, saying, look! And I looked and beheld the Lamb of God, that he was taken by the people; yea, *the Everlasting God,* was judged of the world; and I saw and bear record.

Modern edition, 1 Nephi 11:32:

> And it came to pass that the angel spake unto me again, saying: Look! and I looked and beheld the Lamb of God, that he was taken by the people; yea, *the Son of the everlasting God* was judged of the world; and I saw and bear record.

It is difficult to understand how Joseph Fielding Smith could say that "never has any alteration or addition changed a single original thought" in light of this change and the modern LDS belief that the Father and the Son, while they may be "one God in purpose" are also two separate and distinct beings and separate and distinct Gods, one of which has existed as a God prior to the other. Beyond this, I point your attention to Joseph Fielding Smith's statement that there is "not one change or addition that is not in full harmony with the original text." With reference to the last of the above mentioned changes, the one that occurs at 1 Nephi 11:32, we can find out if the former Church Historian (who was certainly in a position to know) spoke the truth. The handwritten manuscript of the Book of Mormon exists for 1 Nephi 11:32, and it reads just as the 1830 edition as opposed to the modern editions. When we also take into consideration the angel's words recorded in the *Documentary History of the Church* 1:55 where he says that the "translation which you have seen is correct," we are forced to wonder why Joseph Smith would be forced to "edit" this section at a later date. Could it be that his evolving theology forced him to do so?

Changes of an historical nature have been made as well. Seemingly Joseph became confused as to which king was which, and who was supposed to be alive at what time, while dictating the book of Mosiah. On page 200 of the 1830 Book of Mormon we read,

And now Limhi was again filled with joy, on learning from the mouth of Ammon that *King Benjamin* had a gift from God, whereby he could interpret such engravings; yea, and Ammon did also rejoice.

This passage is to be found in the modern edition in Mosiah chapter 21. The problem is fairly obvious, for Mosiah 6:5 reads, "And king Benjamin lived three years and he died." Fifteen chapters later, however, he is alive and well in the 1830 Book of Mormon. The modern edition reads,

[28]And now Limhi was again filled with joy on learning from the mouth of Ammon that *king Mosiah* had a gift from God, whereby he could interpret such engravings; yea, and Ammon also did rejoice.

Who had this gift, Elder Hahn? Was it Benjamin or Mosiah?

The process of editing the text of the Book of Mormon has continued on since the days of Joseph Smith. Mormon scholars such as B. H. Roberts and James Talmage had a hand in this, Talmage doing a good deal of work on the text itself in the 1920s. One of the more interesting changes made in the text of the Book of Mormon can be seen by comparing 2 Nephi 30:6 in the 1979 and 1981 editions:

1979:

[6]And then shall they rejoice; for they shall know that it is a blessing unto them from the hand of God; and their scales of darkness shall begin to fall from their eyes; and many generations shall not pass away among them, save they shall be a *white and delightsome people.*

1981:

[6]And then shall they rejoice; for they shall know that it is a blessing unto them from the hand of God; and their scales of darkness shall begin to fall from their eyes; and many generations shall not pass away among them, save they shall be a *pure and a delightsome people.*

The 1830 Book of Mormon reads the same as the 1979 edition with reference to the change of "white" to "pure" (p. 117). It is my understanding, Elder, that this is not the first time this passage was "edited" in this way. But the fact that it was put into this form (a physical quality being replaced with a moral or a spiritual one) *after* the "revelation" giving the priesthood to the blacks (June 8, 1978) seems to be more than just a "coincidence." Mormon leaders like Bruce R. McConkie and Spencer W. Kimball had cited this passage in its original form *and applied it to the physical property of a dark skin.* Seemingly their "interpretation" was proven in error by the new "revelation" that changed things around.

Some Mormon apologists have alleged that the timing of this change was coincidental, and had nothing to do with the priesthood issue. There is some plausibility to this, for another passage teaching the same doctrine (2 Nephi 5:21) was not changed in the 1981 edition, even though it uses the very same kind of language, and plainly teaches that the "skin of blackness" was placed upon sinful people as a curse. In any case, the text of the Book of Mormon is seen to have undergone purposeful editing with reference to doctrinal and historical subjects. While the *extent* of the editing is not nearly as large as that seen in the *Doctrine and Covenants*, it is nonetheless important.

In light of all this (and there is more that could be said—much more), it is impossible for me to do as you ask, Elder, and pray to God and say, "God, I know that this book is historically inaccurate, and I know that this book contains teachings that are contrary to those doctrines taught in your Word, and I know that Joseph Smith fails the test of a true prophet, and I know that there are many problems with the text showing it to be a modern composition and not an ancient record, and I know that the text of this book has undergone a good deal of editing and changing, but, despite all of that, is it true?" To do so would require me to deny the Christian faith, Elder. I know you probably have not thought of it in that way, but that is the truth. Prayer is vitally important— so important, in fact, that I will not *abuse* the privilege of prayer, (which I believe to be an act of worship that is to be undertaken in solemn adoration), in order to test God and question the revelation of His truth. And may I suggest to you, sir, that it would be wise to question the wisdom of taking a "feeling" that you have gotten by uttering such a prayer and use that as a basis upon which to dismiss all the information I have presented to you?

I would like to talk about one more item with reference to the Book of Mormon. It has to do with the common LDS belief that the Bible actually *prophesies* the coming forth of that book. The two primary passages that are cited are Ezekiel 37:15–17 and Isaiah 29:1–4. Let's look at Ezekiel first:

> [15]The word of the LORD came again unto me, saying,
>
> [16]Moreoever, thou son of man, take thee one stick, and write upon it, For Judah, and for the children of Israel, his companions; then take another stick, and write upon it, For Joseph, the stick of Ephraim, and for all the house of Israel, his companions;
>
> [17]And join them one to another into one stick, and they shall become one in thine hand.

The common LDS interpretation of this passage is that the two sticks represent "scrolls" or "books," the stick of Judah being the Bible, and the stick of Joseph being the Book of Mormon (see, for example, LeGrand Richards, *A Marvelous Work and a Wonder*, p. 66). The two sticks becoming "one" would symbolize the unity of the Book of Mormon and the Bible in their teaching and testimony.

The problem with this kind of interpretation is that it can be used to prove *anything*. Arbitrarily asserting that the "stick of Joseph" means the Book of Mormon is a great error, for the text itself defines and interprets this symbolic action by Ezekiel. First, the word "stick" that is used here means, "stick." I'm not trying to be profound, but if Ezekiel had wished to speak of a scroll, he could have done so quite easily, as there is another Hebrew term that means "scroll" and Ezekiel used it in his book (Ezekiel 2:9, 3:1–3). Often in the prophecy of Ezekiel, God instructs His prophet to enact some symbolic gesture that he is then to explain to the people. A great example of this is in Ezekiel 4:1–5:17, where Ezekiel is to build a little model of the city of Jerusalem and then go through various actions that have symbolic meaning for the city. Here in Ezekiel 37 we have the same thing—Ezekiel is to take two sticks and write upon one of them "Judah" and upon the other "Joseph." He is to put them together in his hand, and they would become one stick. Then, as so often in this book, Ezekiel was to explain to the people the meaning of his symbolic action, which he does in 37:18–22:

> [18]And when the children of thy people shall speak unto thee, saying, Wilt thou not show us what thou meanest by these?
>
> [19]Say unto them, Thus saith the Lord GOD; Behold, I will take the stick of Joseph, which is in the hand of Ephraim, and the tribes of Israel, his fellows, and will put them with him, even with the

stick of Judah, and make them one stick, and they shall be one in mine hand.

²⁰And the sticks on which thou writest shall be in thine hand before their eyes.

²¹And say unto them, Thus saith the Lord GOD; Behold, I will take the children of Israel from among the heathen, whither they be gone, and will gather them on every side, and bring them into their own land:

²²And I will make them one nation in the land upon the mountains of Israel; and one king shall be king to them all: and they shall be no more two nations, neither shall they be divided into two kingdoms any more at all.

Remember that after the death of Solomon two nations existed: Israel to the north, and Judah to the south. Ezekiel often prophecies the *reunification* of the people of God, Israel and Judah together again as one nation. This is what this prophecy is about. If we allow the Bible to define its own terms for us (rather than forcing our own ideas upon it), we see that the two sticks are just that—sticks that represent the nations of Judah and Israel (Ephraim). The significance of Ezekiel's action is explained in verses 21 and 22 as a symbol of the future restoration of the one nation of Israel, the rejoining of Judah and Israel in the last days. The Bible itself identifies the sticks as representing two nations, not as representing two different *records* of two nations. There simply is no reason to accept the LDS interpretation of this passage.

The second biblical reference commonly referred to in support of the Book of Mormon is Isaiah 29:1–4:

¹Woe to Ariel, to Ariel, the city where David dwelt! add ye year to year; let them kill sacrifices.

²Yet I will distress Ariel, and there shall be heaviness and sorrow: and it shall be unto me as Ariel.

³And I will camp against thee round about, and will lay siege against thee with a mount, and I will raise forts against thee.

⁴And thou shalt be brought down, and shalt speak out of the ground, and thy speech shall be low out of the dust, and thy voice shall be, as of one that hath a familiar spirit, out of the ground, and thy speech shall whisper out of the dust.

In a tract entitled *The Mormons and the Jewish People* (which was written by Mormon Apostle LeGrand Richards and published by the

LDS Church), we read the following interpretation of this passage:

> It would appear from these words that Isaiah looked far into the future, "add ye year to year," and beheld the destruction of a people like unto the people of Jerusalem, and that after their destruction, they would "speak out of the ground." Obviously, this could only be possible through a written record. The prophecy stated that the voice of this people would have "a familiar spirit." When the prophets of the Lord speak, they always have "a familiar spirit." This prophecy will be better understood when it is known that the plates from which the Book of Mormon was translated were deposited in a stone box in the Hill Cumorah. . . .

Note that Richards said that "When the prophets of the Lord speak, they always have 'a familiar spirit.' " Then, in his book *A Marvelous Work and a Wonder*, pages 67–68, he cites the same passage from Isaiah and says,

> They would be brought down and would speak out of the ground. Their speech would be "low out of the dust"; their voice would be as one that hath a familiar spirit, out of the ground; and their speech would whisper out of the dust. Now, obviously, the only way a dead people could speak "out of the ground" or "low out of the dust" would be by the written word, and this the people did through the Book of Mormon. Truly it has a familiar spirit, for it contains the words of the prophets of the God of Israel.

So, according to LeGrand Richards, who claimed to be an apostle of Jesus Christ, "When the prophets of the Lord speak, they always have 'a familiar spirit' " and also the Book of Mormon has a familiar spirit, because "it contains the words of the prophets of the God of Israel."

Now, Elder, any beginning Bible student knows what a "familiar spirit" is—but it doesn't seem that LeGrand Richards knew. A familiar spirit is a demonic spirit, a demon. Notice Deuteronomy 18:10–12:

> There shall not be found among you anyone who maketh his son or his daughter to pass through the fire, or that useth divination, or an observer of times, or an enchanter, or a witch, or a charmer, or a consulter with familiar spirits, or a wizard, or a necromancer. For all that do these things are an abomination unto the LORD.

Here are the other occurrences of the Hebrew term *ob* (translated by the King James Version as "familiar spirit"—check them out for yourself):

Leviticus 19:31, 20:6, 20:27; 1 Samuel 28:3, 28:7–9; 2 Kings 21:6, 23:24; 1 Chronicles 10:13; 2 Chronicles 33:6; Isaiah 8:19, 19:3, 29:4.

Clearly this passage has nothing whatsoever to do with the Book of Mormon. It is speaking about the destruction of the city of Jerusalem, and nothing else. We not only see this, but in examining the words of a man who claimed to be an apostle of Christ we find that he knew very little about basic Bible teachings, including the meaning of the term *familiar spirit*. He said that the Book of Mormon has a familiar spirit. Obviously, he was not attempting to say that the Book of Mormon has a demonic spirit, but that is what he ended up saying. This "apostle" was completely wrong about this passage and its meaning—if you cannot trust him on this, what other teachings, that are based solely upon such "apostolic authority," are in error as well?

The Book of Abraham

I remember encountering two Mormon missionaries outside the Mormon temple in Provo, Utah, a few years ago. My companion and I began to talk with them, and in the course of the conversation the topic of the Book of Abraham came up. They had no idea what we were talking about—they did not know what the Book of Abraham was. Seemingly, they are not alone in their ignorance of this small book in the *Pearl of Great Price*. Many LDS today have no idea what the Book of Abraham is about, much less how this one book, more clearly than any other, shows the *error* of believing in Joseph Smith as a prophet.

Many others have taken great time and effort to fully discuss the issue of the Book of Abraham. Jerald and Sandra Tanner's discussion in *Mormonism: Shadow or Reality?* (pages 294–369) is *extensive*. I will not even attempt to summarize all the material that is available on this topic. With the "discovery" of the original papyri fragments upon which Joseph Smith based his "translation" of this little five-chapter book, whole volumes have been published discussing this or that aspect of the issue. Unfortunately, the majority of those volumes had only one purpose—to obscure the fact that Joseph Smith, though he *claimed* to be able to translate the Egyptian characters from the papyri, most obviously *could not*. Mormon apologists have done everything in their power to keep this information from the average Latter-day Saint. Some have latched on to completely unrelated issues in a hopeless attempt to save Joseph Smith from exposure on the basis of his complete mistranslation of the Egyptian language—all to no avail.

There is no need to go into the actual papyri that were turned over to the LDS Church in the late 1960s—anyone who has a copy of the Book of Abraham in the *Pearl of Great Price* has all the information he or she needs to discover that Joseph Smith utterly misunderstood the meaning and significance of the Egyptian papyri that had come into his possession in July of 1835. Here is the story from the *Documentary History of the Church*, 2:235–36:

> On the 3rd of July, Michael H. Chandler came to Kirtland to exhibit some Egyptian mummies. There were four human figures, together with some two or more rolls of papyrus covered with hieroglyphic figures and devices. As Mr. Chandler had been told I could translate them, he brought me some of the characters, and I gave him the interpretation. . . .
>
> Soon after this, some of the Saints at Kirtland purchased the mummies and papyrus, a description of which will appear hereafter, and with W. W. Phelps and Oliver Cowdery as scribes, I commenced the translation of some of the characters or hieroglyphics, and much to our joy found that one of the rolls contained the writings of Abraham, another the writings of Joseph of Egypt, etc. . . .

It is important to note that Smith claimed to *translate* these items, in the same way he had claimed to *translate* the Book of Mormon. If, upon examination, it is discovered that Smith *could not translate* the Egyptian characters that he claimed resulted in the scant dozen pages of the Book of Abraham, how can we believe that he was able to translate the more than 500 pages of the Book of Mormon from "reformed Egyptian"?

The modern editions of the *Pearl of Great Price* include this information at the beginning of the book:

> A Translation of some ancient Records, that have fallen into our hands from the catacombs of Egypt.—The writings of Abraham while he was in Egypt, called the Book of Abraham, written by his own hand, upon papyrus.

If indeed these were the *actual writings of Abraham,* they would constitute the greatest archaeological and historical find of all time. They would pre-date the earliest manuscripts of the Bible by a thousand years and more. The introduction claims that what follows is a *translation* of these records—I keep emphasizing that because, in light of the discovery of the actual papyri themselves, some have attempted to escape the meaning of the word "translate" and have attempted to substitute some other idea to explain Smith's "translation."

Is it very likely that Smith would have found such an incredible treasure in the possession of a traveling showman and his mummies? Probably not, but it is certain that Smith was convinced that he had the writings of Abraham. His "translation" was safe at the time—if there were five people in the United States who could have challenged his "translation," I would be surprised. The study of Egyptian was in its infancy at the time, so claiming to give "translations" by supernatural power was something that could not be tested. Of course, today things are different. We can read Egyptian now, and, as I've mentioned, with the original papyri in our possession, we can find out just how well Joseph Smith did in his "translations." Without getting into all the battles about the papyri, I will give you the translation of the segment thereof that is identified as being the specific portion used by Smith as the basis of the Book of Abraham. Please remember that the Book of Abraham is five chapters long. Smith "translated" those five chapters from the following:

> Osiris shall be conveyed into the Great Pool of Khons—and likewise Osiris Hor, justified, born to Tikhebyt, justified—after his arms have been placed on his heart and the Breathing Permit (which [Isis] made and has writing on its inside and outside—has been wrapped in royal linen and placed under his left arm near his heart; the rest of his mummy-bandages should be wrapped over it. The man for whom this book has been copied will breathe forever as the bas of the gods do. (Klaus Baer, *Dialogue: A Journal of Mormon Thought*, Autumn 1968, pp. 119–20)

What Joseph Smith thought was the writing of Abraham was in fact a common artifact of Egyptian burial ritual—hundreds of examples of this kind of literature are to be found in museums around the world.

But I said I wasn't going to go into the papyri, as that is a rather complex issue. I said that anyone who had a copy of the *Pearl of Great Price* had enough data right there to see that Joseph Smith did not have the slightest idea about what was before him on the Egyptian papyri. This data is to be found in the "facsimiles" that are printed as part of the Book of Abraham. These pictures include an explanation below them, supposedly providing us with Smith's interpretation of what we see in the graphic. By examining these and comparing Smith's explanation, we will see that he was completely in error in his idea of what the Egyptian papyri represented. And, in fact, this is just what some individuals did around the turn of the century—they tried to point out to the LDS people that Joseph Smith, based only on the explanations of the facsimiles in the Book of Abraham, had made many gross blunders in his identifications of the figures in the pictures. However, while the original pamphlet printed on the subject created quite a stir in Utah, it was quickly answered by a Mormon "scholar" and the whole issue sort of "went away." Only later was it discovered that the "scholar" was not a scholar at all, and had *faked* his doctoral degree.

Here is Facsimile #1:

Here is how Smith explains the main characters in this facsimile:

Fig. 1. The Angel of the Lord.
Fig. 2. Abraham fastened upon an altar.
Fig. 3. The idolatrous priest of Elkenah attempting to offer up Abraham as a sacrifice.

If you were to take this facsimile to any expert familiar with Egyptology and Egyptian magic and folklore, and were to ask him to identify the same figures, this is what you would discover:

Figure 1 is actually the soul of Osiris (it should have a human head, but the papyri shows that this section was damaged, and both the bird's head and the human head on the black, standing figure were "drawn in" and that in error). Figure 2 is Osiris lying upon a funeral bier. Egyptians believed that Osiris had been killed by his brother, named Set, and that his body had been discovered by Isis (whom we will meet in a moment) and was embalmed by Anubis, who is Figure 3. Smith made Osiris' soul into the angel of the Lord, turned Osiris into Abraham, and changed Anubis into "the idolatrous priest of Elkenah." The scene depicted here, as I said, is a *common one* in Egyptian funerary literature.

Let's skip to the third of the three facsimiles. Here is what it looks like:

How does Joseph explain this? Here are his words:

Fig. 1. Abraham sitting upon Pharaoh's throne, by the politeness of the king, with a crown upon his head, representing the Priesthood, as emblematical of the grand Presidency in heaven; with the scepter of justice and judgment in his hand.

Fig. 2. King Pharaoh, whose name is given in the characters above his head.

Fig. 3. Signifies Abraham in Egypt as given also in Figure 10 of Facsimile No. 1.

Fig. 4. Prince of Pharaoh, King of Egypt, as written above the hand.

Fig. 5. Shulem, one of the king's principal waiters, as represented by the characters above his hand.

Fig. 6. Olimlah, a slave belonging to the prince.

In reality, this scene (which is found again in other Egyptian funerary texts) shows the god Osiris enthroned toward the left of the picture (figure 1), before whom a man (figure 5) is being led by the goddess Maat (figure 4) and the god Anubis (figure 6). Isis stands behind the throne (figure 2). So, Smith has identified the Egyptian god Osiris as Abraham, the female goddess Maat as a man (the prince of Pharaoh), another female goddess Isis as a male (Pharaoh), and another god, Anubis, as a slave belonging to the prince! It is rather embarrassing to note that the femininity of figures 2 and 4 is rather obvious—how could Smith have missed it? But this may have been one of the only examples of Egyptian drawing he had ever seen, which would explain his missing such an obvious fact. The "Explanation" claimed that the figures above the scene identified various of the people—they do not. They identify the man for whom this papyrus, known as the "Book of Breathings," was made—a man named Hor. The symbols along the bottom read, "O gods of . . . , gods of the Caverns, gods of the south, north, west and east, grant well-being to Osiris Hor, justified. . . ."

While it may be embarrassing to see Joseph Smith's mistakes in identifying the people who are part of these facsimiles, try to remember, Elder Hahn, that these facsimiles are referred to in the body of the text of the Book of Abraham. In Abraham 1:12–14 we read,

> [12]And it came to pass that the priests laid violence upon me, that they might slay me also, as they did those virgins upon this altar; and that you may have a knowledge of this altar, I will refer you to the representation at the commencement of this record.
>
> [13]It was made after the form of a bedstead, such as was had among the Chaldeans, and it stood before the gods of Elkenah, Libnah, Mahmackrah, Korash, and also a god like unto that of Pharaoh, king of Egypt.
>
> [14]That you may have an understanding of these gods, I have given you the fashion of them in the figures at the beginning, which manner of figures is called by the Chaldeans Rahleenos, which signifies hieroglyphics.

If the facsimiles are not what Smith claimed they were, then the text of Mormon Scripture itself is shown to be in grave error, as he connects the text of the Book of Abraham quite obviously with the illustrations we are here examining. How can one believe that the teachings of the Book of Abraham are correct when that text itself refers to false and disproven "interpretations" of these facsimiles? And, by extension, if Smith was able to make errors of this kind in 1835, why not in 1829 when working on the text of the Book of Mormon or later when supposedly receiving "revelation" from God that is in today's *Doctrine and Covenants*? All of Mormon Scripture, then, stands or falls together. These blatant errors in the Book of Abraham reflect on all of Smith's writings.

Here is the second facsimile from the Book of Abraham:

The second facsimile in the book is, to me, the most serious, in that the explanation asserts that it contains very sacred, very secret items that "are to be had in the Holy Temple of God" or "ought not to be revealed at the present time." The explanation is very long, so I will only give relevant sections:

> Fig.   3. Is made to represent God, sitting upon his throne, clothed with power and authority; with a crown of eternal light upon his head; representing also the grand Key-words of the Holy Priesthood, as revealed to Adam in the Garden of Eden, as also to Seth, Noah, Melchizedek, Abraham, and all to whom the Priesthood was revealed.
>
> Fig.   7. Represents God sitting upon his throne, revealing through the heavens the grand Key-words of the Priesthood; as, also, the sign of the Holy Ghost unto Abraham, in the form of a dove.
>
> Fig.   8. Contains writings that cannot be revealed unto the world; but is to be had in the Holy Temple of God.
>
> Fig.   9. Ought not to be revealed at the present time.
>
> Fig. 10. Also.
>
> Figures 12, 13, 14, 15, 16, 17, 18, 19, 20, and 21 will be given in the own due time of the Lord.
>
> The above translation is given as far as we have any right to give at the present time.

The object pictured in Facsimile 2 is actually a *hypocephalus,* a common item of Egyptian funeral literature. It was placed under the deceased person's head, and was said to aid them in making their journey through the netherworld by bathing their bodies in light. Many examples of this kind of hypocephalus are to be found. Rather than explaining the "principles of astronomy" as Smith alleged, this object comes directly from the pagan religions of Egypt. Mormon Egyptologist Michael Dennis Rhoades provided a translation of parts of this facsimile in *BYU Studies,* Spring 1977, page 265. His translation of the edge of the hypocephalus is as follows:

> I am Djabty in the House of the Benben in Heliopolis, so exalted and glorious. [I am] a copulating bull without equal. [I am] that Mighty God in the House of the Benben in Heliopolis . . . that Mighty God. . . .

Figure 8 is supposed to contain writings that "cannot be revealed unto the world but is to be had in the Holy Temple of God," yet Rhoades translates this section (including figures 9, 10, and 11, the entire left middle section) as follows:

O God of the Sleeping Ones from the time of the creation. O Mighty God, Lord of Heaven and Earth, the Netherworld and his Great Waters, grant that the soul of Osiris Sheshonk may live.

The bottom section, which contains figures that Smith claimed "will be given in the own due time of the Lord," actually reads,

May this tomb never be desecrated, and may this soul and its possessor never be desecrated in the Netherworld.

Egyptologists (Mormon and non-Mormon alike) tell us that the deity seen in figure 7 is in reality the god Min. Min is an *ithyphallic deity,* that is, a sexually aroused male deity, as the picture clearly indicates. Min is the god of the procreative forces of nature. The sexually explicit nature of this god has caused embarrassment to Mormon leaders. While the original printing of this hypocephalus appears just as the modern version (Joseph Smith oversaw the restoration of the hypocephalus, which had been damaged, and the preparation of its printing in the *Times and Seasons* of March 15, 1842, as you can see in the *Documentary History of the Church*, Volume 4, pages 519 and 543), beginning at the end of the last century an "edited" version of the Min figure appeared in LDS Scriptures. Note a comparison between the 1966 edition of the *Pearl of Great Price* and the 1981 edition:

1966   **1981**

The modern edition is the accurate one, and shows clearly the pagan origin of these materials. What is Min doing in Facsimile 2? Joseph Smith tells us that he is revealing the grand key-words of the priesthood, with the sign of the Holy Ghost in the form of a dove before him. In reality, he is holding up the "divine flail" in one hand, while being approached not by the Holy Ghost, but by yet another pagan god. The hypocephalus that Joseph had in his possession was damaged at the border so that only the head of the "dove" was visible. So, Joseph had to restore the picture. Did he do so correctly? No, he did not. Below I reproduce for you the same section from another hypocephalus, designated Leyden AMS 62, a hypocephalus that is almost identical in form to the one Joseph Smith utilized:

The being that is approaching Min is not the Holy Ghost in the form of a dove. Rather, it is another ithyphallic figure, specifically, a serpent, probably the Egyptian god Nehebka, presenting to Min the *wedjat-eye*, the symbol of good gifts.

The single LDS scholar who has written the most on the Book of Abraham, Dr. Hugh Nibley, has written of Min:

> As the supreme sex symbol of gods and men, Min behaves with shocking promiscuity, which is hardly relieved by its ritual nature. . . . His sacred plants are aphrodisiacal . . . and he is everywhere represented as indulging in incestuous relationships with those of his immediate family; he had the most numerous and varied entourage of all the gods, consisting mostly of his huge harem. . . . The hymns, or rather chanting, of his worshippers were accompanied with lewd dancing and carousing . . . to the exciting stimulus of a band of sistrem-shaking damsels. (*Abraham in Egypt*, p. 210)

> It must be remembered that Joseph Smith said that this figure represented God sitting on His throne! Incredible as it may seem, intelligent, well-read LDS are fully aware of the true nature of the hypocephalus, including the presence of Min and Nehebka. How do they explain this? Mormon Egyptologist Michael Dennis Rhoades, whose translation of the hypocephalus I cited above, said with reference to the Min figure:

> Joseph Smith mentions here the Holy Ghost in the form of a dove and God "revealing through the heavens the grand key-words of the priesthood." The procreative forces, receiving unusual accentuation throughout the representation, may stand for many di-

vine generative powers, not least of which might be conjoined with the blessings of the Priesthood in one's posterity eternally. (*BYU Studies*, Spring 1977, p. 273)

In other words, since the God of Mormonism is sexually active, begetting children in the spirit-world, and Min is obviously sexually active as well, this, then, is the "connection."

May I suggest, Elder, that Joseph Smith was utterly ignorant of what was represented in the Egyptian papyri that lay before him? Incapable of translating the language, or understanding the significance of the figures, he made things up as he went along, claiming God's direction and inspiration as his guide. In the process he demonstrated his own inability as a "prophet, seer and revelator," for he grossly misidentified each of the items not only in this facsimile, but in the other two as well.

Joseph Smith's defenders today seek to find any connection whatsoever between LDS belief and Egyptian religion, even to the point of seeing in the sexually aroused Min a picture of God upon His throne. But to grasp at this straw is to ignore the biblical testimony to the one true God. Isaiah saw God upon His throne in Isaiah 6:1–10, but instead of an incestuous god, surrounded by lewd dancing girls, the angels surrounded His throne and cried, "Holy, holy, holy." God describes the gods of Egypt as "idols" that tremble before Him (Isaiah 19:1); these false gods will literally be captured by God in His wrath (Jeremiah 43:12). God reveals the worship of these gods to be an abomination that brings His judgment (Jeremiah 44:8), and mentions one Egyptian god by name in speaking of the punishment he will bring to pass against Egypt (Jeremiah 46:25 in any modern translation). Those who worship such gods are "defiled" in God's sight (Ezekiel 20:7–8). The Bible has nothing but utter contempt for the gods of Egypt, which would include the abominable figure of Min, identified by Joseph Smith as his God.

Elder Hahn, I can imagine it is difficult for you to believe what you are reading—but it is just as vital that you remember that at the very beginning I explained to you that I was going to address the topic of Joseph Smith and his claims *only because I desire to share the gospel with you,* and I *must* refute Smith's claims and his teachings because they are standing in the way of your acceptance of the truth. *Please* do not engage in a frantic search for some kind—*any kind*—of "explanation" for Smith's obvious blunders and errors. Rather, recognize the reality of the facts and seek the truth not from Joseph Smith or the system he founded, but from the Word of God, the Bible.

I hope to hear from you soon, Elder. I await your response.

Concerned and praying,

James White

LETTER 9

Come, Let Us Reason Together

Monday, July 9

Dear Elder Hahn,

Your new partner seems like a nice young man. But, I would rather have heard from you. It's not that I think you "owe" me anything for the time I've spent in writing and talking with you—I do this because I see it as a ministry and an avenue of showing my love for Christ and my concern for you. But to simply be told that you do not wish further contact with me seems more than a little unusual. I don't feel that your request has anything at all to do with my personality or the manner in which I have pursued the subjects before us. Rather, I feel that the information I have presented to you is of such a nature as to cause you discomfort. I have challenged your beliefs and in the process you have been faced with tough decisions. That might be painful, or it might just be distracting and bothersome—that all depends upon how seriously you have read my letters and how serious you are about believing that Mormonism is true.

I remember speaking with an acquaintance of mine who was once a Mormon but left the LDS Church when he accepted Christ as his Lord and Savior. While he was on his mission (it was over in England) he encountered people who "rocked his boat" with questions that he could not answer. But, he was counseled to "pray about it" and simply to seek a "stronger testimony." During his mission one of the apostles (as I recall it was Mark E. Peterson) came over and met with the missionaries in the area. He was considered a real theologian—one of those

169

who could answer the tough questions and was great as a speaker. After his presentation a young missionary in the back stood up to ask one of the very same questions that had been thrown at my friend. The answer was quick and sharp: "You needn't worry about those things—talking about them will not help you on your mission. Next!" The missionary sat down rather dazed and bewildered, and everyone else took the cue that asking such questions might not be a good idea.

Just today I listened to a man who left a message on our answering machine (we have a phone message for Mormons). I had been here when he called the first time, and when he began accusing us of being stupid and unaware of LDS beliefs, I picked up the phone and began to talk to him. We spoke for about half an hour. I kept bringing up this fact or that, and all he could say in response was, "Well, you are deceived." At first he berated us for not knowing what we were talking about, but by the end of the conversation, when I was inviting him to meet with me to talk about these things, all he could say was, "Well, you've obviously done your homework, so I'm not going to meet with you." As I said, he called back and tried to respond to just one item I had raised with him when we originally spoke. He started off by saying, "Please don't pick up the phone." He must have called when there was no one here anyway, so he went on. He replied to what I had said and then closed with these rather chilling words (and this is a direct quote of what he said): "I'm not supposed to be in contact with people such as yourself because of the things that you try to make us believe. I am sorry you believe the way you do and have been so misled." Here is a man with whom I attempted to reason—I pointed out to him the fact that it seems much more likely to me that a person who refuses to examine the issues, refuses to face the tough questions, will be "deceived" and misled than a person who is willing to openly discuss and examine the facts. But he wouldn't listen. He never provided a name or way of contacting him—so I pray and leave him in God's hands.

Brigham Young once said something that is actually rather wise:

I say to the whole world, receive the truth, no matter who presents it to you.

Take up the Bible, and compare the religion of the Latter-day Saints with it, and see if it will stand the test. (*Journal of Discourses*, 16:46)

That is what I am challenging you to do, Elder Hahn. I have expressed to you the respect that I have for someone such as you—few people are willing to give of even the barest amount of time, let alone two years of their lives. But what you do brings with it great responsibilities. You are telling people that what you preach is true— yet, if you do not examine these things, and continue to "prove all things, hold fast that which is good" (1 Thessalonians 5:21), you are shirking your responsibilities, and may end up being responsible for leading others into error. That is a heavy weight to carry, Elder Hahn.

I am asking you to meet with me again—just you and me. There is a park about three blocks north and about two blocks west of your apartment—I'm sure you know which one I'm talking about. I believe you mentioned that your "day off," so to speak, is Tuesday. Meet me at that park after sunset. We've been having strange weather this year— 122° at the end of June, and in early July it's actually been under 100° more often than not. But the evenings have been beautiful—and I want to speak with you face-to-face. We should be able to do so without interruption at the park. If you *really believe* that you are doing God's will, you will come and talk to me. I thank you.

Sincerely,

James White

LETTER 10

Meet the Awesome God of the Bible

Wednesday, July 11

Dear Steve,

I can't tell you how much I enjoyed our time together Tuesday evening. When you were delayed I began to wonder if you would come. I was very happy to see you striding across the park. Again, thank you for coming. And, even more so, thank you for your willingness to continue this conversation. I am glad to have had the opportunity of more fully explaining why I feel it is so important.

From the very beginning of my correspondence with you I have mentioned how much I wish to speak to you about the God of the Bible. The very first time I ever met with LDS missionaries this same topic came up. I recall clearly to this day speaking to them of the salvation that is mine, and how it is based not upon the words of a changeable being, or a god who was once a man but had evolved to the status of a god, but upon the words of the never changing, eternal God of the Bible—the Creator of all things, the sustainer of all things, who has always been, and will always be, fully, completely, God. I could rest in that assurance—I knew that God was not going to change, for He had never been anything other than He was—God. They listened intently, Steve, and I hope that God has seen fit to be merciful and to reveal himself to them since that day.

It is difficult to know where to start in even attempting to summarize a few of the more important aspects of the Bible's presentation of God. It is not that the Bible is unclear about God's nature, it is that we are

173

so limited in our capacity to even begin to understand the awesome Being who is presented to us in Scripture. I truly believe you will come to see that the God of the Bible is far removed from the concept of an "exalted man" that you have been taught. God is the Eternal King. To facilitate my presentation, let me break this up into topics.

The Uniqueness of God

The first aspect of God's being is His *uniqueness*. I have already presented to you a good deal of the biblical evidence on this point under the topic of "monotheism" in one of my earlier letters. God is utterly unique—there is none like Him. He even challenges mankind by saying,

> To whom then will ye liken me, or shall I be equal? saith the Holy One. Lift up your eyes on high, and behold who hath created these things, that bringeth out their host by number: he calleth them all by names by the greatness of his might, for that he is strong in power; not one faileth. (Isaiah 40:25–26)

The people of God know that He is unlike anyone or anything else, for He is the Creator of all that is. He is unique, absolute, one-of-a-kind. Note what Jeremiah said:

> Forasmuch as there is none like unto thee, O LORD; thou art great, and thy name is great in might. Who would not fear thee, O King of nations? (Jeremiah 10:6–7a)

And the Psalmist is no less clear:

> The LORD is high above all nations, and his glory above the heavens. Who is like unto the LORD our God, who dwelleth on high, who humbleth himself to behold the things that are in heaven, and in the earth! (Psalm 113:4–6)

Just think about it, Steve—the Psalmist proclaimed that God humbles himself even to look on the things that take place in heaven, let alone on the earth! Here is one who is so far above our imaginations of Him as to defy definition. There is none like Him—none at all. The question of "who is like Him" must be left unanswered, for the answer is too obvious to utter. Isaiah's prophecy exhausted the reaches of human language to describe the incredible, solitary glory of the mighty Jehovah, and still he fell short. Think on what he says in the fortieth chapter:

Who hath measured the waters in the hollow of his hand, and
meted out heaven with the span, and comprehended the dust of the
earth in a measure, and weighed the mountains in scales, and the
hills in a balance? Who hath directed the spirit of the LORD, or
being his counselor, hath taught him? With whom took he counsel,
and who instructed him, and taught him in the path of judgment,
and taught him knowledge, and showed to him the way of understanding? Behold, the nations are as a drop of a bucket, and are
counted as the small dust of the balance: behold, he taketh up the
isles as a very little thing. And Lebanon is not sufficient to burn,
nor the beasts thereof sufficient for a burnt offering. All nations
before him are as nothing; and they are counted to him less than
nothing, and vanity. To whom then will ye liken God? or what
likeness will ye compare unto him? (Isaiah 40:12–18)

Some LDS take all the references to God's hands or eyes or whatever
literally, Steve, but in this passage it is quite *obvious* that such would
be a gross misreading of the intention of Isaiah. None of the questions
asked by Isaiah can be answered—they are purely rhetorical. No one
(but God) has measured the waters in the hollow of His hand, and no
one at all has instructed God or taught Him wisdom. This is the true
God of the Bible—a very different God than one who was indeed taught
wisdom as a little spirit child, or again as a little human being on a
planet far away. This God is unique and totally different. He has never
been instructed because He has always had all knowledge—indeed, He
created all knowledge!

As we examine what the Bible teaches about the one true God I will
ask you often to compare the majestic Being who is presented in the
pages of Scripture with your own beliefs as a Latter-day Saint. I can
only ask you to be honest in answering the question, "Is your God the
same God as is described here in Isaiah, or here in Deuteronomy?" I
know that I see a *vast* difference between the God of Joseph Smith and
the God of Isaiah. Can you honestly say that the God of Mormonism
is unique, one-of-a-kind, or do other gods exist that are just like him,
who exercise dominion over other worlds? If you believe that there were
gods before Jehovah God, you cannot possibly accept the teaching of
the Scriptures that testify to the *solitariness* of the true God.

God Is. . . ?

When Jesus spoke to the woman by the well in Samaria, He spoke
a truth that was known to all. He said, "God is spirit" (John 4:24).

Yes, the King James has "God is *a* Spirit . . ." in its translation. But the original Greek can allow for either translation, and saying "God is *a* Spirit" is not as clear with reference to Jesus' point in this passage. God is not just *a* spirit among *many* spirits, but He is *spirit*. The woman had attempted to engage the Lord in a debate as to *where* people were supposed to worship God—in Jerusalem (as the Jews said) or in Mount Gerizim (as the Samaritans claimed). Jesus' response was that worship—true worship—is performed by those who truly know God, and it takes place *wherever they are*. Worship is not limited to Jerusalem or to Mt. Gerizim. Why? How could God be worshiped *anywhere*? Because God is spirit, and a spiritual being is not limited by physical constraints such as temples or locations.

When the Lord Jesus appeared to the disciples after His resurrection, they thought that they were seeing a "spirit" (Luke 24:38). But when Christ spoke to them, He corrected their misunderstanding:

> And he said unto them, Why are ye troubled? and why do thoughts arise in your hearts? Behold my hands and my feet, that it is I myself: handle me, and see; for a spirit hath not flesh and bones, as ye see me have.

If God then is spirit (or, as the KJV says, "a Spirit"), then He is not limited to a body of flesh and bones. Does the Bible teach otherwise? No, it teaches clearly that God is a spiritual being, not a physical being, in His true nature. Please note, however, that I am not saying that God could not, if He so chose, enter *into* a physical manifestation, as He did numerous times *prior to* the coming of Christ. But God has eternally existed—and He has done so as a spiritual being, not a physical being. The difference between the biblical presentation of God and the Mormon doctrine is clear, for in Mormon theology God is *unable* to exist outside of a physical body—it is part and parcel of his nature. Jehovah is different—He entered into a physical manifestation in Genesis 18 when He visited with Abraham (we know from the rest of Scripture that this was specifically the Son, the Lord Jesus), but it was not a permanent situation. I will talk about the incarnation of the Lord Jesus at a later time.

Spiritual beings are not limited by spatial considerations—God is not limited to one particular "place" where He is to "dwell." As God himself said:

> Am I a God at hand, saith the LORD, and not a God afar off?

Can any hide himself in secret places that I shall not see him? saith the LORD. Do not I fill heaven and earth? saith the LORD. (Jeremiah 23:23–24)

Does God fill heaven and earth, Steve? This concept normally bothers Mormons greatly for they have been taught that this is the "doctrine of the devil." Yet the Bible proclaims this truth. God did not say above that His *influence* fills heaven and earth, but that He *himself* fills heaven and earth. No man can hide from God, for God is *omnipresent*—there is no place where God is not.

Now before I look at other Scriptures that teach this, I want to point something out that seemingly many LDS do not understand. God is unlike us. God is unique, different. But He is also eternal and infinite and unlimited—all things that you and I *are not*. There are things about God that we simply cannot comprehend. Note that I didn't say that we can't *understand* the truth that, for example, God is omnipresent—that He is not limited to one place and one time as you and I are. I understand that, and I hope that you understand that this is what the Scriptures teach as well. But, I cannot *comprehend* how He can exist in that way. I have nothing to compare Him to that would help me to "get a hold of" such an awesome, tremendous God. But it seems to me that many LDS reject that God can exist in this way, not because the Bible does not teach it, but *simply because they won't believe in anything that they can't comprehend.*

Since when did man become the measure of all things? There are lots of thing I can't understand, much less comprehend. Scientists tell me that when two photons are emitted from the same light source they have a particular polarization. If you change the polarization of one, the other will change, too—even if it is billions and billions and billions of miles away. Wow! The best minds in the world scratch their heads at such an oddity of nature, so I'm much more in the dark than they are. But would I be wise to say, "Well, I cannot begin to understand how that is, so I reject that nature exists in this way"? No, I would not. Yet, when it comes to the Creator of both of those photons (who designed them to behave that way in the first place), many are willing to look at His revelation of himself and say, "Well, since it doesn't make sense to me that God is _____ (fill in anything you would like—eternal, omnipresent, triune, anything), then I reject that He exists in that way." Whether God is omnipresent is not dependent upon whether you, or I, believe that He is or not. If He has revealed that He is, then He is, and all that is left is whether we are going to worship Him "in truth" as Jesus said or go our own way in darkness. Whether my puny little mind can even begin to comprehend such an awesome truth is utterly irrelevant to its being true. So, when you see things in Scripture that even rival the "two photon" phenomenon of nature, do not allow yourself to slip into the deadly error of making your own mind the measure of what can and cannot be. "Let God be true, but every man a liar" (Romans 3:4). As God has reminded us before:

> For my thoughts are not your thoughts, neither are your ways my ways, saith the LORD. For as the heavens are higher than the earth, so are my ways higher than your ways, and my thoughts than your thoughts. (Isaiah 55:8–9)

Our pride may stand in the way of our fully recognizing this truth. But it is a truth all the same.

> Whither shall I go from thy spirit? or whither shall I flee from thy presence? If I ascend up into heaven, thou art there: if I make my bed in hell, behold, thou art there. If I take the wings of the morning, and dwell in the uttermost parts of the sea; Even there shall thy hand lead me, and thy right hand shall hold me. If I say, Surely the darkness shall cover me; even the night shall be light about me. Yea, the darkness hideth not from thee, but the night shineth as the day: the darkness and the light are both alike to thee. (Psalm 139:7–12)

This is one of my favorite Psalms. There is no place I can go to get away from God. I have often felt sorry for those who have to limit this passage to simply meaning that God's "influence" fills heaven and earth, so that God is no more "present" with them than the sun is truly "present" in a room into which its light shines. The true God of the Bible is not limited in His presence in this world to simply having an "influence" that acts like a giant information-gathering system while He himself is absent. He is far above such a concept.

God is infinite, limitless, in His Being. This is just one of the many ways in which we, as men, differ from God. You have been taught that God and men and angels are all of one kind of being. "As man is, God once was; as God is, man may become" is the common saying, is it not? But the Bible does not present this kind of teaching at all. Remember God's rebuke of anyone who would think of Him as "one such as yourself" in Psalm 50:21? We would do well to heed His warning. God is God, and man is God's creation, His creature (Isaiah 29:16). He is infinite, unlimited, eternal, while man is finite, limited, locked in time. "It is he that sitteth upon the circle of the earth, and the inhabitants thereof are as grasshoppers; that stretcheth out the heavens as a curtain, and spreadeth them out as a tent to dwell in" (Isaiah 40:22). Would those who are of the "same kind of being" as God be called "grasshoppers" in comparison with God if all that separated them from Him was a period of progression and exaltation? He never intended us to be anything other than what we are—His creations—and He has never been anything other than He is, the one true God.

He Who Inhabits Eternity

The next concept is probably the most amazing truth about God in the Bible—at least it fascinates me, and causes me to bow in awe and wonder every time I consider it. God has said,

> Hast thou not known? hast thou not heard, that the everlasting God, the LORD, the Creator of the ends of the earth, fainteth not, neither is weary? there is no searching of his understanding. (Isaiah 40:28)

Jehovah is the "everlasting God." A literal translation of the Hebrew would be "A God eternal is Yahweh." This is not simply teaching that God has eternally been God (though this is certainly true—Psalm 90:2). The concept is not just that God has been God for a *long time*. If we look at all that these chapters in Isaiah teach, we will discover that God is, in fact, *the Creator of time itself!* Isaiah 41:4 presents this truth, and I shall return to that passage at a later point. Right now I am intent upon understanding how God is the "eternal God." Later Isaiah will say of Him,

> For thus saith the high and lofty One *that inhabiteth eternity,* whose name is Holy; I dwell in the high and holy place, with him also that is of a contrite and humble spirit, to revive the spirit of the humble, and to revive the heart of the contrite ones. (Isaiah 57:15, emphasis added)

God is the one who "inhabits eternity." He inhabits eternity as we inhabit a house. Just as we build houses, so God created eternity itself—time. He is active in time, but just as we are not limited to our houses, so He is not limited to time. The God of the Bible exists *outside* of time! How else could it be if God is the Creator of all that exists? What a tremendous truth! Everything that takes place in time is a present reality to God. Confused? Amazed might be the better adjective. When these kinds of incredible facts of God's existence are proclaimed to men who are still in rebellion against Him, they frequently mock and laugh—but the truth remains the truth in spite of their scorn. God is the great "I Am" (Exodus 3:14). He is *always* the "I Am"—His existence is an eternal "present." There is no future to God—no past, either. He is just as much present at the burning bush of Exodus 3 as He is with you and me right now, Steve. Perhaps a little graphic will help:

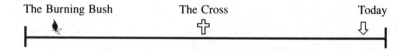

The line represents time itself—it has a beginning and an end. I have marked certain events on the line—the encounter between God and Moses at the burning bush, the crucifixion of the Lord Jesus Christ, and an arrow pointing to the present time. Of course, I have no idea just how "close" we are to the end. I have put us where we are simply for the sake of perspective. Time is going in only one direction, left to right. All of us are "trapped" in this line. But God is not! Imagine now, if you will, that the entire box represents the being of God—He surrounds and envelops all of the line of time. He is present at the burning bush, He is present at the Cross, He is present now. All points in the line are simultaneous in God's sight—a continuous "now."

Seem "incomprehensible" to you? Me, too. And, though I'd like to discuss the reasons for this a little later, I am convinced that outside of the Holy Spirit opening your mind and bringing you into submission to His truth, you will never accept such a stupendous teaching. It is not that the Bible doesn't teach this—we shall see a number of additional passages that assert this very thing as we discuss God as Creator, as Sovereign, etc.,—but that we are unwilling to submit to the truth of God whenever it "infringes" upon our own supposed freedoms. A God like this scares us, because we cannot put Him at a safe distance from

us. We know that we owe such a tremendous God worship and praise—
and we know how far short we fall of thanking Him properly for all
that we have, all that we are.

Isaiah 44:6 says,

> Thus saith the LORD the King of Israel, and his redeemer the
> LORD of hosts: I am the first, and I am the last; and beside me there
> is no God.

God is *both* the first and the last, the beginning and the end. How
could this be if God is not timeless, eternal in His nature and being?
And that is exactly what He is.

I want you to think about some of the results of recognizing this
teaching of the Bible. Mormons have been taught that the Christian
doctrine of God makes God an "ethereal nothingness" or some kind of
"fuzzy, nebulous force" that no one can know. Of course, this is utterly
untrue. We will see that despite the incredibly high and lofty being of
God, He has condescended to have dealings with man—indeed, to enter
into a relationship with man through Jesus Christ—a fact that is all the
more incredible when one realizes the *true nature of God*! But aside
from this, we can see that if God is not locked in time—if time is
actually His creation, so that He rules over it, and is not ruled by it,
then God is *unchanging*. Christian theologians use the term *immutable*
to describe the fact that God simply *cannot* change. How could He?
Change takes place over time, does it not? And if God does not experience a progression of time, then how could He change? Also, if God
is perfect now, and He changes tomorrow, what has happened? Has He
not become *im*perfect? So the Christian doctrine of the changelessness
of God comes directly from the Scriptures that teach that God is eternal
and is the Creator of all that is. The Psalmist wrote,

> Of old hast thou laid the foundation of the earth: and the heavens
> are the work of thy hands. They shall perish, but thou shalt endure:
> yea, all of them shall wax old like a garment; as a vesture shalt
> thou change them, and they shall be changed: But thou art the same,
> and thy years shall have no end. (Psalm 102:25–27)

And James added,

> Every good gift and every perfect gift is from above, and cometh
> down from the Father of lights, with whom is no variableness,

neither shadow of turning. (James 1:17)

The fact that God is unchanging is certainly one of the most *comforting* truths in the Bible. While we may be awestruck at His immutability (since we are so easily changed and experience growth or decay each and every day), we can *rejoice* that God is the eternal God, the unchanging God. He will not be something different tomorrow than He is today. We can trust that since He is just and merciful today, He will be just and merciful tomorrow, too. We can believe in His promises because He has eternally been what He is today. Can you say this about the LDS concept of God, Steve? Has God eternally been what He is today? And though you may not accept the earlier LDS teachings about the *continuing evolution* of God, if you believe that God has ever been in a state of "progression" how can you be *sure* that He will not change again tomorrow? I have confidence in my salvation because it is based upon the words of an unchanging, eternal God. How about you?

The God of the Bible is *perfect.* He lacks nothing, needs nothing, is dependent upon nothing or no one. Since all else that exists does so at His command, then how could He possibly need anything? Therefore, He is perfect. Perfection is part of His nature. If He were to change, or evolve, as Mormon theology has presented it, then He would be *imperfect,* for that which is changing and evolving is either moving toward perfection (which shows that at the present time it is imperfect) or away from perfection (showing the same thing). But Jehovah God is complete, perfect, unchanging.

You may ask, then, how God can be active in the world at all. Does not the Bible speak of God "doing" this or "doing" that? Does this not show that He is acting in time? Yes, it does, but that does not mean that He is *locked into time,* nor that He is experiencing a *progression of time.* Let me explain. I have already alleged that God is the Creator of time itself. Since He created it—all of it—then He is also the one who has determined what will take place *within time.* What we see as God's "actions" in time is, in reality, simply the result of God's eternal *decrees.* God has decreed all things that take place in this universe, and His "actions" in time as we experience them are really the result of what He determined before time itself existed. Amazing, isn't He? Worthy of your awe, your worship, your all. Even some Christians think that this kind of "theology" is dry and boring. But pondering the awesome God of Creation is about the most exciting thing I can think of.

God's decrees, His eternal decisions about how He will rule His creation, are seen in Scripture. Paul wrote to the Ephesians about the salvation that was theirs, and in speaking of how this salvation was given to them solely by God and *not* as a result of their works or worthiness, he described God in a wonderful way. Note what he says:

> In whom also we have obtained an inheritance, being predestinated according to the purpose of him who worketh all things after the counsel of his own will. (Ephesians 1:11)

Did you see how God is described? He is called the one "who worketh all things after the counsel of his own will." All things happen on the basis of God's will, God's decision. He is not simply "reacting" to man, doing His best to keep things going the "right direction." Rather, He is in control, working things out as He determines.

That God has a purpose in all things is seen as well in those passages in Isaiah that by now should be becoming familiar. We read,

> Produce your cause, saith the LORD; bring forth your strong reasons, saith the King of Jacob. Let them bring them forth, and show us what shall happen: let them show the former things, what they be, that we may consider them, and know the latter end of them; or declare us things for to come. Show the things that are to come hereafter, that we may know that ye are gods: yea, do good, or do evil, that we may be dismayed, and behold it together. (Isaiah 41:21–23)

In challenging the false gods, Jehovah lays down two challenges. One is pretty obvious: "Show the things that are to come hereafter." False gods cannot predict the future, since they don't know what the future is. Only the true God knows the future. And how does God know the future? Have you ever wondered about that, Steve? Many Christians have never really given it a lot of thought, either. It is just assumed that He knows—somehow. But we don't have to guess about it. God knows the future because He created time and all that would happen in it. He knows the future because (1) He determined the future when He created all things, and (2) He is present in all points of time, so He is *in* the future just as much as He is here and in the past. So being able to relate future events is something that only the true God can do.

The second challenge, however, is a little harder to notice. The passage reads, "let them show the former things, what they are, that we may consider them, and know the latter end of them." What God is challenging the false gods to do is not just to give us a bare recitation of past events. He is not simply looking for a history lesson. He wants to know the reasons why things happened the way they did. What was the *purpose* of this event or that one? Now there is a challenge! How often we experience things and have no idea why God would bring such a thing to pass. But God knows even if we do not. And the false gods have no more idea of why things happened in the past than we do. They don't know the purposes of God in creation.

Both of these challenges demonstrate that God's decrees determine whatever comes to pass. If they did not, then God could not speak of the purposes of past events, nor could He *certainly* speak of future events. For the God of the Bible, there is nothing unsure about tomorrow. There are no "ifs" in the divine knowledge. What a tremendous God! And how very different than the being described by Mormon writer W. Cleon Skousen in his book *The First 2,000 Years*:

> It is apparent from these and other scriptures that the present exalted position of our Heavenly Father was gradually built up. His glory and power is something which He slowly acquired until today "all things bow in humble reverence." But since God "acquired" the honor and sustaining influence of "all things" it follows as a correlary [sic] that if He should ever do anything to violate the confidence or "sense of justice" of these intelligences, they would promptly withdraw their support, and the "power" of God would disintegrate. That is what Mormon and Alma meant when they specifically stated that if God should change or act contrary to truth and justice "He would cease to be God." Our Heavenly Father can do only those things which the intelligences under Him are voluntarily willing to support Him in accomplishing. (pp. 355–56)

While I agree that God would "cease to be God" if He were ever to act in a way that is contrary to His own nature (an impossibility in and of itself), the *reason* for this is surely vastly different than Skousen would like us to think! God's power is in no way "dependent" upon some community of "intelligences" that pass judgment on God's actions! God's power has eternally been His—He did not "acquire" it over ages of time and change. Rather than being dependent upon "intelligences," the true God of Scripture has eternally been the omnipotent, self-sustaining Creator. All things are dependent *upon Him*, not the other way around!

Creator

The single most often repeated "evidence" of the divinity of the true God is that He is the Creator of all that exists. There can be no question that Jehovah God of Israel claims to be the maker and framer of the entire universe. As the Psalmist said, "The heavens are thine, the earth also is thine: as for the world and the fullness thereof, thou hast founded them" (Psalm 89:11), and in so doing he was echoing that which was known to Israel from the very beginning: "In the beginning God created the heaven and the earth" (Genesis 1:1). From the earliest history of Israel the creatorship and the resultant ownership by God of all the universe was confessed. Deuteronomy 10:14 says,

> Behold, the heaven and the heaven of heavens is the LORD's thy God, the earth also, with all that therein is.

Again in the section of Isaiah where the false gods are exposed as frauds and the true God is set forth, the concept of God being the Creator is emphasized over and over. Isaiah 42:5 is representative of many of these passages:

> Thus saith God the LORD, he that created the heavens, and stretched them out; he that spread forth the earth, and that which cometh out of it; he that giveth breath unto the people upon it, and spirit to them that walk therein. (See also Isaiah 44:24.)

The language used here by God cannot in any way be limited, Steve. The heavens—all the stars, planets, galaxies—the entire universe, is the creation of God. Every human being is God's creation—He makes them alive and gives to them breath. And yes, God is the Creator of their spirits as well. God *forms* the spirits of men—they are creations just as much as anything else. I know this is not what you have been taught, but listen to the prophet Zechariah as he relates God's message:

> The burden of the word of the LORD for Israel, saith the LORD, which stretcheth forth the heavens, and layeth the foundation of the earth, and formeth the spirit of man within him. (Zechariah 12:1)

God's "stretching forth" the heavens is clearly with reference to the creation of the heavens; His "laying the foundation of the earth" is clearly in reference to the creation of the earth; so, his "forming the spirit of man" must also refer to the *creation* of the spirit of man. God does not create spiritual beings by procreation, as in Mormonism. Rather He creates spiritual beings simply by the word of His power. The God of the Bible is the great Creator, not simply an "organizer" of "pre-existing matter" nor a being that is limited to procreation to create spiritual beings. Anything that is not God was created *by* God. Can you say this of the God of Mormonism? No, for you have been taught that matter is eternal, and Joseph Smith claimed that God "never had the power to create the spirit of man at all" (*Teachings of the Prophet Joseph Smith*, p. 354). Which will you believe—the claims of God as seen in Isaiah and Zechariah, or the words of Joseph Smith? As for me, I choose to praise God as the hosts of heaven do, as John tells us in Revelation 4:11:

> Thou art worthy, O Lord, to receive glory and honor and power: for thou hast created all things, and for thy pleasure they are and were created.

Since God created everything, then He has the perfect right to *rule* over everything. If I create something, I have control over that something. It is mine by right. In the same way God, as the Creator, has the perfect and complete right to do with His creation as He sees fit. This concept certainly angers many men who are unwilling to bow before their Creator. Few truths are more hated by men than the fact that God reigns over the universe and can simply do as He pleases with it. But few truths are more clearly taught in the Bible, either. For example, God is called the "King" over and over again in Scripture. He who is a king rules over his kingdom. In the same way, He who is the King of the universe rules as Sovereign over all that exists. The authors of Scripture certainly understood this:

> Wherefore, David blessed the LORD before all the congregation: and David said, Blessed be thou, LORD God of Israel our father, for ever and ever. Thine, O LORD, is the greatness, and the power, and the glory, and the victory, and the majesty: for all that is in the heaven and in the earth is thine; thine is the kingdom, O LORD, and thou art exalted as head above all. (Chronicles 29:10–11)

> The LORD is King for ever and ever: the heathen are perished out of his land. (Psalm 10:16)

> Who is this King of glory? The LORD strong and mighty, the

LORD mighty in battle. . . . Who is this King of glory? The LORD of hosts, he is the King of glory. (Psalm 24:8, 10)

For God is the King of all the earth: sing ye praises with understanding. God reigneth over the heathen: God sitteth upon the throne of his holiness. (Psalm 47:7–8)

But the LORD is the true God, he is the living God, and an everlasting king: at his wrath the earth shall tremble, and the nations shall not be able to abide his indignation. (Jeremiah 10:10)

Which in his times he shall shew, who is the blessed and only Potentate, the King of kings, and Lord of lords; who only hath immortality, dwelling in the light which no man can approach unto; whom no man hath seen, nor can see: to whom be honor and power everlasting. Amen. (1 Timothy 6:15–16)

The king of an ancient nation was the *supreme authority*. The king's word could not be challenged; his plans could not be questioned. So it is with God. While many today do not like the concept of an "ultimate authority" (preferring our own supposed "personal freedom"), the Bible is clear on the fact that God, as the Creator and King of all that is, is *sovereign* over all that is. He will accomplish everything that He intends, and His purposes cannot be frustrated or deterred by anything— including the will of man! There are *many* passages that teach this truth. The Psalmist wrote,

But our God is in the heavens: he hath done whatsoever he hath pleased. (Psalm 115:3)

Whatsoever the LORD pleased, that did he in heaven, and in earth, in the seas, and all deep places. (Psalm 135:6)

Understanding that God is sovereign is a common theme of the "wisdom writer" of the Proverbs, as well. Note these passages:

There are many devices in a man's heart; nevertheless the counsel of the LORD, that shall stand. (Proverbs 19:21)

Man's goings are of the LORD; how can a man then understand his own way? (Proverbs 20:24)

But, as we have already seen, Steve, that tremendous section in Isaiah provides us with some of the richest treasure of truth about God, and here, specifically about His sovereignty. Do you recall back in about my fourth letter to you, when I addressed the Bible's teaching that there is only one true God, that I cited Isaiah 43:10 as one of the most "common" verses that Christians use in showing this truth to Mormons? Well, note what comes immediately after this direct statement of monotheism:

> I, even I, am the LORD; and beside me there is no savior. I have declared, and have saved, and I have shown, when there was no strange god among you: therefore, ye are my witnesses, saith the LORD, that I am God. Yea, before the day was I am he; and there is none that can deliver out of my hand: I will work, and who shall let it? (Isaiah 43:11–13)

Notice that last phrase. In modern terms we would translate it, "I act, and who can reverse (or hinder) it?" When God determines to do something, when He decides to act, who can possibly stop Him? The question is, again, rhetorical, for there is no answer—none can possibly stop God from accomplishing *exactly* what He wills. Earlier in Isaiah we read,

> For the LORD of hosts hath purposed, and who shall disannul it? and his hand is stretched out, and who shall turn it back? (Isaiah 14:27)

Yes, I know exactly what that means, believe me. But I cannot hide from what is in Scripture. Read on:

> I am the LORD, and there is none else, there is no God beside me. . . . I form the light, and create darkness: I make peace, and create evil: I the LORD do all these things. (Isaiah 45:5, 7)

The term *evil* that is used here is placed in contrast with the term *peace* so that it most probably means *calamity* or *distress*. But, the intention of God in uttering these things is clear: Whether it be peace and prosperity, or calamity and disaster, God is in control of what takes place. This is absolutely necessary if *anything* is going to have meaning and purpose, and we have already seen that all things are purposeful. God is working out His will in the world even if we are not sharp enough to figure out *exactly* how God will be glorified in each separate event that takes place.

> Remember the former things of old: for I am God, and there is

none else; I am God, and there is none like me, declaring the end from the beginning, and from ancient times the things that are not yet done, saying, My counsel shall stand, and I will do all my pleasure." (Isaiah 46:9–10)

The true God is able to "declare the end from the beginning" long before the end has even come into view. The true God is able to speak of that which is going to take place. How so? Because His counsel shall stand, and He will do all His pleasure. Can your God say these things? The true God of Creation can. He is the Sovereign King of all that is. This majestic Person demands worship that is undertaken in *truth*. Can a person who has been taught to believe in the god of Joseph Smith possibly worship the true Jehovah in truth? Not when the true God is so utterly and completely *different* than the god of Joseph Smith's final sermons.

One of the truths that flows from God being the Creator of all things, and from His "inhabiting eternity" as we have seen, is that He is *omniscient*—that is, He has all knowledge. I realize that some Mormon writers will speak of God being omniscient. For example, Stephen Robinson, writing in the *Encyclopedia of Mormonism* said,

Latter-day Saints attribute omnipotence and omniscience to the Father. He knows all things relative to the universe in which mortals live and is himself the source and possessor of all true power manifest in it. (p. 549)

Notice that Robinson has to limit God's omnipotence and omniscience to those things "relative to the universe in which mortals live." Since he also admits that God is an "exalted being" it follows that God acquired His knowledge over a period of time, as a part of His exaltation. But, as we have noted already, God did not "acquire" this knowledge over time through some process of learning or progressing as Joseph Smith taught, and as modern Mormons affirm. Rather He has all knowledge because He created all things! Everything there is to know exists only because He allows it to and sustains it! All that is has being and existence because in His eternal wisdom He planned for it. How, then, could there be *anything* that He does not know? Not only this, but if God were to "learn" something, then He would change, and we have already seen that this is an impossibility. As God claimed,

Behold, the former things are come to pass, and new things do

I declare: before they spring forth I tell you of them. (Isaiah 42:9)

Here is a God who knows and understands all things. The Psalmist reveled in this truth:

> Thou knowest my downsitting and mine uprising; thou understandest my thought afar off. Thou compassest my path and my lying down, and art acquainted with all my ways. For there is not a word in my tongue, but, lo, O LORD, thou knowest it altogether. Thou hast beset me behind and before, and laid thine hand upon me. Such knowledge is too wonderful for me; it is high, and I cannot attain unto it. (Psalm 139:2–6)

Can you join with the Psalmist in saying "such knowledge is too wonderful for me; it is high, and I cannot attain unto it"? For some, the fact that God knows *all about them* is downright frightening. But for one who worships this God, it is a comfort indeed. The writer of the letter to the Hebrews certainly agreed on this subject as well, for he wrote,

> Neither is there any creature that is not manifest in his sight, but all things are naked and opened unto the eyes of him with whom we have to do. (Hebrews 4:13)

God has all knowledge—there is nothing He does not know. The Psalmist said that His "understanding is infinite" (Psalm 147:5). What a comfort to know and worship the true God in such an uncertain world!

The Providence of God

I mentioned earlier the common LDS belief that Christians believe in a rather nebulous concept of God and how many feel that their belief in a very human, concrete deity is much more logical. Yet, as we have seen, the Bible is very clear in proclaiming the eternal, infinite, limitless nature of Jehovah. And beyond this, the Scriptures also declare that this God is intimately involved in all that takes place here on earth. He is working out His purpose in the lives of men and the courses of the nations. He is working in this situation between you and me, Steve— He has been from the very beginning. It was not by accident that you and Elder Young were riding through that parking lot that evening right as I was getting out of my car. God had set that appointment from eternity past. The Psalmist expressed it like this:

Let all the earth fear the LORD: let all the inhabitants of the world stand in awe of him. For he spoke, and it was done; he commanded, and it stood fast. The LORD bringeth the counsel of the heathen to nought: he maketh the devices of the people of none effect. The counsel of the LORD standeth forever, the thoughts of his heart to all generations. (Psalm 33:8–11)

It is not men's plans that will in the end be "established," but God's. This is true of nations, it is true of leaders, it is true of the worker on the farm or the peasant woman on the street. All of creation experiences God's providential care and control. No king, no matter how mighty or powerful, is outside of God's command. God is described as the one who "bringeth the princes to nothing; he maketh the judges of the earth as vanity" (Isaiah 40:23). Not only is His control exercised in this area, but the natural elements—wind, rain, and sun—obey His command at *all* times, too. The Psalmist said,

He sendeth forth his commandment upon earth: his word runneth very swiftly. He giveth snow like wool: he scattereth the hoarfrost like ashes. He casteth forth his ice like morsels: who can stand before his cold? He sendeth out his word, and melteth them, he causeth his wind to blow, and the waters flow. (Psalm 147:15–18)

But while there are many who are willing to confess this kind of general sovereignty of God, few are willing to go as far as the Scriptures go in describing the control of God over one particular area—the very actions of men themselves. When the truth of God begins to impinge upon man's supposed freedom, men begin to rebel with intense hatred. The Bible, however, is clear on the subject. For example, when Abimelech took Abraham's wife at Gerar, Jehovah kept him from sinning in the matter. The Bible says,

And God said unto him in a dream, Yea, I know that thou didst this in the integrity of thy heart; for I also withheld thee from sinning against me: therefore suffered I thee not to touch her. (Genesis 20:6)

God *withheld* Abimelech from sinning! Does God truly have this kind of power? Yes, He does. "The king's heart is in the hand of the LORD, as the rivers of water: he turneth it whithersoever he will" (Proverbs 21:1); "A man's heart deviseth his way: but the LORD directeth his steps" (Proverbs 16:9). Here is a God who is not simply taken up with the "big things" but is involved in each and every happening on earth and in the heavens above. As I pointed out before, Steve, this is due to the fact that God is the Creator of all things, *including time and all the actions therein.* His providential activity in this world is the *result* of His eternal plan and decree. What a tremendous God!

One last example of God's providence—Isaiah 10:5–7. Note here how God uses an evil people (the Assyrians) to punish His people, and how He does so in such a just and righteous way as to be able to hold the wicked Assyrians responsible for their behavior:

> O Assyrian, the rod of mine anger, and the staff in their hand is mine indignation. I will send him against an hypocritical nation, and against the people of my wrath will I give him a charge, to take the spoil, and to take the prey, and to tread them down like the mire of the streets. Howbeit he meaneth not so, neither doth his heart think so; but it is in his heart to destroy and cut off nations not a few.

The Assyrians came against Israel and destroyed her. They had no idea they were fulfilling God's design and that He in fact was working out His plan through them. Yet, at the same time, they were to be held responsible for what they did. The Assyrians were incredibly wicked people—brutal and harsh. God used their wickedness to accomplish His goals, His plans, and in doing so showed His holiness and power!

Holiness, Wrath, Goodness, Mercy, and Grace

If all we knew of God is that He is in control of all things and is our Creator, we might indeed have good reason to despair, for we know how often we have rebelled against Him. But God has revealed much more about himself than just this, though all else we know of God (and anything else for that matter) must be based upon the truths we have already seen. Mormonism shows us all too well what happens when we attempt to build an edifice upon a cracked and broken foundation— just so, if we do not understand God's eternity, His unchanging nature, and His absolute sovereignty over all things, we will end up making serious errors later on in understanding how God acts in this world, especially with reference to how God saves men and brings them into a proper relationship with himself.

Before we can get to the wonderful truths of God's mercy and grace, we must recognize God's holiness and his wrath against sin. The God of the Bible is *holy*. The Scriptures again are clear on this fact:

> Give unto the LORD the glory due unto his name; worship the LORD in the beauty of holiness. (Psalm 29:2)

> Thy testimonies are very sure: holiness becometh thine house, O LORD, for ever. (Psalm 93:5)

I would strongly suggest that you find the time, Steve, to sit down in some quiet place and *slowly* read through the sixth chapter of the book of Isaiah. Then read it again. Try to envision what Isaiah saw on that day. Listen as the angels cry over and over again, "Holy, holy, holy is the LORD of hosts!" Notice how Isaiah immediately recognizes his own sin when he sees the *Holy God of Israel*. With that in mind, remember the words I quoted earlier from Mormon Apostle Orson Pratt from his book *The Seer*:

> The Gods who dwell in the Heaven from which our spirits came, are beings who have been *redeemed* from the grave in a world which existed before the foundations of this earth were laid. They and the Heavenly body which they now inhabit were once in a fallen state. . . . And thus, as their world was exalted from a temporal to an eternal state, they were exalted also, *from fallen men to Celestial Gods* to inhabit their Heaven forever and ever." (p. 23, emphasis mine)

This Holy, eternal God who sits upon the throne in Isaiah 6 was once a fallen, sinful creature upon another planet? Is this what we are to believe the Bible teaches? *Surely not!* It may have been the god of Joseph Smith's final years, but it is *not* the God of the Christian!

God's holiness is not simply limited to His moral perfection—His holiness is related as well to His absolute "otherness," or, as we saw before, His utter *uniqueness*. That which is holy is separate, distinct. God is separate, distinct—He is not to be confused with the creation itself. Have you noticed that this truth is also compromised in Mormon theology, Steve? The God of the LDS faith is not *separate* from the creation! In fact, not only can it not be said that He is the creator of *all* that exists, but if one believes that He was once a fallen man who lived upon another planet, then He was, at least for a time, *dependent* upon other things. If He is a man like you and me, then we know that we are not holy in the sense of being separate or unique. No, the god of Mormonism is certainly not the Jehovah of the Bible.

Because God is holy, He cannot abide the presence of evil. Evil, though it exists with His permission, and functions to serve a purpose, is still abhorrent to Him. He *must* punish evil if He is to be *just*. Please note that I am not saying that God is limited by what we *think* is justice. We are often wrong in our ideas. Rather, God is the very definition of what is right, what is just. He loves righteousness and justice. Note a few more Scripture passages:

> He loveth righteousness and judgment [justice]: the earth is full of the goodness of the LORD. (Psalm 33:5)

> The king's strength also loveth judgment [justice]; thou dost establish equity, thou executest judgment [justice] and righteousness in Jacob. (Psalm 99:4)

God's holiness and righteousness results in *wrath against sin*. Many in today's world think that this concept is antiquated—we need an "up-to-date" God, or so they think. But such men do not have the slightest idea of what God is truly like—His eternal nature, His holiness, His purity—and they are even less likely to honestly admit the depth and wickedness of their own personal sin. Show me a person who is unconcerned about God's punishment of sin and I'll show you a person who doesn't know God or themselves very well at all. "God judgeth the righteous, and God is angry with the wicked every day" (Psalm 7:11). God's wrath is responsible for many of the judgments that take place in our world—of course, we do not see this, for we do not see His hand in control of the wind or the waves, but it is true nonetheless.

In light of God's holiness and His wrath against sin, we can begin to recognize the incredible *depth* of God's mercy and grace in having anything at all to do with sinners, let alone providing a way for them to have forgiveness and eternal life! But, to properly discuss God's grace and mercy, we must speak about He who is Mercy, Grace, and Truth—the Lord Jesus Christ. I would like to hold that discussion long enough to ask you to respond to this material, and allow me to attempt to answer any questions or objections you might have. Then I would like to discuss my Lord and Savior with you.

In closing, Steve, I want to ask you to go back and read this letter over again before forming your final questions or thoughts. Ponder the Scriptures that I have referenced. Look them up as well in the New American Standard Bible and the New International Version that I gave to you when we met—some of these passages in the King James use very archaic language that might make some of these things a little more difficult to grasp. But most importantly of all, realize that we are bound to accept God's truth about himself—we cannot "edit" Him down to fit into *our* limited concepts. Even someone as tremendously knowledgeable as the Apostle Paul, when he finished reviewing God's works in this world, had to simply throw up his hands and cry,

O the depth of the riches both of the wisdom and knowledge of God! how unsearchable are his judgments, and his ways past finding out! For who hath known the mind of the Lord? Or who hath been his counselor? Or who hath first given to him, and it shall be recompensed unto him again? For of him, and through him, and to him, are all things: to whom be glory forever. Amen. (Romans 11:33–36)

To which I add my own "amen." May you be blessed as you seek His will and His truth.

In Christ Jesus,

James White

But the Bible Says . . .

Monday, July 16

Dear Steve,

Yes, I have been accused of being a frustrated author. More than once my correspondence with an individual has grown to what might be called "monumental proportions." And yes, you are right, my last letter allowed a good bit of "me" and my excitement about the awesome God of the Bible to show through. I'm not ashamed to admit that I love talking about God and thinking about His tremendous majesty. Some folks are just very emotional about God but don't go beyond that— personally, I am most emotional in the sense of worship/adoration when I ponder the magnificent truths of Scripture about who God is and what He has done. I think that is what the Psalmist was saying when he wrote,

> O LORD our Lord, how excellent is thy name in all the earth, who has set thy glory above the heavens! . . . When I consider thy heavens, the work of thy fingers, the moon and the stars, which thou hast ordained; What is man, that thou art mindful of him? and the son of man, that thou visitest him? (Psalm 8:1, 3–4)

It will *always* amaze me that such a great and magnificent God would love and care for a sinner like me. All of eternity does not contain enough time for me to thank Him for His grace toward me.

But, I'm getting a little ahead of myself. Your note contained some questions that I feel I need to get to before we move on to other topics.

Basically, given all I said in the previous letter, you had three questions:

1) If God can actually stop someone from sinning, why doesn't He?
2) If God is really "sovereign" and everything that takes place does so because of His decrees, because of His command, then doesn't this make Him responsible for evil?
3) Doesn't the Bible present God as "repenting" of an action, hence showing that He changes His direction according to what happens—especially in response to men's actions?

The first two questions are connected in my thinking, and I will address them together before getting to the third.

I'd like to start by laying down a general principle and going from there—a principle that is demonstrated most clearly in the crucifixion of Jesus Christ. The actual act of nailing the sinless Lord Jesus Christ upon the wooden cross was, we would both agree, a horribly sinful one. The men who were responsible—not just the soldiers, but Herod, Pilate, and the Jewish leaders who falsely accused Jesus—were guilty of a tremendous crime, a heinous evil. They *sinned* in what they did.

Yet, we also know that no single action in all of history has resulted in such tremendous *glory* being given to God. I know that many LDS have been taught to view the cross as little more than an instrument of death, yet Paul could write, "but God forbid that I should glory, except in the cross of our Lord Jesus Christ . . ." (Galatians 6:14). God's plan of redemption included the cross, and as such it is an action that is holy and right and perfect and just. On the cross sin and death were defeated once and for all, and the way of salvation for God's people was secured.

So we see in the cross an incident in which men's sinful actions resulted in God's glory. God used those sinful men (who certainly did not have pure motives for what they did) to accomplish His will. In fact, the early Church once gathered and prayed and said,

> The kings of the earth stood up, and the rulers were gathered together against the Lord, and against his Christ. For of a truth against thy holy child, Jesus, whom thou hast anointed, both Herod, and Pontius Pilate, with the Gentiles, and the people of Israel, were gathered together, *for to do whatever thy hand and thy counsel determined before to be done.* (Acts 4:26–28)

Did you catch that last phrase? What Herod, and Pilate, and the Jewish leaders did was *exactly what God had determined beforehand would be done!* How else could it be? Jesus is described in Revelation 13:8 as "the Lamb slain from the foundation of the world." If it was not eternally God's plan that the Son was to die as the sacrifice for the sins of God's people, how could He be described as the Lamb *slain from the foundation of the world*? So here we see what seems to me to be the classic example of a single action in time—the crucifixion of Christ—and the role of both man and God in it. The men who acted did so voluntarily—God did not have to "force them" to do what was evil. Their intentions, from the start, were evil. But God's intentions in the same act were pure and holy. While God eternally predestined this action which involved human guilt and sin, He did so for the holiest and purest reasons. The ultimate goal was the salvation of God's people, which brings glory to God's name.

How does this help me to answer your first two questions? Well, in answer to the first question, it points out that while God could indeed stop all men from sinning (just as He could have stopped Pilate from sentencing Christ to death, or could have frozen the soldier's hand in midair so that the nails could not be driven into the Lord's hands), He does not do so because He has a *purpose* in all that takes place in this world, including those actions that are sinful! We normally do not know the specific reason in each and every instance, but we can be confident that God is working out His eternal plan and, in the end, justice and righteousness will be established. I am reminded of King Nebuchadnezzar in the book of Daniel. He did something that was quite sinful—He lifted up his heart in pride and engaged in idolatry. As a result, God struck him with insanity so that he went about like an animal in the forest. But, when his sanity returned to him, he saw the foolishness of his ways. His sin was used by God to teach him a lesson, which he expressed in the following words:

> And I blessed the Most High, and I praised and honored him that liveth forever, whose dominion is an everlasting dominion, and his kingdom is from generation to generation: And all the inhabitants of the earth are reputed as nothing: and he doeth according to his will in the army of heaven, and among the inhabitants of the earth, and none can stay his hand, or say unto him, What doest thou? (Daniel 4:34–35)

Your second question is closely related to this one. Yes, if God had so chosen, He could have kept evil from ever existing. Yet, He did not. Why not? He had a purpose to accomplish, and, in His infinite wisdom He saw that the existence of evil was proper to His accomplishing His own desire. In the final analysis, greater good and glory will exist because of the existence of evil than if it had never existed at all. I can't tell you much more than that, for God has not revealed anything more than that. Yes, I know that "latter-day revelation" addresses the issue of *why* things are the way they are, yet we have already seen that the LDS concept of God is so far removed from the biblical one that the two cannot possibly have their origin in the same Being, the Holy Spirit of God.

Your third question is a little more difficult to answer—not because the Bible is not clear on the subject, for it is, but because the answer lies in a realm that neither you or I can possibly fully understand—eternity itself.

> God is not a man, that he should lie, neither the son of man, that he should repent: hath he said, and shall he not do it? Or hath he spoken, and shall he not make it good? (Numbers 23:19)

Yet, as you pointed out, we find the Bible saying that God "repented of the evil" He planned to execute (e.g., Jonah 3:10). In fact, a supposed "classical contradiction" is to be found in 1 Samuel the fifteenth chapter, verses 29 and 35:

> And also the Strength of Israel will not lie *nor repent;* for he is not a man, that he should repent.

> And Samuel came no more to see Saul until the day of his death; nevertheless, Samuel mourned for Saul. And the LORD *repented* that he had made Saul king over Israel.

The same Hebrew term, *nacham*, is used (though in different forms) in both verses—so how are we to understand this? We are to do what we learned before and allow the context to speak for itself. When Samuel is speaking to Saul in verse 29 he is speaking of the *differences* between God and man. One of those differences is that men change their minds and vacillate back and forth, even to the point of lying (note that Numbers 23:19 uses the same language). God will not lie nor repent in this sense. Yet, God is not a robot, and even though all that takes place does so at His command, He is still grieved and pained by the sinfulness of men. In 1 Samuel 15:35 the statement about God's repentance is preceded by a statement that Samuel, though he never saw Saul again until his death, mourned for him. So, too, God felt anguish and "sighed deeply" (the literal meaning of the term) with reference to Saul's wickedness as well. Saul was a tragic character indeed for both God and Samuel to experience mourning and sadness over him.

But all of that aside, do we not see God "changing His mind" in the Bible, even at the encouragement of men? How shall we understand this? Many are willing to just simply say, "Well, it is obvious that God has changed His mind and gone a different path," but few have thought through what this would mean. If I personally am forced to change my mind about a certain action, I have to admit that I did not have the proper foresight to avoid the situation in the first place. While that is perfectly understandable for me, can we possibly charge God with a lack of foresight? Is God so slow-witted as to make a rash promise and then have to go back and, upon calmer reflection, change His mind? Certainly this is not true of the God of the Bible that we examined in my previous letter, Steve! So how are we to understand this?

I said above that the answer to this question lies in a realm that you and I cannot comprehend—the realm of eternity. The problem is not with God, nor with His Word, but with you and me. We see things only as they occur in time, one thing after another, cause and effect, on and on down through history. But, as I've pointed out, God isn't like that. What happens in time is the result of His creation of time and all else. When we see Him acting, we are seeing Him only "from one side," so to speak—the side of time. So, we are only going to get a very distorted view. It would be like watching a play in only one dimension—only seeing a "sliver" of the whole stage and trying to figure out what was going on. In the same way, when we see God at work, we must be careful not to violate His Word and make wrong inferences that result in contradictions.

At the same time, we also need to realize that God's speaking to us is like my speaking to my infant daughter—frequently I say some rather silly things simply because right now her understanding is limited (though expanding at an *alarming* rate!). While it may bruise our egos a good bit, we are far less than infants when compared with the great Jehovah—and for Him to even deem it proper to communicate with us in such a way that we can understand Him is pretty amazing. So, in some instances (especially where we are prone to make mistakes because we cannot comprehend eternity nor the nature of His dwelling in that realm), God speaks to us "with a lisp" as John Calvin put it, as we would talk with a child. Let me give you an example.

Last week I fell down and broke my left arm. Now, when I had the arm in a sling, my children wanted to know what had happened. How wise would I be to say, "Well, kids, I have a non-displaced fracture of the head of the radius"? They probably would have said, "But what did you do to your arm?" I didn't tell them about non-displaced fractures and didn't even try to describe the difference between the radius and the ulna or anything else about anatomy or physiology. I told them, "Daddy fell down and broke the bone in his arm." Not very technical, not very specific, but it communicated the basic message.

When God brought the message of destruction to the city of Ninevah by the means of His not-so-happy prophet Jonah, He did so for a purpose. It was His purpose that the city repent, and it did. God had planned and decreed what happened all along—He didn't change. But, from our perspective, it *looked* like He had said He was going to do one thing but ended up doing another. See, it is *our perspective* that causes the problem, not God's actions. He speaks to us simply and basically, so that we can understand. We couldn't understand a full dissertation on the relationship of time and eternity—so He doesn't give us one. But, at the same time, we would be very, very foolish to say that God changes or that His Word is contradictory simply because we *cannot* fully understand God's working in the world. We may stand up in our pride and charge God with error, but such would simply be yet another manifestation of our inherent sin and rebellion.

You did mention one other thing that I wanted to respond to. You mentioned that in your talking with people who claim to be Christians you have not heard such an emphasis upon the sovereignty of God before—in fact, you have heard people speak much more about the "free will of man" than you have about the free will of God! Such is, sadly, a very accurate observation, Steve. It is uncommon to hear men speaking about the sovereignty of God. We are much more likely to emphasize our own "freedom" at the expense of God's, and that is simply part and parcel of what sin does to the heart of man. But I hope you recognize that truth is not determined by "majority vote." Even if there was almost no one who believed that God is absolutely sovereign over all things it would remain true simply because the Bible *says* that it is true. There are many truths in the Word that men are not terribly fond of, but those truths remain vital all the same. You will see the vast difference a belief in the sovereignty of God makes when we get to the topic of the grace of God and salvation.

I hope these thoughts have been of assistance to you, Steve. I, too, am looking forward to discussing the Lord Jesus Christ with you. Leave me a message on my recorder if it would be okay to go ahead and move right into that issue.

In Christ Jesus,

James

The Truth About Jesus Christ

Thursday, July 19

Dear Steve,

So you liked my daughter's guest appearance on the answering machine? Actually, it wasn't planned. My wife has never figured those things out, and keeps pressing buttons she shouldn't, and well, you ended up listening to a discourse on something that was obviously important to an 18-month-old little angel—and no, being a parent doesn't help you figure out exactly what she is saying. You will find that I have repaired the phone message so you needn't be concerned about calling the next time! Kids are so much fun—my wife and I really enjoy them.

Yes, I would love to share with you my belief in Jesus Christ—nothing is more pleasurable than that! And yes, I will be careful to compare and contrast my belief with the Mormon perspective just as you requested. To do so, however, I will have to define the LDS position so that I can then present the biblical teaching of Christ in response. Even that will not be easy, for I will still have to ask your indulgence to hold off some aspects of the discussion of Christ for a later letter. Here is my proposal as to how to handle this topic:

First, I will deal with the *person* of Jesus Christ. I will contrast LDS teaching about Christ being the literal spiritual and physical offspring of God the Father (Elohim), as well as those concepts connected with His being the Creator of all things and His "premortal relationship" as our spirit brother. I will compare these LDS teachings with the biblical presentation of Christ.

Second, I will deal with the Mormon doctrine of the atoning work of Christ on Calvary. I will in that letter deal with the concept of "blood atonement" as well, again presenting the biblical view of this issue— I think you will be a little surprised about some of the things I have to say there. I will also deal with the subject of Christ's role as our *only* High Priest, and will probably need to deal with the LDS concept of the priesthood at the same time. So, with that, let's move into the LDS teaching about Christ.

First let me say something about the importance of this topic. I can't tell you how many times when sharing with a Mormon person this kind of conversation has taken place:

"It sounds like you are saying we are not Christians, right?"

"Yes, that is what I am saying."

"But that's absurd! Not only is the name of Christ in the name of our church, but we believe in Jesus Christ!"

"Which one?"

"What do you mean, 'which one'? There is only one Jesus."

"Right, there is only one Jesus—but there are many *false* Christs being taught today. The Jehovah's Witnesses teach that Jesus is Michael the Archangel. Are they wrong in that belief?"

"Of course—Jesus isn't Michael the Archangel."

"I agree—and neither is He the spirit brother of Lucifer as you believe. A Jesus who is Michael the Archangel, or a Jesus who is the spirit brother of Lucifer, is a *false Christ*. Since we are saved by Jesus Christ, it is obvious then that we *cannot* be saved by a Christ who does not exist, can we? Therefore, if one believes in a false Christ, one will not be saved, and any system of religion that would teach falsehood about Christ is not a Christian faith."

We *cannot* be saved by a Christ who does not exist, Steve. What we believe about Christ is absolutely *vital* because I think it is self-evident that Christ defines Christianity! Jesus certainly thought so. When disputing with the Jews in John chapter 8, He said to men who were standing right in front of Him,

> Ye are from beneath; I am from above: ye are of this world; I am not of this world. I said, therefore, unto you, that ye shall die in your sins: for if ye believe not that I am *he*, ye shall die in your sins. (vss. 23–24)

The Jews who were coming against the Lord Jesus certainly believed certain things about Him—they believed, for example, that He was a man. But, obviously, believing that Jesus was simply a man is not enough. If Jesus had only claimed to be a prophet they probably would have accepted Him as such—but accepting Christ as a prophet is not enough. If Jesus had only claimed to be the Messiah they might have even accepted that—but He didn't stop there, and accepting Jesus *simply* as the Messiah is not enough, either. No, Jesus did not leave them with too many options—He claimed to be God himself! At the end of this chapter He will make it clear by saying, "Before Abraham was, I am!" The Jews picked up stones to stone Him for this statement (8:58–59), for it was all too clear what He meant by "I am." He was claiming to be their God, Jehovah! That, to their ears, was pure blasphemy.

But back in John 8:24 Jesus had said to them, "unless you believe that I am *He,* you shall die in your sins" (New American Standard). Did you note that "He" is in italics (as it is also in the KJV)? The term is not in the Greek original—in fact, Jesus says the same thing here that He says in 8:58, "I am"! Unless one believes that Jesus is the "I am," that person will die in his/her sins. Those are not my words, those are the Lord Jesus' words—and strong ones they are indeed! You might say, "But I do believe that Jesus is Jehovah." But you do not believe what the Bible says about Jehovah. Aside from Jehovah there is no God (Isaiah 45:5). To accept LDS teaching about the "plurality of Gods" is to undercut all that the Bible teaches about God, and, as a result, about Christ. A Christ who is just one god among many is still a false Christ, Steve.

With that understood, let's get to the topic at hand. As we discussed earlier, in current Mormon theology the Father is identified as Elohim and the Son, Jesus Christ, is Jehovah. We have already seen that this distinction is antibiblical in that it is directly contradictory to what the Bible reveals about God. But it is important to keep this distinction in mind to understand the LDS concept of Christ. (I keep saying "current Mormon theology," Steve, because originally Joseph Smith taught a different concept, and Brigham Young yet another—the current belief about Elohim and Jehovah did not develop until early in this century.)

The Mormon Jesus is Elohim's firstborn spirit child in the pre-existence. I have here the pamphlet you gave me when we first met entitled *What the Mormons Think of Christ.* On pages 6 and 7 we read:

In this conversation our Lord boldly directed the Pharisees to consider the very heart and core of Christianity. Is he really the Son of God, as we are the sons of mortal fathers? Or was he just another religious teacher, of whom there were many among the Jews in that day? Or was he the greatest moral and spiritual teacher of all ages, though not the literal, personal offspring in the flesh of that exalted, personal being who is God our Father? . . .

Their state of blind rejection of revealed truth was not of a different variety than that found among equally sincere, religious people today. Many reliable surveys have been made among present-day ministers and laymen, inquiring relative to a belief in Christ as the literal Son of God. Few have knowledge that he is such, literally, personally, actually, as other men are the sons of mortal parents.

The pamphlet is clear in saying that Christ is the *literal* offspring of God the Father. We will note later the fact that this is to be taken *both* with reference to his premortal existence as well as his physical existence. But specifically in reference to his supposed "spiritual begetal," the pamphlet goes on to say,

Christ is the Firstborn. Obviously, he did not have this distinction as pertaining to his birth into mortality, for many millions preceded him in birth upon this earth.

But it must not be forgotten, however little the doctrine is known and believed in the Christian world, that all men lived in a premortal estate before they were born into this world; all were born in the premortal existence as the spirit children of the Father. Christ as the firstborn spirit child; and from that day forward he has had preeminence in all things. (p. 22)

The writer goes on to cite Colossians 1:15 as evidence of this, not understanding that the term translated "firstborn" in the Greek language is not referring here to the idea of birth at all, but to the concept of rulership, preeminence, having the first place in all things. He who "created all things" (Colossians 1:16–17) is not himself a created, or begotten, being.

Bruce R. McConkie wrote in his book *Mormon Doctrine*,

Christ is the *Firstborn*, meaning that he was the first Spirit Child born to God the Father in pre-existence. (p. 281)

And Joseph Fielding Smith added,

THE FIRSTBORN. Our Father in heaven is the Father of Jesus Christ, both in the spirit and in the flesh. Our Savior is the Firstborn in the spirit, the Only Begotten in the flesh. (*Doctrines of Salvation*, 1:18.)

Doctrine and Covenants 93:21 teaches the same thing:

And now, verily I say unto you, I was in the beginning with the Father, and am the Firstborn.

God the Father, Elohim, begot a son with one of his celestial wives—the spirit child's name was Jehovah, or Jesus. You and I, supposedly, were also begotten by God the Father and one of his celestial wives. (Indeed, does not the LDS hymn entitled "O My Father" say in the third stanza, "In the heavens are parents single? No; the thought makes reason stare! Truth is reason, truth eternal, tells me I've a mother there"?) So we see that according to LDS teaching, Jesus Christ entered into spiritual existence as a spirit child of God the Father. To make the contrast between LDS teaching and biblical doctrine more complete, I might express it this way: Elohim, an exalted man, as a father begot a spirit son, Jehovah, by one of his celestial wives. That son was Jesus.

Flowing from this, then, is the concept that the Mormon Jesus is the spirit brother of you and me, since we both would have the same father in heaven—Elohim. Not only this, but since the Mormon Church teaches that Lucifer was also one of the premortal offspring of God the Father, then Jesus and Lucifer are *spirit brothers*. This is certainly a teaching that (1) is highly offensive to most Christians, and (2) is not understood or known by many LDS. I can't tell you how often some Mormon person has said to me, "Well, that shows how little *you* know about what *we* believe!" So that we have no misunderstandings, I give you the following citations:

Thus it is shown that prior to the placing of man upon the earth, how long before we do not know, Christ and Satan, together with the hosts of the spirit-children of God, existed as intelligent individuals, possessing power and opportunity to choose the course they would pursue and the leaders whom they would follow and obey. (James Talmage, *Jesus the Christ*, p. 8)

The appointment of Jesus to be the Savior of the world was contested by one of the other sons of God. He was called Lucifer, son of the morning. Haughty, ambitious, and covetous of power and glory, this spirit-brother of Jesus desparately [sic] tried to become the Savior of mankind (Milton R. Hunter, *The Gospel Through the Ages*, p. 15—this book was "written and published under the direction of the General Priesthood Committee of the Council of the Twelve of the Church of Jesus Christ of Latter-day Saints.")

Comparing the following quotations from McConkie's *Mormon Doctrine* brings out the same teaching:

> The *devil* . . . is a spirit son of God who was born in the morning of pre-existence. (p. 192)

> Christ is the *Firstborn,* meaning that he was the first Spirit Child born to God the Father in pre-existence. (p. 281)

> Christ, the Firstborn, was the mightiest of all the spirit children of the Father. (p. 590)

And if all of that wasn't enough (and I've met a few LDS for whom it *wasn't*), the *Ensign* magazine, an official publication of the LDS Church, ran a "Questions from Readers" in the June 1986 edition. While this section always has a statement that reads, "Questions of a general gospel interest answered for guidance, not as official statements of Church policy," it is clear that when it comes to doctrinal issues, the Church would not publish something out of line with its own views. In this issue the following question is asked:

> How can Jesus and Lucifer be spirit brothers when their characters and purposes are so utterly opposed?

Part of the response is as follows:

> On first hearing, the doctrine that Lucifer and our Lord, Jesus Christ, are brothers may seem surprising to some—especially to those unacquainted with latter-day revelations. But both the scriptures and the prophets affirm that Jesus Christ and Lucifer are indeed offspring of our Heavenly Father and, therefore, spirit brothers. . . . But as the Firstborn of the Father, Jesus was Lucifer's older brother. (p. 25)

So far we have the teaching that Jesus is (1) the firstborn spirit offspring of an exalted man, Elohim, God the Father, and (2) that he is the spirit brother of not only all mankind, but of Lucifer as well. Two more items are necessary for this particular letter. Next, I need to address the rather sensitive issue of the LDS concept of the means by which the physical body of Jesus Christ was begotten.

When I first began to study LDS theology, I was somewhat confused by a particular question. How could Mormons handle the fact that Jesus Christ is called the "only-begotten Son"? I noted that Mormon missionaries, when using the phrase, would almost always add something to it by saying, "the only-begotten of the Father *in the flesh.*" I never thought to stop them and ask just what they meant by that. Fortunately, the answer was to be found in LDS writings. Again, since I don't know your particular position on this (I've met Mormons who have *vehemently* denied the doctrine I am about to lay out for you), I am going to take the time to really nail down the position through a number of citations. Please be patient—this is important. Let's start with some of the older LDS leaders from last century.

> When the Virgin Mary conceived the child Jesus, the Father had begotten him in his own likeness. He was *not* begotten by the Holy Ghost. . . .
>
> . . . Now, remember from this time forth, and for ever, that Jesus Christ was not begotten by the Holy Ghost. I will repeat a little anecdote. I was in conversation with a certain learned professor upon this subject, when I replied, to this idea—"if the Son was begotten by the Holy Ghost, it would be very dangerous to baptize and confirm females, and give the Holy Ghost to them, lest he should beget children, and be palmed upon the Elders by the people, bringing the Elders into great difficulties." (Brigham Young, *Journal of Discourses*, 1:50–51)

Aside from the incredible blasphemy that anyone can see in Young's remarks, the point is that it was the Father who begot Christ.

> When the time came that His first-born, the Saviour, should come into the world and take a tabernacle, the Father came Himself and favoured that spirit with a tabernacle instead of letting any other man do it. The Saviour was begotten by the Father of His spirit, by the same Being who is the Father of our spirits, and that is all the organic difference between Jesus Christ and you and me. (Brigham Young, *Journal of Discourses*, 4:218)

> This matter was a little changed in the case of the Savior of the world, the Son of the living God. The man Joseph, the husband of

Mary, did not, that we know of, have more than one wife, but Mary the wife of Joseph had another husband. On this account infidels have called the Savior a bastard. This is merely a human opinion upon one of the inscrutable doings of the Almighty. That very babe that was cradled in the manger, was begotten, not by Joseph, the husband of Mary, but by another Being. Do you inquire by whom? He was begotten by God our heavenly father. (Brigham Young, *Journal of Discourses*, 11:268)

. . . but it was the personage of the Father who begot the body of Jesus; and for this reason Jesus is called "the *Only* Begotten of the Father;" that is, the only one in this world whose fleshly body was begotten by the Father. There were millions of sons and daughters whom He begot before the foundation of the world, but they were spirits, and not bodies of flesh and bones; whereas, both the spirit and body of Jesus were begotten by the Father—the spirit having been begotten in heaven many ages before the tabernacle was begotten upon the earth.

The fleshly body of Jesus required a Mother as well as a Father. Therefore, the Father and Mother of Jesus, according to the flesh, must have been associated together in the capacity of Husband and Wife; hence the Virgin Mary must have been, for the time being, the *lawful* wife of God the Father: we use the term *lawful* Wife, because it would be blasphemous in the highest degree to say that He overshadowed her or begot the Saviour unlawfully. It would have been unlawful for any *man* to have interfered with Mary, who was already espoused to Joseph; for such a heinous crime would have subjected both the guilty parties to death, according to the law of Moses. But God having created all men and women, had the most perfect right to do with His own creation, according to His holy will and pleasure; He had a lawful right to overshadow the Virgin Mary in the capacity of a husband, and beget a Son, although she was espoused to another; for the law which He gave to govern men and women was not intended to govern Himself, or to prescribe rules for his own conduct. It was also lawful in Him, after having thus dealt with Mary, to give Mary to Joseph her espoused husband. Whether God the Father gave Mary to Joseph for time only, or for time and eternity, we are not informed. Inasmuch as God was the first husband to her, it may be that He only gave her to be the wife of Joseph while in this mortal state, and that He intended after the resurrection to again take her as one of his own wives to raise up immortal spirits in eternity. (Mormon Apostle Orson Pratt, *The Seer*, p. 158)

You should really read all of pages 158–59 of *The Seer*. There is much more on the subject that could be presented. We see, then, that the early LDS leadership was quite open and frank on their teaching that God the Father was the *literal* parent of the body of Jesus Christ. Modern LDS writers are not much less open:

> CHRIST NOT BEGOTTEN OF HOLY GHOST. I believe firmly that Jesus Christ is the Only Begotten Son of God in the flesh. He taught this doctrine to his disciples. He did not teach them that He was the Son of the Holy Ghost, but the Son of the Father. . . . Christ was begotten of God. He was not born without the aid of Man, and *that Man was God*! (Joseph Fielding Smith, *Doctrines of Salvation*, 1:18)

Under the topic "Only Begotten Son" in *Mormon Doctrine*, Bruce R. McConkie wrote,

> These name-titles all signify that our Lord is the only Son of the Father in the flesh. Each of the words is to be understood literally. Only means *only;* Begotten means *begotten;* and Son means *son*. Christ was begotten by an Immortal Father in the same way that mortal men are begotten by mortal fathers. (pp. 546–47)

McConkie also taught this in a later book entitled *The Promised Messiah*:

> Some words scarcely need definition. They are on every tongue and are spoken by every voice. The very existence of intelligent beings presupposes and requires their constant use. Two such words are *father* and *son*. Their meaning is known to all, and to define them is but to repeat them. Thus: A son is a son is a son, and a father is a father is a father. I am the son of my father and the father of my sons. They are my sons because they were begotten by me, were conceived by their mother, and came forth from her womb to breathe the breath of mortal life, to dwell for a time and a season among other mortal men.
>
> And so it is with the Eternal Father and the mortal birth of the Eternal Son. The Father is a Father is a Father; he is not a spirit essence or nothingness to which the name Father is figuratively applied. And the Son is a Son is a Son; he is not some transient emanation from a divine essence, but a literal, living offspring of an actual Father. God is the Father; Christ is the Son. The one begat

the other. Mary provided the womb from which the Spirit Jehovah came forth, tabernacles in clay, as all men are, to dwell among his fellow spirits whose births were brought to pass in like manner. There is no need to spiritualize away the plain meaning of the scriptures. There is nothing figurative or hidden or beyond comprehension in our Lord's coming into mortality. He is the Son of God in the same sense and way that we are the sons of mortal fathers. It is just that simple. Christ was born of Mary. He is the Son of God—the Only Begotten of the Father. (pp. 468–69)

In *The Teachings of Ezra Taft Benson* we read,

> A fundamental doctrine of true Christianity is the divine birth of the child Jesus. This doctrine is not generally comprehended by the world. The paternity of Jesus Christ is one of the 'mysteries of godliness' comprehended only by the spiritually minded. . . . Thus the testimonies of appointed witnesses leave no question as to the paternity of Jesus Christ. God was the Father of Jesus' mortal tabernacle, and Mary, a mortal woman, was His mother. He is therefore the only person born who rightfully deserved the title "the Only Begotten Son of God". . . .
>
> The Church of Jesus Christ of Latter-day Saints proclaims that Jesus Christ is the Son of God in the most literal sense. The body in which he performed His mission in the flesh was sired by that same Holy Being we worship as God, our Eternal Father. Jesus was not the son of Joseph, nor was He Begotten by the Holy Ghost. He is the son of the Eternal Father. (pp. 6–7)

Robert A. Rees served as bishop of the Los Angeles First Ward. He gave a sacrament meeting talk on April 29, 1990, and provided an article to *Dialogue* that is found in the Winter 1991 issue. It is entitled, "Bearing Our Crosses Gracefully: Sex and the Single Mormon." In it we find the following:

> Mormons differ from other Christians in our literal belief that we are begotten of God spiritually and that Christ was begotten of him physically. Paul says in Acts that we are God's offspring (17:28–29). We believe that our spiritual conception was sexual just as we believe that Christ's mortal conception was. Elucidating the latter, James E. Talmage says, "That child to be born of Mary was begotten of Elohim the Eternal Father, not in violation of natural law, but in accordance with a higher manifestation thereof." (1986, 81)

Finally, we turn to the new *Encyclopedia of Mormonism* for these words:

> It is LDS doctrine that Jesus Christ is the child of MARY and GOD THE FATHER, "not in violation of natural law but in accordance with a higher manifestation thereof" (*Jesus the Christ*, p. 81). (Vol. 2, p. 729)
>
> For Latter-day Saints, the paternity of Jesus is not obscure. He was the literal, biological son of an immortal, tangible Father and Mary, a mortal woman. . . . Jesus is the only person born who deserves the title "the Only Begotten Son of God" (John 3:16, Benson p. 3). He was not the son of the HOLY GHOST; it was only through the Holy Ghost that the power of the Highest overshadowed Mary.

I don't think you could get any plainer than that! I have met a few Mormons that I like to call "minimalists." That is, if you can't show them a direct text out of Mormon scripture, they won't even attempt to defend it, even though they might believe it. Some of them have tried to deny that the LDS Church teaches that God the Father is *literally and physically* the parent of the child Jesus. The above quotes, all taken from apostles and prophets of the LDS Church, teach otherwise. It is certainly understandable why some Mormons are embarrassed by the doctrine, for, in bold and frank terms, they are teaching that Elohim, God the Father, had sexual intercourse with Mary, resulting in her pregnancy and the birth of Jesus Christ. There are many problems with such a teaching, two of the most obvious being (1) Mary, according to LDS teaching, would be the *spirit child* of Elohim in the first place, resulting in an incestuous union, and (2) the miracle of the virgin birth was that Mary was a virgin at the time of the birth. In Mormonism all you can say is that she was a virgin at the time of conception, which in and of itself is hardly a miracle.

Other LDS, however, are much more open about this teaching. I was caught utterly flat-footed one day outside of the west gate of the LDS temple in Salt Lake during the General Conference. A tall man, about fifty years of age, came striding across West Temple Drive. I could tell he was in a hurry, but in my best tracting style I offered him a gospel tract. You could tell he thought for a moment, and then came to a halt.

"Do you know what is wrong with you guys?" he said to me and the other volunteers standing with me. I've heard just about every answer to that question, but wasn't prepared for what he had to say.

"Sir?" I replied.

"You think sex is dirty!" Those who know me, Steve, will tell you that I am rarely left speechless, but this time I just stood there, staring. "You don't believe that God the Father could have had sex with Mary and that it could be a holy, righteous thing," he continued. I managed to say something about not thinking that sex was dirty, and trying to go into a discussion of the nature of God, but he wasn't about to be reasoned with. "That really is your problem. This church (he said pointing to the tabernacle) is the true one, and you are just too blind to admit it." With that he turned and strode through the gate. I looked at the other volunteers and said, "Well, at least he was honest about it—more than you can say for most!" And so I come to the last LDS belief about Christ (for this letter anyway). It has really been covered before—back when I discussed with you the doctrine of God and the Bible's absolute monotheism. Jesus Christ, as a resurrected being today, is a god in LDS thought. But, it must be honestly recognized that he is simply one god among many, many gods. He is one god among three gods for this planet—and there was a god ruling the planet that the god of this planet lived on ages ago; and there was a god before him, and yet another god before him, so that there are, literally, a nearly unlimited number of gods out there—what sets Jesus Christ apart from the rest? His dominion, in comparison with one of these gods that has been a god for a far longer time, would be minuscule and hardly remarkable. Is this the "Alpha and Omega" of the Bible, the Almighty ruler of creation? Hardly. The polytheism of the LDS Church robs the Lord Jesus Christ (not to mention the Father and the Spirit) of His rightful honor. My Jesus holds everything that exists ANYWHERE together—without Him, it would all come flying apart. Is that the same Christ you proclaim?

So here we have the LDS doctrine of the *person* of Christ. Let's turn to the Bible and find out what that inspired book teaches about Christ and how this compares with what we have just reviewed.

The first truth of Scripture about Jesus Christ is that *He has eternally existed as God.* Jesus is no created being; the eternal Son did not enter into existence at a particular point in time. Christ was not born as a "spirit child" then had to undergo growth and development until attaining some level of exaltation or power. The Lord of glory has always been—He is eternal. Let's look at just a few of the passages that teach this.

When Micah prophesied of the coming of the Messiah, he wrote,

> But thou, Bethlehem Ephratah, though thou be little among the thousands of Judah, yet out of thee shall he come forth unto me that is to be ruler in Israel; whose goings forth have been from of old, *from everlasting.* (Micah 5:2, emphasis mine)

The Apostle John taught the same truth:

> In the beginning was the Word, and the Word was with God, and the Word was God. The same was in the beginning with God. All things were made by him; and without him was not anything made that was made. (John 1:1–3)

Note, Steve, that the Word (who is identified as the Lord Jesus Christ in verse 14) "was in the beginning with God." The Greek text underlying this translation is very expressive, in that the verb used does not refer to a point in time at which the Word *began* or *came into existence,* but instead it refers to continuous action in the past—no matter how far into the past you wish to push this "beginning" the Word *was already in existence.* The Word is *eternal.* The description given here is certainly not in harmony with the LDS concept mentioned above. When passages like these are presented to Mormons, my experience is that the all-encompassing context of these passages is automatically limited to "just this planet." The beginning spoken of by John is limited to the beginning of this planet—not to the beginning in the *absolute* sense obviously meant by John. That John is not limiting his meaning to just this planet is clear by the fact that he goes on to teach that "all things were made by him; and without him was not anything made that was made." *Nothing* exists outside of Christ's creative action—*nothing!* I will look more at the fact that Christ is the Creator of all things, but for now the point is clear that if Christ is the Creator, He must be eternal and exist prior to all other things.

Jesus identified himself as Jehovah God in John 8:58 when He said, "Before Abraham was, I am." Jehovah, as we have already seen, is the "eternal God" (Isaiah 40:28). How then can LDS teachers say that Jesus is the spiritual offspring of Elohim when the Bible says that Jehovah *is* the eternal Elohim?

Jesus Christ is the "Alpha and Omega, the beginning and the end, the first and the last" (Revelation 22:13). Even though Mormon Scriptures also make this identification of Christ (D&C 19:1), modern LDS belief forces a drastic redefinition of the clear meaning of this phrase. A god who is the spiritual offspring of another god who is also the spiritual offspring of yet another god from ages past, is *not* the Alpha and Omega! Such a god could not possibly be called "the beginning" nor "the end," let alone the "first and the last." The true Jesus Christ of Scripture is the eternal Jehovah, not the spirit child of an exalted man.

One of the clearest means the Holy Spirit used in Scripture to reveal the eternal nature of the Lord Jesus was through the Bible's teaching that Jesus Christ is the Creator of all things. Mormons confess that this is true. Even *What the Mormons Think of Christ* makes this clear on pages 12–14. But when Mormons are pressed, they have to severely limit the meaning of "all things." Note what Paul says in Colossians 1:16–17 with reference to Christ:

> For by him were all things created, that are in heaven, and that are in earth, visible and invisible, whether they be thrones, or dominions, or principalities, or powers—all things were created by him, and for him; and he is before all things, and by him all things consist.

Paul is extremely specific and exhaustive in defining the sphere of Christ's creatorship. He just about exhausts the limits of the language to speak of that which Christ created. Christ created *all things*. What does this mean? It means all things in heaven and in earth (that's everything), whether those things are visible or invisible (that's everything), thrones, dominions, principalities, or powers (that includes all spiritual beings and powers in existence *anywhere*). *All things* were created *by* Christ. *All things* were created *for* Christ. Christ is *before all things* (again showing His absolute eternal nature), and by him all things "consist" or "hold together." Without the Lord Jesus, nothing would exist. Without the Lord Jesus, nothing would have purpose. Without the Lord Jesus, everything would cease to exist. He is holding all things together by the word of His power (Hebrews 1:3). Is this not exactly what the Bible teaches about Jehovah God? It is. Jehovah God created all things alone (Isaiah 44:24) yet the Bible teaches that Jesus created all things (John 1:3).

When Mormons are faced with the *expansiveness* of Christ's creative activity, they are quick to limit His work to simply that which is "relevant to this earth." Where does the Bible limit Christ's work? Nowhere. So why are LDS people so quick to say "Christ created all things relevant to this earth" rather than simply confessing, with Paul and John and the writer of Hebrews, that Christ is the Creator? Because the truth of Christ's being the Creator of all things causes insurmountable problems for LDS theology. For example, if Jesus Christ is the Creator of *all things*, this would mean that He created all worlds wherever they might be—look to the sky and see all the stars and realize that Christ created them all and upholds them by His power. But, Mormonism teaches that Jesus' spiritual parent, Elohim, was once a man who lived on a planet, and all this *prior to* Elohim's exaltation to godhood and the "birth" of the spirit child Jehovah! How could Jesus Christ create the planet upon which His father lived as a man *before Jesus was even begotten as a spirit child*? And we can go backwards from there— what about Christ's "grandparent," the god who gave birth to Elohim before Elohim was a man? Did that god not also live upon a planet? And who created that planet? According to the Bible, it was Jesus Christ. But how could this be? So you can see why the work of Christ as Creator has to be severely limited by LDS theology, for if Christ were the Creator of all things , then He would be the only true and eternal God. That *is* what the Bible teaches, but it is *not* what the LDS Church teaches.

The fact of Christ's position as the maker of heaven and earth also causes severe problems for the Mormon doctrine of the "pre-existence" as well as the teaching that Jesus is the "spirit brother" of Lucifer. As the quotes above demonstrate, the Mormon concept is that Jesus is the *first* of the many millions of spiritual offspring of Elohim, making Jesus one of the "spirits of men." Yet, the Bible teaches that Jehovah is the *Creator* of all things, *including* the spirits of men! Notice Zechariah 12:1:

> The burden of the word of the LORD for Israel, saith the LORD, who stretcheth forth the heavens, and layeth the foundation of the earth, and formeth the spirit of man within him.

If Jehovah is one of the spirits of men, how can He be the one that forms the spirits of men? Clearly, the Jehovah of the Bible is vastly different than the LDS concept! And since we do agree that Jesus is Jehovah, then it is utterly impossible that Jesus is a "spirit child" of

Elohim in some premortal existence.

We also see that it is impossible to teach that Jesus is the spirit brother of Lucifer if indeed Christ is the Creator of all things. In Colossians 1:16 we saw that all things, *including* the spiritual realm (thrones, principalities, dominions, powers), were created by Christ. Lucifer (Satan) would be included in that realm, and would therefore be the *creation* of Christ rather than His "spirit brother." Anything that exists that is not God was created by God, and Lucifer is included in that. Indeed, it seems that Satan is being addressed under the title of the "king of Tyre"("Tyrus" in the KJV) in Ezekiel 28:13–15 (compare Isaiah 14:12–17), and Jehovah says,

> Thou hast been in Eden, the garden of God; every precious stone was thy covering, the sardius, topaz, and the diamond, the beryl, the onyx, and the jasper, the sapphire, the emerald, and the carbuncle, and gold: the workmanship of thy tabrets and of thy pipes was prepared in thee *in the day that thou wast created.* Thou art the anointed cherub that covereth; and I have set thee so: thou wast upon the holy mountain of God; thou hast walked up and down in the midst of the stones of fire. Thou wast perfect in thy ways from the day *that thou wast created*, till iniquity was found in thee.

If Satan is indeed in view here (and we would have to ask how the king of Tyre was in the garden of Eden or was an "anointed cherub" if Satan is not the one being addressed), then it is clear that he is a *created being,* for this fact is repeated twice. Therefore, if he is a created being, then Jesus Christ created him. How, then, could Jesus Christ be the spirit brother of His own creation?

So we have seen that the Lord Jesus of the Bible is (1) eternal, not created or "begotten" at some point in time in the past, and (2) is the Creator of all things, including Lucifer and the very spirits of men. The next concept raised by the Mormon doctrine of Christ is His virgin birth. The classic texts are to be found in Matthew 1:18 and Luke 1:35:

> Now the birth of Jesus Christ was on this wise: When, as his mother, Mary, was espoused to Joseph, before they came together, she was found with child of the Holy Ghost.

> And the angel answered and said unto her, The Holy Ghost shall come upon thee, and the power of the Highest shall over-shadow thee: therefore also that holy thing which shall be born of

thee shall be called the Son of God.

The *means* of Mary's pregnancy is not in doubt—the Holy Ghost began the pregnancy by supernatural means. The Holy Ghost did not have to use sexual means to begin the process of growth—God created us, and He knows full well how we function. Mary was still a virgin, having known no man, including an "exalted man," at the time of the birth of Christ. This is the miracle of the virgin birth of the Lord Jesus. No human agency brought about His birth—Mary was the passive recipient of the eternal Word who "became flesh" within her.

The main problem with the LDS concept is tied in with the Mormon doctrine of God. Bruce R. McConkie made this clear when he spoke of the terms *father* and *son* being *literally* applied to the Father and the Son. The fact that God is utterly unique and that such an application of human terms to the eternal God *must* result in error is missed by LDS leaders. The relationship of the Father and the Son must be defined by God's revelation, not by our understanding of human relationships. For example, since the Son is clearly eternal in His existence, then how can we understand *father* and *son* as literal descriptions? My son Joshua is not as old as I am, obviously. I begot him at a point in time. But the Son has eternally existed, and therefore was not "begotten" by a "father" at a point in time. The terms *Father* and *Son* are meant to communicate something else—something about the intimate, close and personal relationship that exists between the Father and Jesus Christ. But to force *human* and, therefore, *creaturely* functions and forms upon the nature of God is a grave error. While Mormons are quick to recognize the symbolic descriptions of God elsewhere (such as God's "wings" or His "feathers," (Psalm 91:4), when it comes to these terms they insist upon literality, even when the Bible clearly makes such an interpretation an impossibility. Since we have already seen how the Bible denies that God is an exalted man, the entire concept of the physical begetting of Jesus Christ by the Father is seen to be a false teaching based upon a grave misunderstanding.

The true Jesus Christ, Steve, is not one god among many, many gods. He is not your "spirit brother" but He *is* your Creator. Your spirit brother cannot save you. Your Creator can. Jesus Christ is worthy of your worship for He has eternally existed as God, He created all things, and upholds all things by His power. This is the true and living Jesus Christ. Would you like to know Him?

Next time I will address the atoning work of Christ and His priesthood, along with any questions you might have. I'm looking forward to hearing from you.

In Him,

James White

The Atonement and the Priesthood of Christ

Wednesday, July 25

Dear Steve,

My what a busy week! Sorry I haven't gotten back to you sooner. Let me dive right into your questions, answer them, and move into the subject of the atonement of Jesus Christ and His priesthood.

First, you asked about two references, Jeremiah 1:4–5 and Job 38:7. The first reads,

> Then the word of the LORD came unto me, saying, Before I formed thee in the belly I knew thee; and before thou camest forth out of the womb I sanctified thee, and I ordained thee a prophet unto the nations.

And the second passage needs a little context, so I will cite Job 38:1–7:

> Then the LORD answered Job out of the whirlwind and said, Who is this that darkeneth counsel by words without knowledge? Gird up now thy loins like a man; for I will demand of thee, and answer thou me. Where wast thou when I laid the foundations of the earth? Declare, if thou hast understanding. Who hath laid the measures of it, if thou knowest? Or who hath stretched the line upon it? Whereupon are its foundations fastened? Or who laid its cornerstone when the morning stars sang together, and all the sons of God shouted for joy?

Both passages are commonly cited by LDS people in defense of their doctrine of pre-existence. Yet, an examination of the texts demonstrates that they are ill fit for such a use. First, the passage in Jeremiah simply says that God had *chosen* Jeremiah as a prophet before his birth. The term translated *to know* (as in "I knew you") in the Hebrew is often used in the sense of *to choose*, not simply to *know* in a sense of *familiarity with*. For example, when God speaks of Israel in Amos 3:2, He says, "You only have I *known* of all the families of the earth. . . ." Did God only *know* about Israel—did He not also know about Egypt, or Assyria, or Babylon? Of course—but only Israel was *chosen* to be His people. The same is true here in Jeremiah 1:5—the term *knew* is paralleled with two other terms—God *sanctified* him and *ordained* him. All speak of God's sovereign predestination of Jeremiah to the office of a prophet. Nothing here suggests that Jeremiah had a pre-existence in which he was familiar with Jehovah.

The second passage is even more clearly unsuitable for a defense of pre-existence. If you would take the time to read the entire chapter, you would find that it is one long unanswerable question—one huge rhetorical demonstration of the foolishness of a man who would question God and His workings in the world. Job can't answer any of these questions that he is asked, and in fact, having been utterly crushed under the weight of this awesome revelation of God that extends through the next chapter, he finally is forced to say,

> Behold, I am vile; what shall I answer thee? I will lay mine hand upon my mouth. Once have I spoken; but I will not answer; yea, twice; but I will proceed no further. (Job 40:4–5)

It doesn't seem God felt that was enough, because He continues on with His questioning in Job 40:6-41:34, and Job answered saying,

> I know that thou canst do every thing, and that no thought can be withheld from thee. Who is he who hideth counsel without knowledge? Therefore have I uttered that which I understood not; things too wonderful for me, which I knew not. (Job 42:2–3)

So when God asked Job where he was when "the morning stars sang together, and all the sons of God shouted for joy" Job had no answer *because he wasn't there*! To use this to say that Job was one of the "sons of God" mentioned in the passage is to miss the obvious. "Sons of God" in the Old Testament refers to the angels of God, His creations, not to some group of pre-existent spirit children. So, as you can see, Steve, these two passages, so often quoted by LDS people, do not in any way teach the concept of pre-existence.

You also asked about the relationship of the Father and the Son in reference to Jesus being the Creator, yet the Father also being the Creator. Remember what I had mentioned before concerning the doctrine of the Trinity—it is based upon three biblical teachings: (1) There is only one God, (2) there are three Persons described as God—the Father, the Son, and the Spirit, and (3) all three Persons share fully and completely that being that is God. The final point would primarily be concerned with the deity of Christ and the Spirit since few people deny the deity of the Father! Also, remember the very important distinction I brought out between the terms *being* and *person*. Rocks have being, but they are not personal. There is one being of God, eternal and infinite, yet there are three Persons who share that one being. And, I've already warned you about "importing" human concepts into your understanding of God, such as understanding "person" in human terms.

Now, in reference to your question, since Creation is the work of God generally, it is not surprising to see the Father, the Son, and the Spirit all described as having a part in that work. Since the name "Jehovah" is used of all three divine Persons, and Jehovah created all things, then all three Persons were in some way involved in the creative act. Only the Mormon insistence on forgetting the absolute unity of the being of God results in your misunderstanding. A person informed only by the Bible and not by Joseph Smith would not have a difficulty seeing the unity of the work of God.

I hope that is satisfactory with reference to your questions. I will now move on to the subject of the atonement of Christ.

Bruce R. McConkie said of the atonement:

> To atone is to ransom, reconcile, expiate, redeem, reclaim, absolve, propitiate, make amends, pay the penalty. Thus the atonement of Christ is designed to ransom men from the effects of the fall of Adam in that both spiritual and temporal death are conquered; their lasting effect is nullified. . . . *Immortality* comes as a free gift, by the grace of God alone, without works of righteousness. *Eternal life* is the reward for "obedience to the laws and ordinances of the Gospel". . . .
>
> Because of the atonement and by obedience to gospel law men have power to become the sons of God in that they are spiritually begotten of God and adopted as members of his family. (*Mormon Doctrine*, pp. 62, 65)

According to this and other statements by Mormon leaders, the work of Christ "saves everyone" in the sense that all men will be resurrected because of the atonement, no matter what their personal lives were like or if they had repented of their sins or not. This is "universal salvation" and is given simply on the basis of God's grace (I hope to discuss this with you more fully at a later time under the broad topic of the Gospel of grace). But I hope you realize that most Christians would not use the term *salvation* simply with reference to physical resurrection. We do not believe that the resurrection of the unjust for their judgment is part of "salvation," nor that the atonement of Christ was necessary for them to be resurrected at all. But aside from that difference, McConkie also states that the atonement seems to make *possible* the gaining of eternal life, which is defined as the "reward for 'obedience to the laws and ordinances of the Gospel.' " Without getting deeply into the topic of salvation and the gospel, gaining eternal life in Mormon thought is the same as gaining "exaltation," and this is *not* by grace alone but grace coupled with obedience to laws and ordinances that are supposedly a part of the Gospel plan (see *Mormon Doctrine*, page 671). So the atonement does not, in and of itself, accomplish this "higher" salvation, this personal exaltation, but it simply makes it a *possibility*.

Much could be said about the LDS doctrine of the atonement. One unique concept has to do with the idea that the atonement began in the Garden of Gethsemane, when Christ's sweat was, "as it were great drops of blood falling down to the ground" (Luke 22:44). D&C 19:18 takes this to mean that Christ did indeed "bleed from every pore" and hence the idea that the atonement began at this point. However, I would just note in passing that we read in the Bible that we are saved and redeemed not by the blood of the garden but by the blood shed on the cross (Colossians 1:20), and that it is without the *shedding* (not *sweating*) of blood that there is no remission of sins (Hebrews 9:22).

I am also reminded of a talk given by Elder Boyd K. Packer at the General Conference in April of 1977 entitled "The Mediator." In his talk Elder Packer told a parable of a person who was in debt and could not pay his bill. A mediator appears and offers to pay the debt. I pick up at this point:

> The mediator turned then to the debtor. "If I pay your debt, will you accept me as your creditor?"

"Oh yes, yes," cried the debtor. "You save me from prison and show mercy to me."

"Then," said the benefactor, "you will pay the debt to me and I will set the terms. It will not be easy, but it will be possible. I will provide a way. You need not go to prison."

Later Packer identifies the mediator as Christ, and we as the debtors. He says,

The extension of mercy will not be automatic. It will be through covenant with Him. It will be on His terms, His generous terms, which include, as an absolute essential, baptism by immersion for the remission of sins.

And later he added these words,

He also makes possible redemption from the second death, which is the spiritual death, which is separation from the presence of our Heavenly Father. This redemption can come only to those who are clean, for no unclean thing can dwell in the presence of God. (*Ensign*, May 1977, pp. 55–56)

The concept that we somehow continue to owe the debt of sin even after our "salvation" is one that we will discuss later. Till then, I note especially that the *atonement of the Lord Jesus, according to the Church of Jesus Christ of Latter-day Saints, does not bring about full and complete salvation outside of the works of man*. Such things as baptism and "continued obedience to gospel ordinances and principles" are required for the atonement to be effective.

But what is for me the most striking, and indeed the most disturbing aspect of LDS teaching about the atonement of Christ is that of the doctrine of "blood atonement." I have broached this topic with many LDS and have received a wide variety of explanations about this belief, even to the point of denial that it is taught by Mormonism. Since there are some LDS who don't seem to be aware of this teaching, I will again make sure that my "ducks are in a row" and provide you with a number of citations that demonstrate this teaching. I will proceed chronologically, going back to the man who spoke the most about this doctrine, Brigham Young, the second president of the LDS Church.

On March 16, 1856, Brigham Young preached a sermon in the

Tabernacle in Salt Lake City. Here is an excerpt from that sermon. I will let it speak for itself:

> You say, "That man ought to die for transgressing the law of God." Let me suppose a case. Suppose you found your brother in bed with your wife, and put a javelin through both of them, you would be justified, *and they would atone for their sins,* and be received into the kingdom of God. I would at once do so in such a case; and under such circumstances, I have no wife whom I love so well that I would not put a javelin through her heart, and I would do it with clean hands. But you who trifle with your covenants, be careful lest in judging you will be judged. (*Journal of Discourses,* 3:247, emphasis mine)

A scant six months later he preached yet another sermon and said,

> I say, that there are men and women that I would advise to go to the President immediately, and ask him to appoint a committee to attend to their case; and then let a place be selected, *and let that committee shed their blood.*
>
> *We have those amongst us that are full of all manner of abominations, those who need to have their blood shed, for water will not do, their sins are of too deep a dye.*
>
> You may think that I am not teaching you Bible doctrine, but what says the apostle Paul? I would ask how many covenant breakers there are in this city and in this kingdom. I believe that there are a great many; and if they are covenant breakers we need a place designated, *where we can shed their blood. . . .*
>
> *We have been trying long enough with this people, and I go in for letting the sword of the Almighty be unsheathed, not only in word,* but in deed. . . .
>
> Brethren and sisters, we want you to repent and forsake your sins. And you who have committed sins that *cannot be forgiven through baptism, let your blood be shed, and let the smoke ascend,* that the incense thereof may come up before God *as an atonement for your sins,* and that the sinners in Zion may be afraid. (*Journal of Discourses,* 4:49–51, emphasis mine)

Young was even more explicit later that day:

> There are sins that men commit for which they cannot receive forgiveness in this world, or in that which is to come, and if they had their eyes open to see their true condition, they would be per-

fectly willing *to have their blood spilt upon the ground,* that the smoke thereof might ascend to heaven as an offering for their sins; and the smoking incense *would atone for their sins,* whereas, if such is not the case, they will stick to them and remain upon them in the spirit world.

I know, when you hear my brethren telling about cutting people off from the earth, that you consider it is strong doctrine; but it is to save them, not to destroy them. . . .

. . . I know that there are transgressors, who, if they knew themselves, and the only condition upon which they can obtain forgiveness, would beg of their brethren *to shed their blood,* that the smoke thereof might ascend to God as an offering to appease the wrath that is kindled against them, and that the law might have its course. I will say further: I have had men come to me and offer their lives to atone for their sins.

It is true that the blood of the Son of God was shed for sins through the fall and those committed by men, *yet men can commit sins which it can never remit.* . . . There are sins that can be atoned for by an offering upon an altar, as in ancient days; and there are sins that the blood of a lamb, of a calf, or of turtle doves, cannot remit, *but they must be atoned for by the blood of the man.* (*Journal of Discourses,* 4:53–54, emphasis mine)

Five months later Brigham Young returned to his topic once again:

. . . When will we love our neighbor as ourselves? . . . Now take a person in this congregation who has knowledge with regard to being saved in the kingdom of our God and our Father, and being exalted, one who knows and understands the principles of eternal life . . . and suppose he is overtaken in a gross fault, that he has committed a sin that he knows will deprive him of that exaltation which he desires, and that he cannot attain to it *without the shedding of his blood,* and also knows that by *having his blood shed he will atone for that sin,* and be saved and exalted with the Gods, is there a man or woman in this house but what would say, "shed my blood that I may be saved and exalted with the Gods"?

. . . Will you love your brothers and sisters likewise, when they have committed a sin that cannot be atoned for without the shedding of their blood? Will you love that man or woman enough to *shed their blood*? That is what Jesus Christ meant. . . .

I could refer you to plenty of instances *where men have been righteously slain, in order to atone for their sins.* I have seen scores

and hundreds of people for whom there would have been a chance
(in the last resurrection there will be) if their lives had been taken
and their blood spilled on the ground as a smoking incense to the
Almighty, but who are now angels to the devil. . . . I have known
a great many men who have left the Church for whom there is no
chance whatsoever for exaltation, *but if their blood had been
spilled,* it would have been better for them. . . .

This is loving our neighbor as ourselves; if he needs help, help
him; and if he wants salvation and it is necessary *to spill his blood
on the earth in order that he may be saved, spill it.* . . . That is
the way to love mankind. (*Journal of Discourses*, 4:219–20, emphasis mine)

I must admit to being sickened simply by typing these quotations,
Steve. No Christian heart can possibly hear this kind of incredibly false
teaching without cringing in horror. But allow me to "head you off at
the pass," so to speak. I know that all of those references are well over
a hundred years old. But does the modern LDS Church still believe in
this kind of doctrine? It most certainly does! Read the words of Joseph
Fielding Smith, Prophet of the LDS Church from 1970–1972 just as
they appear in his book *Doctrines of Salvation*, Volume 1, pages 134
and 135:

But man may commit certain grievous sins—according to his
light and knowledge—that will place him beyond the reach of the
atoning blood of Christ. If then he would be saved he must make
sacrifice of his own life to atone—so far as in his power lies—for
that sin, for the blood of Christ alone under certain circumstances
will not avail.

ATONEMENT AND SINS UNTO DEATH. Joseph Smith taught that
there were certain sins so grievous that man may commit, that they
will place the transgressors beyond the power of the atonement of
Christ. If these offenses are committed, then the blood of Christ
will not cleanse them from their sins even though they repent.
Therefore their only hope is to have their own blood shed to atone,
as far as possible, in their behalf. This is scriptural doctrine, and
is taught in all the standard works of the Church.

Bruce R. McConkie, in *Mormon Doctrine*, also stated that the "true
doctrine of blood atonement is simply this":

1. Jesus Christ worked out the infinite and eternal atonement

by the shedding of his own blood. He came into the world for the purpose of dying on the cross for the sins of the world. By virtue of that atoning sacrifice immortality came as a free gift to all men, and all who would believe and obey his laws would in addition be cleansed from sin through his blood. . . .

2. But under certain circumstances there are some serious sins for which the cleansing of Christ does not operate, and the law of God is that men must then have their own blood shed to atone for their sins. Murder, for instance, is one of these sins; hence we find the Lord commanding capital punishment. Thus, also, if a person has so progressed in righteousness that his calling and election has been made sure, if he has come to that position where he knows "by revelation and the spirit of prophecy, through the power of the Holy Priesthood" that he is sealed up unto eternal life (D&C 131:5), then if he gains forgiveness for certain grievous sins, he must "be destroyed in the flesh," and "delivered unto the buffetings of Satan unto the day of redemption, saith the Lord God." (pp. 92–93)

It seems that modern LDS leaders like Joseph Fielding Smith and Bruce R. McConkie agree with Brigham Young on the doctrine of blood atonement! This concept seems alive and well in the modern LDS Church. Of course, the *practice* of blood atonement cannot be carried out by the Mormon Church today, though there certainly is evidence that it was practiced during the days of Brigham Young. With reference to this McConkie wrote these rather chilling words:

This doctrine can only be practiced in its fullness in a day when the civil and ecclesiastical laws are administered in the same hands. (*Mormon Doctrine*, p. 93)

Since many Mormons believe that in the end times the civil and ecclesiastical laws *will* be administered by the same hands, such a concept is certainly frightening in its ramifications.

I shall hold my rebuttal of this doctrine until I have had an opportunity of presenting what the Bible teaches about the atoning work of Jesus Christ. For now it will be sufficient for me to state that anyone who could believe or teach such a concept knows little or nothing about the work of Christ on the cross. Indeed, I will close my presentation of the LDS concept of the atonement by noting the words of Joseph Smith with regard to his teaching that animal sacrifices would be reinstituted in the future:

It will be necessary here to make a few observations on the doctrine set forth in the above quotation, and it is generally supposed that sacrifice was entirely done away when the Great Sacrifice [i.e., the sacrifice of the Lord Jesus] was offered up, and that there will be no necessity for the ordinance of sacrifice in future: but those who assert this are certainly not acquainted with the duties, privileges and authority of the priesthood, or with the Prophets. . . .

These sacrifices, as well as every ordinance belonging to the Priesthood, will, when the Temple of the Lord shall be built, and the sons of Levi be purified, be fully restored and attended to in all their powers, ramifications, and blessings. (*Documentary History of the Church*, 4:211)

Amazingly, this section is quoted with approval by McConkie in *Mormon Doctrine*, p. 666. The concept that there could possibly be any more sacrifices by the "priesthood" is so far removed from biblical teaching (note the entire argument of the book of Hebrews), and so foreign to the Christian mind, that it is difficult to fully grasp what I have just presented above. Allow me to move on quickly to biblical truth about the work of Jesus Christ.

The Finished Work of Christ on Calvary

Entire books have been written on this subject, and I have no intention of adding yet another in this letter. I will limit my discussion of the atonement to those points where we differ greatly in our understanding.

The death of Jesus Christ on the cross accomplished *atonement*. We agree on that. But what does atonement mean? How are we to understand this? Briefly, the Bible uses a number of terms to describe the effect of the death of Christ. Some of these terms include *forgiveness, righteousness* (or *justification*), *redemption, reconciliation,* and *propitiation*. It teaches that these things flow *necessarily and surely* from the work of Christ. What do I mean by this? I mean that the death of Christ actually accomplishes the forgiveness, justification, redemption, and reconciliation of those for whom it is made, *without any outside considerations*. The death of Christ is not "incomplete" without the addition of "other works" such as your own acts of obedience. The sacrifice of Christ is not dependent upon Steve Hahn or James White for its effectiveness.

One of the major differences between us is that you seem to believe that the death of Jesus Christ simply makes complete salvation a *possibility* rather than a *reality*. In other words, you believe that the death of Christ "opens the way" of salvation, but it does not in and of itself *accomplish* salvation. It removes barriers (sin) but does not actually save anyone in the fullest sense, for outside of your acts of obedience, such as baptism, and continued obedience to gospel rules and principles, it is helpless to save you fully. Not only this, but it seems that if you follow the counsel of Brigham Young or Bruce R. McConkie, you further believe that there are certain sins that the blood of Christ is unable to remit—that your own blood, however, *is* able to bring forgiveness of this sin.

Steve, let's look first at the fact that there is no sin that is beyond the atoning blood of Christ, no sin so heinous, so evil, that the blood of Christ is *insufficient* to bring about forgiveness. Let's look at what the Bible says:

> For it pleased the Father that in him should all fullness dwell; and, *having made peace through the blood of his cross,* by him to reconcile all things unto himself; by him, I say, whether they be things in earth, or things in heaven. (Colossians 1:19–20)

Did Christ just make peace *possible* or did He actually *make peace* by the blood of His cross?

> And you, being dead in your sins and the uncircumcision of your flesh, hath he quickened together with him, having forgiven you *all trespasses;* blotting out the handwriting of ordinances that was against us, which was contrary to us, and took it out of the way, *nailing it to his cross.* (Colossians 2:13–14)

Was it *some* of our trespasses that were nailed to the cross? Was it only those trespasses that were *not grievous enough* to require the blood of the sinful man to be shed that were nailed to the cross? Or was it *all* our trespasses, all our sins?

> But if we walk in the light, as he is in the light, we have fellowship one with another, and the blood of Jesus Christ, his Son cleanseth us from *all sin.* (1 John 1:7)

Does John teach that the blood of Jesus Christ cleanses from *some* sin, or *all* sin? And how are we redeemed, forgiven? Peter answers that question:

> Forasmuch as ye know that ye were not redeemed with corruptible things, like silver and gold, from your vain conversation received by tradition from your fathers, *but with the precious blood of Christ,* as of a lamb without blemish and without spot. (1 Peter 1:17–18)

The shed blood of Christ is the basis upon which God justifies or makes righteous those who believe in Christ, as Paul wrote,

> Being justified freely by his grace through the redemption that is in Christ Jesus, whom God hath set forth to be a propitiation through faith in his blood, to declare his righteousness for the remission of sins that are past, through the forbearance of God; to declare, I say, at this time his righteousness, that he might be just, and the justifier of him who believeth in Jesus. (Romans 3:24–26)

I will deal with this more later, but the two terms *justification* and *to make righteous* mean the same thing in the New Testament. They translate the same Greek word. So, if one wishes to be made righteous, to be justified in God's sight, the only way in which this can happen is through the death of Jesus Christ. Why is this? Because Christ *took our place.* He was our perfect *Substitute.* He took our sins upon himself— *all of them!* In doing so, He provided for us full and complete salvation. Paul wrote:

> For he hath made him to be sin for us, who knew no sin; that we might be made the righteousness of God in him. (2 Corinthians 5:21)

The sinless Lamb of God "was made to be sin for us," and what was the result of this? We are made the righteousness of God *in Him,* that is, in Christ and in Him alone. That is where one finds righteousness and nowhere else—*in Christ Jesus.* He took my place so that His death results in the forgiveness of my sins. Elsewhere Paul wrote,

> But God commendeth his love toward us, in that, while we were yet sinners, Christ died *for us.* Much more then, *being now justified by his blood,* we shall be saved from wrath through him. For if, when we were enemies, we were *reconciled to God by the*

death of His Son, much more, being reconciled, we shall be saved by his life. (Romans 5:8–10)

The Bible says that Christ died *for* us. The preposition in the Greek language can be properly translated "in behalf of" as well as "for." Christ died in behalf of me, in my place, even while I was yet a sinner. So, I have been justified, made righteous, *by His blood.* I am righteous before God, Steve, not because of anything that *I have done,* but because of what *Christ did!* I have been reconciled to God, not by my actions, not by my works of righteousness, but by "the death of His Son." Jesus Christ's death is what makes me righteous and reconciles me to the Father.

As I've been just briefly looking at some of these passages of Scripture, you've probably noticed a consistent theme in them all—that is that salvation is totally and completely of God—God is the one who saves, the one who brings men to himself. Yes, that's exactly what I am saying. And with reference to the atonement, I am clearly and openly asserting that the death of Christ alone is sufficient to bring about full salvation for those who believe in Him. The passages above make that clear, yet in your pamphlet *What the Mormons Think About Christ* on pages 19–20 we read,

> Christians speak often of the blood of Christ and its cleansing power. Much that is believed and taught on this subject, however, is such utter nonsense and so palpably false that to believe it is to lose one's salvation. For instance, many believe or pretend to believe that if we confess Christ with our lips and avow that we accept him as our personal Savior, we are thereby saved. They say that his blood, without any other act than mere belief, makes us clean.

Possibly, when this writer referred to the "many" who believe this, he was referring to the Apostle Paul who wrote Romans 3:24–26 and 5:8–10 above? I would rather believe what Paul said than what this pamphlet says. Of course, I will later deal with the nature of true saving faith (it is the gift of God) and much more on salvation—but right now I want to turn from the clear biblical teaching that Christ's death *actually and really* brings about forgiveness and reconciliation to the LDS concept that the blood of Christ cannot atone for all sins.

Joseph Fielding Smith said in the citation above from his book *Doctrines of Salvation* that there are certain sins that place the person "beyond the reach of the atoning blood of Christ." In this situation, "the blood of Christ alone . . . will not avail." And he went on to say that these sins place the transgressor "beyond the power of the atonement of Christ." Steve, what is beyond the reach of the atoning blood of Christ? For what sin will the blood of Christ not avail? What could possibly place one "beyond the power of the atonement of Christ"? Is the atonement provided by the shed blood of the sinless Lamb of God limited? Certainly not, yet the Mormon doctrine of blood atonement teaches just that! It would be one thing to say that there are certain sins that are simply *too great* to be forgiven (even though this in and of itself would be incorrect as well), but to say that there are certain sins that the blood of Christ is not *sufficient* to forgive that your own sinful blood *can* atone for is something else completely!

And right here is one of the most dangerous errors of Mormon theology. The death of Jesus Christ atones for sin because He, as the sinless substitute, was not under the penalty of sin; therefore, He could take the place of those who were powerless to save themselves. Since He was an infinite Person, Jehovah God in the flesh, His death was infinite in its value. But Mormon leaders teach that the blood of a sinful, condemned man has power to atone for his own sins. How can this be? If my blood can atone for *anything at all,* why then did Christ have to die? If my death can bring forgiveness of sins, then why send Christ to be my substitute? The shedding of my blood, Steve, could not atone for spitting on the sidewalk, let alone for some great and grievous sin that is so horrid it is beyond the power of the atonement of Christ! Can you see how this doctrine makes the blood of a sinful, vile person like me *more powerful* than the blood of the Lamb of God? Such a teaching shows how *deeply* the atonement of Christ is misunderstood in Mormonism. *Only* the death of Christ has the ability to bring forgiveness of sins. *Only* the death of Christ can bring full and complete salvation. It is the death and resurrection of Christ *alone* that saves—any and all actions of man, whether they be through religious ceremonies and works, or even the shedding of one's own blood, cannot in any way add to the finished and completed work of Jesus Christ. That is why Joseph Smith's teaching about the reinstitution of animal sacrifices under the auspices of the priesthood in the millennium is so false—animal sacrifices were but a picture of the final work of Christ. Why go back to the old shadows, the symbols, when the reality has come? Such is in fact a *denial* of the finished work of Christ on Calvary.

Yes, I admit it—you can tell I am just a little emotional about this issue. I'm probably not writing in quite my normal way. I try to remain "scholarly," but when it comes to the death of my Lord, and the *all-sufficiency* of His work, I do allow my emotions to at least influence my use of italics and exclamation points! And when doctrines like the LDS teaching of blood atonement, and its clear denial of the power of the blood of Christ, are in view—well, there are some things that are important enough to cause a little escalation in the voice and the blood pressure.

Now you may stop me here and ask about Matthew 12:31–32. It reads:

> Wherefore I say unto you, All manner of sin and blasphemy shall be forgiven unto men: but the blasphemy against the Holy Ghost shall not be forgiven unto men. And whosoever speaketh a word against the Son of man, it shall be forgiven him: but whosoever speaketh against the Holy Ghost, it shall not be forgiven him, neither in this world, neither in the world to come.

This is surely the most popular section used in "defense" of blood atonement, though, upon even a cursory examination, we see that it is hardly suited for such a task. First, the passage says that this "unpardonable sin" is just that—unpardonable. There is *no forgiveness* for it—none. Shedding the blood of a person who has committed the unpardonable sin will not change that situation—they will not be forgiven. So it is clear to see that Jesus was not teaching the Mormon doctrine of blood atonement here.

So what then was He teaching, you ask? Does He not here contradict what 1 John 1:7 said, that His blood cleanses us from *all* sin? No, He doesn't. Let's look at the passage to see how this is so.

Just before these words of Jesus, He had cast out a demon. The Pharisees had come to Him and accused Him of casting out demons by the power of the prince of demons, Beelzebul, or Satan. This charge provides the background for understanding verses 31 and 32. The Pharisees had identified the working of the Holy Spirit of God with the power of Satan—they called God the devil.

Jesus identifies this act, that of calling that which is good, evil, the unpardonable sin. Why is it unpardonable? Is it unpardonable because it is so serious that even the sacrifice of Christ cannot atone for it? No, that is not the case.

When one blasphemes the Holy Spirit, he (or she) is cutting himself off from the presence and work of the Spirit. When one rejects the work of the Holy Spirit (by attributing it to evil, as the Pharisees had done), one is cut off from His convicting power. Remember that the Bible teaches us in John 16:8 that one of the roles of the Holy Spirit is to bring conviction of sin to the heart of man—not only conviction that results in regeneration (being born again), but even conviction to those who will never turn to God. The Spirit is actively involved in convicting the world of its sin, and, I would add, God by His Spirit is actively involved in *curbing* the existence of evil and suppressing the natural tendency of man toward evil. Be that as it may, the Holy Spirit is the one who convicts man of his sin. When one blasphemes the Spirit, one is showing that one is no longer being convicted by the Spirit—such a person has become so twisted, so perverse, as to be able to identify the work of the Spirit as the work of Satan (or vice versa). Such a person is cut off from the convicting influences of the Spirit of God. This is what makes the unpardonable sin unpardonable—it is not the *seriousness* of the sin itself, but the *effect* that it has. One cannot ask forgiveness of sin unless one is convicted by the Holy Spirit. When one is cut off from His convicting power, one cannot any longer even ask for pardon, hence the unpardonableness of the sin.

Now you may ask who would commit this kind of sin. First, we can see that the person would have to be terribly twisted, calling what is obviously good, evil, and what is obviously evil, good. Isaiah put it this way:

> Woe unto them who call evil good, and good evil; that put darkness for light, and light for darkness; that put bitter for sweet, and sweet for bitter! (Isaiah 5:20)

The most likely candidates for this in my opinion, Steve, ironically, are religious people—the very ones who have the most "light" in which to walk are the ones who can become so twisted as to commit this sin. I have seen, sadly, such people involved both in cults, and more often, atheism. I have debated atheists who once were professing Christians, and such people, by their own statements, are likely candidates for the unpardonable sin, and most definitely fall in the category of the ones spoken of in Hebrews 6:4–6.

The point of all of this is to say that the unpardonable sin is not one that by its gross severity is beyond the reach of the atonement of Christ—it is unforgivable because of the position it places the sinner in, one from which he cannot, and will not, ever cry for forgiveness.

Originally I pointed out that the atoning death of Christ accomplishes that which it was intended to accomplish *without the additional works of man*. Now aside from the whole works/faith issue, you may well be saying, "Now wait a minute—don't Christians believe that Christ died for everyone, and therefore if the death of Christ accomplishes the redemption of all for whom it was made, then are not all saved, even in your sense of the term?" I hope you don't mind this, but a few months ago I put together a little article entitled "Was Anyone Saved at the Cross?" As it answers that question directly, I will provide its text for your consideration. It will also help you to understand more about my doctrine of salvation as well.

"Was anyone saved at the cross? Did the death of Jesus Christ actually and really save anyone at all?" Various answers have been given to this question down through the ages. The answers fall into three categories:

1. A "universalistic" perspective: From this perspective, Christ died in behalf of every single man, and His death, aside from every single other consideration, brings about eternal salvation. If Christ has taken one's sins, then there no longer remains any grounds for God's judgment or wrath, hence all for whom Christ died will be saved. Since no works of man are needed or required, all men will be saved.

2. The view of many different groups: The second group gathers together many, many different beliefs which agree on this one item: Christ's death was for all men, yet, His death alone does not actually save anyone, and is not complete in and of itself. Rather, Christ's death *makes salvation possible* for anyone who will do certain things—some saying that people must only believe to make the atonement "effective," others arguing for baptism, laying on of hands, sacraments, penances, ceremonies, all sorts of "good works," and almost every possible combination of the above. What unites this group is the concept that the death of Christ, being universal in scope (that is, Christ died for *all* men) is *incapable* of saving anyone outside of man's actions.

3. The "Reformed" view: The third group is similar to the first, in that they assert that the death of Christ, outside of any human actions, saves those for whom it is made. Christ's death as the perfect Substitute means that all those for whom He died are thereby forgiven, redeemed, and, since their sins are taken away on the cross, they cannot possibly be punished for them. *All those for whom Christ died are by that action*

saved, and cannot possibly fail of receiving eternal life. The difference, however, lies in the fact that the Reformed view says that Christ died substitutionarily in behalf of God's people, God's elect, *and not for every single human being.* The Reformed view presents a definite, specific, or limited view of the *extent* of Christ's work.

Examination of These Views

All Christians who look to the Bible as the Word of God can dismiss the first position immediately, for the Bible is very clear in proclaiming the fact that not all men will be saved, not all will be brought into a proper relationship with God through Jesus Christ. Rather, there will be those who suffer eternal punishment, separated from God (Matthew 25:46, 2 Thessalonians 1:9, etc.). But what of the remaining views? The two positions are seen to differ on some very fundamental questions: For whom did Christ die? What is the result of His death? What was His intention in going to the cross? The only way to resolve these questions is to go to God's Holy Word, the Bible.

The Reason Christ Came

Why did Christ go to Calvary? What was His reason for coming to earth at all? Jesus answered this plainly in Luke 19:10 when He said, "For the Son of Man came to seek and to save the lost." His was a mission of seeking, *and saving,* the lost. Note that He does not say that He came "to make a way possible" but to *actually save sinners.* The same is taught by the Apostle Paul in 1 Timothy 1:15: "It is a faithful saying: Christ Jesus came into the world to save sinners." So it is plain to see that Christ came to save sinners, and He did this by His sacrificial death on the cross of Calvary. Yet, we must ask, did He accomplish the purpose for which He came? The Reformed position says that He did. The other perspective suspends judgment, asserting that Christ's death was not intended, in and of itself, to save sinners, but to only make a way of salvation *possible.* Where does the Bible teach this? And upon what basis can one say that the death of Christ is in need of "further actions" on the part of men in order for it to become effective?

The Result of Christ's Work at Calvary

The Bible tells us that the death of Christ accomplished certain things. His death brings about forgiveness of sins (not just the possibility of forgiveness) and makes a person righteous (justified) in God's sight (Romans 3:24–25). By the death of Christ men are *reconciled* to God (Romans 5:8–11, Colossians 1:21–22), and are *redeemed* (Ephesians 1:7). All other blessings of salvation are dependent upon, and flow from, the atoning work of Christ. When Christ dies for someone as their substitute, they are by that action redeemed, forgiven, reconciled, justified, and sanctified. Their salvation is made complete, as the writer of Hebrews said, "But he, on the other hand, because he abides forever, holds his priesthood unchangeably, hence, he is able to save completely those who come unto God by him, as he lives forever to make intercession on their behalf" (Hebrews 7:24–25) and later, "But when Christ appeared as high priest of the good things to come, he entered through the greater and more perfect tabernacle not made by hands, that is, not of this creation, neither did he enter the holy place once for all through the blood of goats and calves, but through His own blood, having obtained eternal redemption" (Hebrews 9:11–12).

Did Christ truly obtain eternal redemption or did He only make it a theoretical possibility? Was the death of Christ a real atonement, complete and finished, or was it simply the first step, incomplete, resulting not in a *finished* salvation but a *possible* redemption? The biblical answer seems clear. What happens to a person for whom Christ dies? The writer of Hebrews again teaches, "By this will we have been sanctified through the offering of the body of Jesus Christ once for all. . . . For by one offering He has perfected forever those who are sanctified" (Hebrews 10:10, 14). Note that the believer has been sanctified, and how? Through the offering of the body of Jesus Christ *once for all*. And what does verse 14 assert? By that one offering Christ *has perfected forever* those who are sanctified. Indeed, if Christ's death accomplishes what the Bible here teaches, and one does not believe that all shall be saved, then one *must* believe that Christ's atonement was *specifically* for a certain people—God's people.

For Whom Did Christ Die?

"The Son of Man did not come to be served, but to serve, and to give His life a ransom for many"(Matthew 20:28*). Christ came to save sinners, and He did this by giving His life as a "ransom for many."

---

*All verses in this section are quoted from NASB.

Who are these "many"? This would be the same group spoken of by Isaiah the prophet in Isaiah 53:11, "By His knowledge the Righteous One, my Servant, will justify the many, as He will bear their iniquities." They are Christ's sheep, as He said, "I am the good shepherd; the good shepherd lays down His life for His sheep . . . even as the Father knows Me and I know the Father; and I lay down My life for the sheep" (John 10:11, 15). (Not all are Christ's sheep—John 10:26.) Together they are the Church, the body of Christ: ". . . just as Christ loved you, and gave Himself up for us . . . husbands, love your wives, just as Christ also loved the church and gave Himself up for her . . ." (Ephesians 5:2, 25). They are called Christ's "friends" in John 15:13, and "His people" in Matthew 1:21—"And she will bear a Son, and you shall call His name Jesus, for it is He who will save His people from their sins."

They are believers who look forward to Christ's coming, as Paul wrote to Titus, "[We are] looking for the blessed hope and the appearing of the glory of our great God and Savior, Christ Jesus; who gave Himself for us, that He might redeem us from every lawless deed, and purify for Himself a people for His own possession, zealous for good deeds" (Titus 2:13–14). Finally, the Bible clearly identifies this people for whom Christ died, and who are, by His death, sanctified, as "the elect of God." Paul wrote, "What then shall we say to these things? If God is for us, who is against us? He who did not spare His own Son, but delivered Him up for us all, how will He not also with Him freely give us all things? Who will bring a charge against God's elect?" (Romans 8:31–33).

All these passages teach us that Christ's death had a *specific purpose,* a *particular goal*, and that was the salvation of God's elect, God's people. As we have seen, Christ's death accomplishes that which God intended.

Is It Important?

Surely the atonement of Jesus Christ is central to Christian belief. The truth about *what* Christ did on the cross, and why He did it, should be important to those who name the name of Christ. The definite, specific atonement of Jesus Christ is consistent with the Bible's teaching of the absolute sovereignty of God in the matter of salvation: God elects, chooses to save, not on the basis of what any man does or will do, but purely on the basis of His own mercy and will (Romans 9:16–18). Since this is so, Christ's death would logically only be for those to whom God has chosen to be merciful. The result of this is the wonderful truth that all the honor and glory for salvation goes to God and to God alone. He is seen to be powerful to save, for the death of Christ accomplishes that which He intends. On the other hand, if we deny this truth, we are left presenting the death of Christ as something incomplete and ineffective, lacking the power to bring about salvation outside of man's response, man's actions. Rather than a sovereign God who calls men to himself, we present a God who would really *like* to save men, but is constantly frustrated by their actions, their will. Is this the God of the Bible? (Psalm 115:3, 135:6)

I hope you will think about these things, Steve. I know that the position taken here is not the most common one you might encounter going door to door. However, I think you will see that the position I take is consistent with the doctrine of God that I have presented previously. I look forward to a time when we can sit down and talk about these subjects. But now, let me move directly into the subject of the priesthood.

The Priesthood Issue

As you know, the Church of Jesus Christ of Latter-day Saints claims to be the only true church on earth today. Part of this claim is to be seen in the vital LDS doctrine that they, and they alone, hold the true priesthood authority. Supposedly the Aaronic priesthood was conferred on Joseph Smith and Oliver Cowdery on May 15, 1829, and then, sometime in June of the same year, Peter, James, and John supposedly appeared and conferred the Melchizedek priesthood upon them. We have seen already, of course, that Joseph did not claim to hold the priesthood until *after* the founding of the Church in 1830, and that he was more than willing to "edit" previously written revelations to "insert" the concept of the priesthood so that it *appeared* to have been a part of his original teachings (i.e., Section 27 of the D&C being a prime example). I believe that this is a major issue that anyone who would defend the LDS concept of "priesthood authority" cannot ignore.

When Christians attempt to confront the teachings of the LDS Church, the frequent response of the Mormons is, "What is your authority?" Mormons truly believe that they have a special authority from God as presented by the priesthood. But, the question I must ask is this—does the Bible support these ideas? Does the Bible present a special priesthood authority as the Mormon Church claims? Let's examine this idea from the perspective of Holy Scripture.

The Aaronic Priesthood

The presentation of the Aaronic priesthood as found in the Bible demonstrates clearly that Aaronic priests were ordained to that position in quite a different way than LDS men are today. If you will take the time to read through Exodus chapter 29 and Leviticus chapter 8, you will discover a *very different* rite of ordination presented there. I have asked Mormon elders who claimed to have been ordained *in the exact same way as all Aaronic priests were ordained in the past* if they went through a seven-day period of consecration, and had blood placed upon their right ear, their right thumb, and their right big toe (Leviticus 8:23). Most thought that ordination to the priesthood involved little more than a ceremony of laying hands upon their heads—something that is actually *missing* from the true ordination of Aaronic priests in the Bible. Not only this, but the duties of the Aaronic priests were also inconsistent with those of the priests of Mormonism (see Leviticus chapters 4 through 10). What is even more important for our purposes is the fact that the requirements for the biblical Aaronic priests are very different from those of Mormon teaching. The priesthood of Aaron is reserved solely and eternally for the descendants of Aaron. Where does the Bible teach this? One of the most obvious places is in Numbers, chapter 16.

Numbers 16 tells the story of the rebellion of Korah, Dathan, and Abiram. Korah was a Levite, but was not of the family of Aaron. They rebelled against Moses, claiming that "all the congregation is holy" and that Moses and Aaron had taken "too much" upon themselves (16:3). They desired to "come near" unto God, which was the sole function of the priesthood with Aaron as the High Priest. You can read the story for yourself, but in short, God caused the ground to open up and swallow Korah and those who followed him. Upon the event of their destruction, we read,

> To be a memorial unto the children of Israel, that no stranger, which is not of the seed of Aaron, come near to offer incense before the LORD; that he be not as Korah, and as his company: as the LORD said to him by the hand of Moses. (Numbers 16:40)

And later we can listen as God speaks to Aaron and says,

> Therefore thou and thy sons with thee shall keep your priest's office for every thing of the altar, and within the veil; and ye shall serve: I have given your priest's office unto you as a service of gift: and the stranger that cometh nigh shall be put to death. (Numbers 18:7)

Obviously, one who was not of the tribe of Levi and the family of Aaron could not hold the priesthood authority. You, Steve, are not even Jewish, let alone of the tribe of Levi or the family of Aaron. How then can you claim to hold the Aaronic priesthood?

I know—when we look at LDS practice we find that in the individual's "Patriarchal blessing" he is told to what tribe he belongs. Normally, the tribe is that of Ephraim or Manassah—personally, in all the times I have asked concerning this issue, I have never encountered any Mormon who claimed to be of the tribe of Levi, let alone the family of Aaron. Clearly, then, you must not be claiming to hold the *same* priesthood as spoken of in the Bible, as very few of the members of the LDS Church are Jewish in lineage! The most telling objection to be raised to the entire idea of a modern, functioning Aaronic priesthood is the simple teaching of the New Testament that in the one-time sacrifice of Jesus Christ the entire sacrificial system, along with its priesthood duties, was *fulfilled* and completed. To go back to the old system is to undo the work of Jesus at Calvary! For example—the veil of the Temple in Jerusalem was torn in two from top to bottom when Christ died (Matthew 27:51). This veil had stood for the separating wall between God and man that was bridged but once a year by the *one* high priest (yes, *one* high priest, not many as the LDS Church has. Jesus Christ is our *only* high priest, and anyone claiming to be a "high priest" is usurping His position, Hebrews 7:26–28) when he offered the sacrifice of atonement for the people (Leviticus 16, Hebrews 9:7). Christ, however, offered the final sacrifice and in doing so opened the way *permanently* for all who would come to God by Him. Christ did not do away with the priesthood; rather He *fulfilled* it. Its purpose was done, finished, completed. Hebrews 7:12 says that there has been a "change" in the Aaronic priesthood. The Greek term indicates that the Aaronic priesthood has been completed. As Dr. A. T. Robertson, one of the greatest Greek scholars America has ever produced, said in reference to this verse,

God's choice of another kind of priesthood for His Son, left the Levitical line off to one side, forever discontinued, passed by "the order of Aaron." (*Word Pictures in the New Testament*, Vol. 5, p. 383)

Since this is so, anyone today who wishes to revive the old ways of the Aaronic priesthood woefully misunderstands the work of Christ on the cross (Hebrews 9:10–28). Sadly, as we saw above, this is exactly the situation with the leaders of the LDS Church, Joseph Smith in particular.

In passing, I might mention to you, Steve, that should you think that John 15:16 ("Ye have not chosen me, but I have chosen you, and ordained you . . .") refers to the ordination of the apostles and the granting to them of some special authority, I would like to point out that the word translated *ordained* in 15:16 is simply a synonym for *chosen* that is translated in modern versions as *appointed*. It has no reference whatsoever to the idea of a special religious ordination of priests.

The Melchizedek Priesthood

Much more important than the Aaronic priesthood in Mormon thought is the "Holy Priesthood after the Order of the Son of God" or the "Melchizedek Priesthood." This priesthood,

> . . . comprehends the Aaronic or Levitical Priesthood, and is the grand head, and holds the highest authority which pertains to the priesthood . . . and is the channel through which all knowledge, doctrine, the plan of salvation and every important matter is revealed from heaven. (*Mormon Doctrine*, p. 476)

Obviously this supposed authority is very important to the LDS Church. But again, does the Bible support such a teaching?

Let's first examine the qualifications of the "Melchizedek" priest as given in the Bible. Hebrews 7:3 tells us that Melchizedek was "without father, without mother, without descent, having neither beginning of days, nor end of life. . . . " Only Melchizedek and Christ meet those qualifications, for this priesthood is unique—no one but Melchizedek and Christ has ever held it. Indeed, Hebrews 7:3 also makes clear that Melchizedek is only *like* the Son of God—he was not the pattern that Jesus followed by, rather he was a *type*—the mere reflection of the full expression of the Son of God. This priesthood is also seen, on the basis of this passage, to be one that is not passed on from one to another—there were no "Melchizedek" priests between Genesis 14 and the coming of the Lord Jesus. Melchizedek did not "give" the priesthood to Jesus (or anyone else for that matter); it was Jesus' by right.

The work of the Melchizedek priest is seen in Hebrews 7:24–25, where the Bible says,

> But this man (Jesus), because he continueth ever, hath an unchangeable priesthood. Wherefore, he is able also to save them to the uttermost that come unto God by him, seeing he ever liveth to make intercession for them.

The priesthood Jesus holds is His *unchangeably* or *permanently*. Some translate it by the word *intransmissable*, indicating that no one else can hold this priesthood. Though some would argue with the translation of the word, the fact is clear that the person holding this priesthood by right of eternal life is able to save completely those who come unto God by him—a claim that few Mormons would knowingly make. That doesn't mean that I haven't had a few stand before me and say, "Well, if that is what the Melchizedek priest can do, then I can do it." What about you, Steve? Do you claim to be able to "save to the uttermost" those who come unto God by you? I certainly hope not, for you know that you cannot. However, if the LDS Church is going to declare that it has this priesthood, it must face the fact that it is professing to have that which, according to the Bible, is the property of Jesus Christ alone.

A passage that is frequently cited in this discussion is Hebrews 5:6 which mentions the order of Melchizedek. The LDS Church teaches that this indicates that there was an order of priests after Melchizedek—that this is a priesthood that is passed on much like the Aaronic. The whole point of the discourse, however, is just the opposite—the priesthood of Jesus is superior to that of Aaron and one of the reasons is that it is *not* passed from one to another. It is not invested in men who will die, but is given only to the One who has died and lives forever, the Lord Jesus Christ! To miss the point is to misunderstand the entire argument of Hebrews! It must also be pointed out that the word translated "order" means "of the same kind" or "nature, quality, manner, condition, appearance." It does not refer to a lineage of priests, but rather to the *kind* of priest. It must again be stressed that Jesus' priesthood is His uniquely and that *no one* can claim to hold what is His by right as the one great High Priest, the one Mediator between God and man (1 Timothy 2:5). Therefore, the LDS Church's claim to hold this priesthood is without biblical basis or historical basis, and far more importantly, it strikes at the very core of the work and office of the Lord Jesus Christ.

Well, Steve, I think it is about time we got to the final and important issue—the gospel of Jesus Christ. What has come up to this point is very important—vital even—to a proper understanding of the gospel. I'd like you to do me a favor—when you write back, define for me just what the gospel is, and what it involves. Then we can discuss the Bible's presentation of this all-important matter. I look forward to hearing from you soon.

In Christian concern,

James White

The Gospel of the Grace of God in Christ Jesus

Monday, July 30

Dear Steve,

A few years ago I sat down in the second bedroom of my apartment and began a letter to an Elder Wolf. I had begun talking with this young man a few weeks earlier. He seemed like a very honest, sincere person, much like you. I wrote late into the night with nothing but the light of a small computer screen by which to see. I was talking to him about grace—God's infinite and unlimited grace, and how it was so difficult for men to believe in a plan of salvation that was based completely on God, and not on man. I can only pray that he read that letter under the guidance of the Spirit of God and that he is today one of those who acknowledges the truth of God's grace.

The most difficult truth of the Bible for man to accept is that God is the one who saves men. No, I didn't say that God simply provides a way for men to be saved, but that God actually *saves* sinners! One writer was able to condense the essence of the gospel of Christ down to three words: God saves sinners. When he did that, this writer was contrasting the biblical gospel against the much more common "type" of gospel message that can only say that "God wants to save sinners, tries to save sinners, but in the final analysis, is only able to save those sinners who help Him to do it." That is one of the most basic differences between the Christian gospel and the religions of men—all religions, in one way or another, teach that man is responsible for somehow "getting" to God. They differ as to just how man is supposed to accomplish this—some present elaborate systems of religious ritual and works. Others commend inward reflection and meditation. Still others teach us to empty ourselves so that we can be "dissolved" into the unknown. But in each and every instance, God is seen as the goal of human action and achievement—salvation is seen as the work of man whereby he strives and struggles to please God in this way or that.

Even in much of popular evangelicalism it is the same way. God is presented as the all-loving Father who has provided a way for men to come to Him. He has sent His Son to die for all men, so that, *if men so choose*, they might take advantage of this plan and come to Him. God does not actually save anyone, for in the final analysis, outside of the human initiative, outside of man's choosing, God is utterly helpless to save a single individual. Even if a person believes that God provides 99 percent of the plan, that still leaves the entire process up to man. If man refuses, God is stymied, utterly unable to accomplish His desired goal of saving man.

You have probably run into a lot of well-meaning people who have presented the gospel to you in this way, Steve. I believe that the vast majority of these folks just haven't thought through what they are saying. Many of these do not realize what the Bible says about the nature of God as the absolute sovereign ruler of the universe, or, even if they do, have not realized that their belief in a salvation that is dependent upon the decision or "free will of man" contradicts in my view the biblical teaching about God. Whatever the reason, I again direct your attention not to the teachings of men, but to the teachings of the Word of God, the Bible.

God saves sinners. What a tremendous truth! God brings men to himself. He is not thwarted by His small creations—if He intends to bring a soul to salvation, He can accomplish the desire of His heart. He is no impotent sovereign waiting helplessly for man's response, but as the Creator of all things He brings to pass His will in each and every life. *God saves sinners.* Note that it is *God* who does this. He is the one who "works all things after the counsel of his will" (Ephesians 1:11). He is the one who from eternity past decided to create the world and all that is in it, and to join a certain people to Jesus Christ (Ephesians 1:4). God is the author of the plan of salvation, and He is the finisher of the plan of salvation—from beginning to end, God is in charge.

God saves sinners. He does not simply call sinners, He actually *saves* sinners. He brings them into a relationship with himself. He gives them faith and repentance, and causes them to trust in Him. He justifies them, redeems them, reconciles them, all through Jesus Christ. They have eternal life through faith in Christ (John 5:24), not through any work of their own.

God saves sinners. Who does He save? *Sinners.* Men who are spiritually dead (Ephesians 2:1), who are not seeking after God (Romans 3:11), who are the sworn enemies of God (Romans 8:7–8). These sinners are utterly and completely incapable of saving themselves, utterly and completely incapable of even availing themselves of a "plan" if it were offered to them. They are not simply spiritually "sick," they are spiritually *dead.* Dead as the proverbial doorknob. These are the ones God saves. Sinners—like you and me.

Let me begin discussing the gospel of the grace of God in Christ Jesus in a way that will probably be rather strange to you—let me talk first about God's role in salvation, then about the nature and state of man outside of Christ.

God, the Author of Salvation

When we spoke of the God of the Bible, I emphasized to you His utter *uniqueness* and His absolute *sovereignty* over all things. We saw many Scriptures that directly taught this truth. Yet many who would on one level agree that the Bible teaches God's sovereignty on another level deny this truth by believing that when it comes to man's salvation, for some reason God abandons His throne and allows man to call the shots. I will wait until later to speak with you about what I feel is the real reason that so many do this, why so many are comfortable with a God who "tries real hard" to save men but, in a majority of the cases it seems, fails in reaching His goal. For now, let's follow the pattern we have developed over the past month or so and go to God's Word. I am embarrassed by the richness of material that I could present to you on this topic—but to facilitate our discussion, I will limit myself to a "perfect number" of passages—seven—on the topic of God's sovereignty in the salvation of man.

One of the classic sections of Scripture on the topic of salvation is to be found in Paul's letter to the Ephesians, chapter 1, verses 3 through 12:

> Blessed be the God and Father of our Lord Jesus Christ, who
> hath blessed us with all spiritual blessings in heavenly places in

Christ: according as he hath *chosen us in him before the foundation of the world*, that we should be holy and without blame before him in love: having *predestinated* us unto the adoption of children by Jesus Christ to himself, according to the good pleasure of his will, to the praise of the glory of his grace, wherein he hath made us accepted in the beloved. In whom we have redemption through his blood, the forgiveness of sins, according to the riches of his grace; wherein he hath abounded toward us in all wisdom and prudence; having made known unto us the mystery of his will, according to his good pleasure which he hath purposed in himself: that in the dispensation of the fullness of times he might gather together in one all things in Christ, both which are in heaven, and which are on earth; even in him: in whom also we have obtained an inheritance, *being predestinated according to the purpose of him who worketh all things after the counsel of his own will*: that we should be to the praise of his glory, who first trusted in Christ.

Allow me, if you will, to point out briefly the major aspects of this tremendous passage. Note first that over and over again Paul uses the phrase "in Christ" or "in Him." If anything can be said about salvation other than it is the work of God, it would be that it is the work of God *in Christ*. Salvation is wrapped up in the work of Christ, centered on the Person of Christ. Outside of Christ, there is no salvation. Secondly, take notice of the verbs in this passage—if you will examine them closely, you will see that *God is the one who is active in this passage.* God is the doer, man the receiver, the one acted upon.

Paul begins by asserting that God chose us, His people, in Christ Jesus "before the foundation of the world." This was God's choice, not man's. God was not simply "reacting to" men's decisions that He could *foresee* in the future. Rather, God chose us in Christ, and determined to make us holy and without blame—in other words, to make us like Christ (Romans 8:29). He goes on to say that God "predestined" (in our more modern language) us to adoption as sons by Jesus Christ. There is no use in attempting to escape the language that the Apostle uses here—predestination is predestination, not simply "foreordination" as many LDS understand it. God chose a people in Christ, and predestined them to adoption as sons. He did not predestine a *plan* but a *people*, the people of God.

On what basis did God choose the men and women that He will draw to himself in salvation? Was it on the basis of works that they would do? Did He look into the future and see that some people would be more "worthy" than others? Did He foresee that some people would do all the works required and on this basis choose them? Certainly not—God's eternal decisions are not based upon or determined by the actions of man in time! Not only this, but Paul tells us upon what basis God chose certain men and women—"according to the good pleasure of his will" (v. 5). That doesn't go over too well with most folks, does it? But Paul said what he meant—the basis of God's predestinating grace is simply the good pleasure of His will. God's choice is not based upon men's actions, men's works, men's worthiness. It is based solely upon His will, His mercy, His grace. Yes, I know this is completely opposite of what you have been taught about grace, works, and salvation. But follow along and see if this is not exactly what the Bible teaches.

In verse 6 Paul tells us the outcome of God's eternal predestination: the praise of the glory of His grace. That is why God has chosen to save sinners. When God saves a sinner, the glory of His *grace* is praised. If salvation were in the least bit "of man," if it were based even the slightest upon man's obedience to various rules and regulations (or maybe "ordinances and principles"?), then God's grace would not be praised for the salvation of sinners. But the Bible will have nothing of this—God saves by His grace and mercy, and therefore the glory of His grace is praised when men are brought to salvation.

Steve, how do you have redemption, the forgiveness of your sins? You would probably say that without the sacrifice of Christ, there would be no forgiveness, and I agree. And you would say that without the grace of God, there would be no forgiveness, and I agree. But you would also say that there are certain things that you must do to *obtain* that forgiveness, that redemption—such things as repentance, faith, baptism, and "continued obedience to gospel ordinances and principles" throughout the time of your mortal probation, right? But Paul says that we are redeemed, forgiven of our sins, solely on the basis of the "riches of his grace." Do God's riches need the addition of your works? Is the treasury of God's grace so small that without the additional "good works" of mankind it is insufficient to "cover the check" of man's forgiveness? May it never be! We have forgiveness solely and completely on the basis of grace—I did *not* say that we have access to a "plan" whereby we can gain forgiveness for ourselves by God's grace, but that we actually *have* forgiveness on the basis of God's grace. There is a vast *and eternal* difference between the two.

Paul goes on to assert that we have obtained an "inheritance" not on the basis of our worthiness or our works, but simply because we have been predestined "according to the purpose of him who worketh all things after the counsel of his own will" (Ephesians 1:11). An inheritance in the Kingdom of God is not given on the basis of our works or righteousness, Steve. It is not given only to those who pass a certain kind of test or reach a certain goal. An inheritance in the Kingdom of God is the gift of God given to undeserving men simply because it is God's purpose to demonstrate His love and mercy in doing so (Ephesians 2:7).

And what is the result of this gracious action of God? It is again that we might be to the "praise of his glory." Salvation is all of God so that all of the praise might go to God. If even a small portion is dependent upon man, then man is deserving of part of the glory that comes from salvation. But we have nothing of which to boast, for our salvation is based solely upon God's actions.

When Paul wrote to the Church at Thessalonica, he said,

> But we are bound to give thanks always to God for you, brethren beloved of the Lord, because God hath from the beginning chosen you to salvation through sanctification of the Spirit and belief of the truth: whereunto which he called you by our gospel, to the obtaining of the glory of our Lord Jesus Christ. (2 Thessalonians 2:13–14)

Who chose these "beloved brethren" for salvation from the beginning? God did. And how does God bring their salvation about? He does so through "sanctification of the Spirit" and "belief in the truth." God has ordained certain means by which He brings about the salvation of His people, the elect. God has not chosen to save men outside of Jesus Christ. He has decided to save them through the sanctifying work of the Spirit (the Spirit sets us apart, makes us holy, and works in our lives so that we seek God's will, do good works, all those things that are part and parcel of an obedient child of God) *and* through belief in the truth. No one is saved in falsehood. God does not bring people to salvation through error and lies, but through faith, belief, in the truth. God calls us unto this sanctification and truth by the gospel (v. 14).

Why has God decided to call men unto himself by the preaching of the gospel of grace? I have no idea—that is how He decided He would be glorified in the greatest way, and that is enough for me. The Word teaches it, and I believe it to be true. And let me make sure you understand two things about this: First, *all* those who are saved are sanctified by the Spirit. The Spirit works in the lives of all the redeemed to bring about holiness and obedience. You have been taught that works of obedience are necessary *to bring about salvation* while the Bible teaches that these works of obedience, these good works, *are the work of the Spirit in those who are saved.* As we will see over and over again, the LDS emphasis upon works is the truth *in reverse!* Yes, there are good works in the Christian life—but every single good work, every single obedient act of the child of God is accomplished through the power and work of the Spirit of God as He is working out our sanctification! We will probably need to return to this later. Secondly, many people (not just Mormons), when faced with the biblical teaching of the eternal predestination and election of God's people unto salvation, immediately ask, "Then why should we go out and proclaim the gospel to anyone if God has already decided who He is going to save?" But as you can see from this passage in 2 Thessalonians, God has decided that He is going to bring about the salvation of His people in a particular way—through the proclamation of the gospel of Christ and the exhortation to repent from sin and turn to God. So those who accept the Bible's teaching about God's sovereignty *do not* as a result stop sharing, witnessing, and working to bring glory to God. In fact, if I did *not* believe that God is sovereign in the matter of salvation, I would not have extended our conversation as long as I have. In fact, I probably would not have bothered to engage these topics with you at all! Why? Because if I felt that it was up to me to somehow *convince* you that I am right and you are wrong, or if I had to somehow argue you into accepting the gospel, I would despair of ever succeeding. But I know that in the final analysis God is the one who saves, and the Holy Spirit is the one who can open your eyes to His truth. So I can simply seek to glorify God by sharing with you, and leave the results to the only one who knows men's hearts—God himself.

To this point I have limited myself to the teachings of Paul the Apostle. As some LDS have an almost "anti-Paul" attitude (I don't know if you do or not—I have just encountered a large number of LDS folks who really don't like Paul very much), let's turn to the teaching of Jesus Christ on this subject. In Matthew 11:27 we read,

> All things are delivered unto me by my Father: and no man knoweth the Son, but the Father; neither knoweth any man the Father, save the Son, and he to whomsoever the Son will reveal him.

The Lord Jesus here indicates that to know the Father, one must go through the Son (John 1:18). No man can bypass Jesus Christ in coming to know the Father, for the Father has chosen to reveal himself only in the Son. So who can know the Father? Only those to whom the Son wills to reveal Him. Christ claims exclusive right as "revelator" of the Father. But to whom does the Son will to reveal the Father? All men? To answer that, let's turn to the discourse in Capernaum in John chapter 6. Beginning with verse 37 we read,

> All that the Father giveth me shall come to me; and him that cometh to me I will in no wise cast out. For I came down from heaven, not to do mine own will, but the will of him that sent me. And this is the Father's will which hath sent me, that of all which he hath given me I should lose nothing, but should raise it up again at the last day. And this is the will of him that sent me, that every one that seeth the Son, and believeth on him, may have everlasting life: and I will raise him up at the last day.

And then in verses 44–45,

> No man can come to me, except the Father which hath sent me draw him: and I will raise him up at the last day. It is written in the prophets, And they shall be all taught of God. Every man therefore that hath heard, and hath learned of the Father, cometh unto me.

It seems impossible to really follow the Lord's words here without a solid understanding of the absolute sovereignty of God. The very first phrase of verse 37 makes this clear—"All that the Father gives me shall come to me." The Father is pictured as the "owner" of all men, and He "gives" to the Son a particular people. The Lord Jesus states this truth boldly—*all* that the Father gives to Him *will come* to Him. There is no doubt, there is no hesitation, no "contingency." He does not say "I *hope* that all the Father gives Me will come to Me," nor "I will try My best to make all those who are given to Me by the Father come to Me." He states a fact—all who are given by the Father will come to the Son. On the flip side of this, the one who comes to Christ (obviously as a result of the Father having given him to the Son) will never be cast out. No one who comes to Christ (the true, living Jesus Christ), will ever be cast out and lost. God is able to save all those who trust in Jesus.

But the Lord goes on to describe just why the believer in Him is secure in his position. He says that He has come down from heaven to do the will of the Father. Certainly, Steve, we can agree that if anything can be said of Christ, it is that He *always* does the will of the Father, right? So what is the will of the Father of which Jesus is speaking? He says, "that of all that he hath given me I should lose nothing, but should raise it up again at the last day." The will of the Father for the Son is that the Son lose *nothing* of what the Father has given Him. Instead, the Son will raise up those who are His at the last day—a synonym in this chapter for "eternal life," as we will see in the next verse. So will the Son do the will of the Father, Steve? If so, then all who are given by the Father to the Son will be raised up and given eternal life. What tremendous security for the one who has looked to Christ and Christ alone for salvation! My relationship with Him is as sure as the Son's obedience to the Father!

Jesus further describes the will of the Father by saying that everyone who sees, or looks upon, the Son, and believes in Him, should have eternal life. What does it mean to look on Christ and believe in Him? Is this an action of which everyone is capable? Or does it require the supernatural agency of the Spirit of God? In verse 44, Jesus answers this question by saying that *no man* is even *able* to come to Him unless the Father draws him. Outside of the work of the Father in drawing men *no one would ever believe in Christ*. Do you understand this, Steve? Do you accept the Lord's words? Do you really believe that outside of the Father's drawing that *no man* can come to Christ? Can you see how this points out God's absolute sovereignty in salvation? Can you also see how it makes the concept of man's adding anything to his own salvation by works an utter impossibility? If we are not even able to come to Christ for salvation outside of the Father's drawing us to Him, how can we possibly say that we have to do this work, or undergo that religious action, prior to our salvation? As we saw in the preceding passages, the Bible is clear on the fact that God is the one who saves, and He does so only through Christ Jesus. God enables men to believe in Christ, and draws them to Him. God is the power behind it all.

When Paul wrote to Timothy he asserted the same truth with reference to the salvation he and Timothy (and all Christians) share:

> Be not thou therefore ashamed of the testimony of our Lord, nor of me his prisoner: but be thou partaker of the afflictions of the gospel according to the power of God; who hath saved us, and called us with an holy calling, not according to our works, but according to his own purpose and grace, which was given us in Christ Jesus before the world began. (2 Timothy 1:8–9)

Who saves Christians? God. This salvation is described as a "holy calling." On what basis are Christians called? On the basis of their works, their worthiness, their merit? No, not on any human basis at all, but on the basis of God's own purpose and grace—nothing more. And when was this grace granted to us? Was it granted to us in response to anything we did? No, for it was granted to us in Christ Jesus "before the world began." As we've already discussed, Steve, you and I were not around when the world began, so to think that this mercy was given to us on the basis of anything we have done, are doing, or might do in the future is utterly false, for this grace is granted to God's people *before God's people even entered into existence*! From God's perspective, the actual salvation of His people is an eternal reality. It is a completed work. Yes, we experience our salvation in time—before God by His Spirit regenerated me, caused me to be born again, I was a "child of wrath" just as anyone else (Ephesians 2:1–3). But my eternal salvation was not in doubt, not in question, even before I was born. God had willed it, and it will therefore take place. Is that not what Paul wrote to the Romans?

> For whom he did foreknow, he also did predestinate to be conformed to the image of his Son, that he might be the firstborn among many brethren. Moreover whom he did predestinate, them he also called: and whom he called, them he also justified: and whom he justified, them he also glorified. (Romans 8:29–30)

Some have called this the "Golden Chain of Redemption." It goes like this:

Foreknown ◊ Predestined ◊ Called ◊ Justified ◊ Glorified

Each link in the chain leads inexorably to the next—all who are foreknown are predestined. All who are predestined are called. All who are called are justified. All who are justified are glorified. Note that this is all done in past-tense language. From God's viewpoint, this is a finished process, and He did it *all*. Not much room for boasting by man, is there? None indeed. The term *foreknow* refers to God's gracious choice to enter into relationship with His people—elsewhere it is simply described as the "good pleasure of His will." God decides to save His people, and therefore predestines them, calls them, justifies them, and glorifies them. It is God's work from beginning to end. God is truly the author of our salvation.

But let us move on to the last passage I wish to bring to your attention on this topic at this time. It is also found in Paul's epistle to the Romans chapter 9, verses 10 through 24. This is not an easy passage (I've had people get up and leave a class I was teaching just for reading this section!), so please read it over slowly—maybe more than once.

> And not only this; but when Rebecca also had conceived by one, even by our father Isaac; (For the children being not yet born, neither having done any good or evil, *that the purpose of God according to election might stand, not of works, but of him that calleth;*) it was said unto her, The elder shall serve the younger. As it is written, Jacob have I loved, but Esau have I hated.
>
> What shall we say then? Is there unrighteousness with God? God forbid. For he saith to Moses, *I will have mercy on whom I will have mercy,* and I will have compassion on whom I will have compassion. So then *it is not of him that willeth, nor of him that runneth, but of God that showeth mercy.* For the scripture saith unto Pharaoh, Even for this same purpose have I raised thee up, that I might show my power in thee, and that my name might be declared throughout all the earth. *Therefore hath he mercy on whom he will have mercy, and whom he will he hardeneth.* Thou wilt say then unto me, Why doth he yet find fault? For who hath resisted his will? Nay but, O man, who art thou that repliest against God? Shall the thing formed say to him that formed it, Why hast thou made me thus? Hath not the potter power over the clay, of the same lump to make one vessel unto honor, and another unto dishonor? What if God, willing to show his wrath and to make his power known, endured with much longsuffering the vessels of wrath fitted to destruction: and that he might make known the riches of his glory on the vessels of mercy, which he hath afore prepared unto glory, even us, whom he hath called.

I warned you it is a tough passage. Men have, over the centuries, devised a number of ways to get around the clear import of these words, but most have just found it more convenient to *ignore* what Paul here asserts. Possibly it is because we don't like being compared to a lump of clay—this God is so far above us that we can't even begin to question His doings. I am not going to go "verse by verse" through it—Paul was more than clear enough on his own. But I did want to point out to you that almost every single objection that is raised against God's sovereignty in salvation (i.e., as I would translate verse 16, "therefore it does not depend upon the one who wills or the one who runs, but upon God, the one who shows mercy") is raised, and answered, by Paul in this passage. Do you find yourself raising the same objections to what I have said to you? Do you say that this would mean God is unrighteous in not saving everyone (v. 14)? Do you question how God could hold men responsible for their rebellion against Him when He has eternally decreed what shall come to pass (v. 19)? And does your heart and mind rebel and say, "But that isn't a good enough answer" (i.e., the answer given in verses 20 through 21)? So when you throw these questions back at the Scriptures, are you not showing that you are opposing what is being taught there? Is that where you really want to be, opposing God's Word? I would hope not.

So the first of two vitally important foundations has been laid—God is sovereign in the matter of salvation. It is not dependent upon the works of man, the striving of man, the choice of man. It is God's work. Now on to the second aspect that will be vital to our final discussion of the gospel of Christ—the nature of man.

Man in Sin

The flip side of the sovereignty of God in salvation is the *total inability of man*. The two go hand-in-hand, for the one who hates God's sovereignty will most probably have a very high view of his own capabilities and status. Few men *like* to be told about how evil they are, or how helpless they are. But the Bible is plain and clear on this topic as well. Let's look at a few passages that show us, sometimes painfully, who we really are outside of Christ Jesus.

Paul's epistle to the Romans does not start out in chapter one with the tremendous truths of God's election and predestination—Paul waits until chapters eight and nine for that. Why? He has something else to deal with first, and that is man in his sin. Just about the entire first chapter is devoted to a discussion of man's sin. He asserts in that passage that man is without excuse; that God has given sufficient revelation of

His nature to hold man responsible to worship Him and give Him thanks (Romans 1:20–21). But what does man do? He "suppresses" the truth about God, and instead worships created things rather than the Creator himself. He engages in idolatry—the worship of *anything* other than the true God, the Creator of all things. What does man worship? Anything—birds, reptiles, beasts, even man himself. Have you stopped to think that this would apply equally well to an "exalted man" such as the god of Joseph Smith?

As a result of this rebellion against God, God gives man over to his sin. The catalog of sinful actions and attitudes provided by Paul in Romans 1:24–31 is depressingly accurate in describing men down through the ages. Since men did not like to "retain God in their knowledge, God gave them over to a reprobate mind" we are told (1:28). This reprobate mind is the common property of all men—every single person who has not been made a new creation in Christ Jesus (2 Corinthians 5:17) has this reprobate mind. While it may manifest itself in different ways and in different levels of evil, the reprobate mind is still there, and it is dead-set against submitting to the true and living God.

After pointing out the sin that is common in all the world, Paul moves on to deal with the Jews, who, by their religious attitudes and possession of the commandments of God, considered themselves to be different than the rest of the world, and therefore blessed by God and His grace. But Paul shows them that they, too, just like everyone else, are condemned as sinners, transgressors of the law, without hope. In fact, he finally pulls together a number of quotations from the Old Testament into a single, sweeping condemnation of the sin of man. Here is what he says:

> As it is written, There is none righteous, no, not one: There is none that understandeth, *there is none that seeketh after God.* They are all gone out of the way, they are together become unprofitable; there is none that doeth good, no, not one. Their throat is an open sepulchre; with their tongues they have used deceit; the poison of asps is under their lips: Whose mouth is full of cursing and bitterness: Their feet are swift to shed blood; Destruction and misery are in their ways: And the way of peace have they not known. *There is no fear of God before their eyes.* (Romans 3:10–18)

A dismal portrait, is it not? But those of us who are honest with ourselves know how true it is. There is none righteous, none who understands. In fact, man is so blinded by his sin, so enslaved to evil, that there is not even one single person who seeks after God (verse 11)! Can you accept this statement? There is no such thing as a "God-seeker." Oh yes, I know many who are "seeking after truth," too. But the Bible teaches that they are in reality seeking after their own selfish ends, not the true God. It is one thing to seek after "truth" so as to find comfort or peace or happiness; it is another to seek the true God and to worship Him and give oneself over to Him. The first any man can do; the second only the person who has been renewed by the Spirit of God can do.

Jeremiah was given a penetrating ability to look into the human heart. He asked,

> Can the Ethiopian change his skin, or the leopard his spots? then may ye also do good, that are accustomed to do evil. (Jeremiah 13:23)

What does Jeremiah mean? Well, we know the Ethiopian cannot change the color of his skin, and neither can the leopard change the spots on its coat. So, neither can those who are accustomed to doing evil, do good. Certainly men are accustomed to doing evil, so outside of God's Spirit making them new creations, how can they do good? And if you continue to believe that men must do certain good works *before* they are saved, *before* they are regenerated or justified, how do you explain this biblical teaching that contradicts your position? Unless God changes your heart, Steve, you can't do truly good works! Salvation must come *first*, *then* we can do good works so as to glorify God, not "earn" what is in fact a free gift of God—full and complete salvation. Jeremiah also said,

> The heart is deceitful above all things, and desperately wicked: who can know it? (Jeremiah 17:9)

I discussed this with you when I first wrote to you about your "testimony." The human heart is a rebel against its God—evil lurks in its dark shadows. Who then can know it? Who can trust it? Until the light of the Spirit shines in that heart, it remains in darkness.

Paul described the situation man is in like this:

> And you hath he quickened [made alive], *who were dead in trespasses and sins;* wherein in time past ye walked according to the course of this world, according to the prince of the power of

the air, the spirit that now worketh in the children of disobedience: Among whom also we all had our conversation in times past in the lusts of our flesh, fulfilling the desires of the flesh and of the mind; and were by nature the children of wrath, even as others. (Ephesians 2:1–3)

Man is *dead in sin*. Paul does not say he is simply "sickened" by sin, or "weakened" by sin, but that he is *dead* in sin. What difference does it make? A great deal. If a man is just weak or sick, he can call out for help, or can try to move toward assistance. He can go to a doctor for medicine or surgery. Frequently the illustration of a drowning man is used. The person in the water struggles fiercely to keep from going down, while waving frantically to a ship, seeking a life-preserver or other assistance. This is how man in his sin is viewed by man—but not by the Bible.

A dead man does not have the options mentioned above. He cannot call out for help, for he is dead. He cannot move toward assistance, for he is dead. Neither medicine nor surgery can save him. He is not struggling in the water, yelling for help. He is at the bottom of the ocean—as one writer put it, he's shark food. Dead and gone. Paul used the same terms elsewhere:

And you, *being dead in your sins and the uncircumcision of your flesh,* hath he quickened [made alive] together with him, having forgiven you all trespasses. (Colossians 2:13)

Both in Colossians and Ephesians Paul says that it was God who "made us alive." Well, most people don't have any problem with the idea that only God can make someone alive, or, in this case, raise someone from the dead. But what does this mean? It means that God must act first in salvation, for man, being dead in trespasses and sin, is not about to initiate his own resurrection to life! Therefore, any system that says that man must do anything *before* God regenerates (causes to be born again) or *before* God responds in salvation, has missed the boat on *both* the sovereignty of God (making God dependent upon man) and the inability of sinful man who is dead in sin! That is why Jesus said that no man is *able* to come to Him unless the Father draws him, or as He said in John 6:65, unless "it were given unto him of my Father." Does this not also show you the error of the entire understanding of the LDS faith with regard to the gospel?

If man is dead in sin, and is utterly dependent upon God to bring him to spiritual life, then it follows that both *faith* and *repentance* must be gifts of God. And this is exactly what we find in Scripture as well. Faith and repentance, being spiritual activities, can only be undertaken by men and women who are no longer spiritually dead! So, not only are we dependent upon God for our spiritual life, but for faith and repentance as well. Where does the Bible teach this? Well, with reference to repentance we read in Romans 2:4,

> Or despisest thou the riches of his goodness and forbearance and longsuffering; not knowing that the goodness of God leadeth thee to repentance?

It is the goodness of God that leads us to repentance, not our own desires or works. Furthermore we read in 2 Timothy 2:25,

> In meekness instructing those that oppose themselves; if God peradventure will *give them repentance* to the acknowledging of the truth.

And in Acts 5:31,

> Him hath God exalted with his right hand to be a Prince and a Savior, *for to give repentance to Israel*, and forgiveness of sins.

But the most clearly presented argument is found again in the eighth chapter of Romans, verses five through eight:

> For they that are after the flesh do mind the things of the flesh; but they that are after the Spirit the things of the Spirit. For to be carnally minded is death; but to be spiritually minded is life and peace. Because the carnal mind is enmity against God: for it is not subject to the law of God, neither indeed can be. So then they that are in the flesh cannot please God.

Either one is carnally minded, or spiritually minded—there is no middle ground. Unless one is born again, one is carnally minded. Therefore, Paul teaches that such a person is at "enmity" with God—he is an enemy of God, at war with Him. Such a person's mind is not subject to the law of God, and in fact, it can't be! The result of this situation? Those who are "in the flesh" cannot please God. Until one is made "spiritually minded" by the Spirit of God, one cannot please God.

Now, is repentance pleasing to God? Is God pleased when men and women repent of sin? Of course. So if it is impossible for a "natural man," a "carnal man" to do that which is pleasing to God, then does it not follow that a man must be made "spiritually minded" *before* he can repent? Indeed it does.

The same can be said of true, *saving* faith. It is plainly said to be the work of God in man—a gift of His Spirit. Grace, faith, and love were poured out abundantly upon Paul (1 Timothy 1:14). Faith is wrapped up in that which is a "gift of God" in Ephesians 2:8–9. 1 John 5:1 indicates that everyone who believes that Jesus is the Christ *has already been born again*—that is, that regeneration *precedes* faith. And Galatians 5:22 speaks of "faith" as one aspect of the "fruit of the Spirit."

You will note that I spoke of *saving* faith just now. I am talking about a supernatural gift of God that causes a person to believe, trust, and cling solely to Jesus Christ as Savior. I am not talking about a mere tipping of the hat toward God, a brief intellectual assent to the facts of the gospel, but a life-changing, disciple-making faith that radically alters a person's outlook and life. Only God can give that kind of faith. And it is on the basis of that kind of faith that God freely justifies sinners.

I want to go into the topic of justification, but I see that I have again gone long, and I was just informed by a knock on the bedroom door that there are two little munchkins waiting for Daddy to come and tickle them for a while before heading to bed. I never knew that tickling little kids could be so much fun until I had my own. I shall send this with the morning's mail and try to do my best to find time again tomorrow to take up where I have left off.

In Christian service,

James White

Faith, Justification, and Works

Tuesday, July 31

Dear Steve,

I hope you don't mind "rapid-fire" letters, but I didn't want you to think I had forgotten about you, so I wanted to get that letter out, while at the same time I didn't want to have to "rush" the extremely important discussion of justification, either. I hope this arrangement will be acceptable to you. As I promised in my last letter, I am picking up with the topic of justification as it is defined in the Bible.

Let's begin by defining what we are talking about when we speak of justification. The Greek term as used by Paul in the New Testament was borrowed from the Roman legal system. When a prisoner was found not guilty he was said to be *dikaios*, righteous. It referred to a person having the right relationship to the court and to the law. It speaks of a whole relationship, one in which there is no sin or transgression. In English, we translate the term in two different ways. We can use the term *justification* or its verbal form *to justify*, or we can use the term *righteousness* or its verbal form *to make righteous*. There is no difference between the two terms as they are found in the New Testament, since both are translating the same Greek word. To be just is to be righteous, to have justification is to be made righteous.

A person who is righteous in God's sight is one who has a "right relationship" to God. Obviously, then, if one has been justified, then one has been forgiven, for the presence of unforgiven sin would preclude the possibility of calling a person "just" or "righteous." All the impediments to a proper relationship with God have been removed. This is what it means to be justified.

There is another term that is so frequently used in conjunction with justification that I need to mention something about it before we get too deeply into a study of the Scriptures. It is probably the most beautiful term in the Bible, at least in my opinion. It is the term *grace*. It is important that I take a moment to look at the word, for it is terribly misunderstood in Mormon thinking. As I mentioned earlier, you believe in two different kinds of salvation. The first is universal or general salvation which is basically the same as resurrection. Bruce R. McConkie commented,

> Immortality is a free gift and comes without works or righteousness of any sort; all men will come forth in the resurrection because of the atoning sacrifice of Christ. . . . In this sense, the mere fact of resurrection is called *salvation by grace alone*. Works are not involved, neither the works of the Mosaic law nor the works of righteousness that go with the fulness of the gospel. (*Mormon Doctrine*, p. 671)

But I am not talking to you simply about rising from the dead. I am talking to you about what the New Testament teaches—how one obtains full and complete salvation. I am not talking about exaltation, as there is no such thing taught in the Bible. I am talking about being with Christ for eternity, walking with God, being right with Him.

McConkie went on to talk about "exaltation" and explained,

> Salvation in the celestial kingdom of God, however, is not salvation by grace alone. Rather, it is *salvation by grace coupled with obedience* to the laws and ordinances of the gospel. . . . Immortality comes by grace alone, but those who gain it may find themselves damned in eternity. (*Mormon Doctrine*, p. 671)

So the "highest" form of salvation in Mormon thought is not based solely on God's grace, but instead requires works of law—continued obedience to the "laws and ordinances of the gospel" (whatever they might be).

Back when I was talking about the theological errors in the Book of Mormon, I cited 2 Nephi 25:23 as an example of this, for it contains the phrase, "for we know that it is by grace that we are saved, after all we can do." At the time I said that we are not saved by grace *after all we can do,* but that we are saved by grace *in spite of all we have done*! But the terrible misunderstanding of what grace is can be seen most clearly in what must be the saddest statement I think I have ever read in LDS literature. It again comes from Bruce R. McConkie:

> Grace is granted to men proportionately as they conform to the standards of personal righteousness that are part of the gospel plan. (*Mormon Doctrine*, p. 339)

Here a Mormon apostle tells us that grace is granted to men in proportion to their personal righteousness—the more "righteous" you are, the more grace you receive. I admit that McConkie was just following Joseph Smith's own views, as seen in the Book of Mormon:

> Yea, come unto Christ, and be perfected in him, and deny yourselves of all ungodliness; and if ye shall deny yourselves of all ungodliness, and love God with all your might, mind and strength, then is his grace sufficient for you, that by his grace we may be perfect in Christ. (Moroni 10:32)

Please note that this passage teaches that one must *first* deny oneself of *all* ungodliness, and love God with *all* of one's might, mind, and strength, so that the grace of God can become effective. I hope, Steve, that you really do not believe that. Nothing could be further from the biblical truth. "But where sin abounded, grace did much more abound," Paul taught (Romans 5:20). I cannot deny myself of ungodliness and love God truly without God's grace. If God's grace is dependent upon man's actions as Moroni 10:32 teaches, we are all lost, without hope.

Grace is favor that is granted without any reference to the worthiness of the recipient. In fact, grace is not just "unmerited favor," it is in fact "*de*merited favor" in the sense that not only do we not merit God's mercy and love, but we instead merit His anger and wrath for our sin. But, despite what we are really worthy of, God's grace gives us something else. Grace is free by definition. If the object of grace did something to deserve it, it would no longer be grace. Grace cannot be bought, purchased, or demanded. Grace must be given by God solely because He wants to give it, and for no other reason. Grace is the opposite of merit, the opposite of works. As Paul said in Romans 11:6, "And if by grace, then it is no more of works; otherwise grace is no more grace." You can't mix grace and works. Grace plus works is dead, being meaningless.

Graphically it would look like this:

GRACE ◄——————————————————————————► WORKS

So McConkie's idea that grace is granted *in proportion to* some standard of "personal righteousness" is the opposite of the truth, for grace is not at all related to personal righteousness or worthiness—instead, grace *produces righteousness in the life of the believer!* As in all of salvation, first it is the work of God (grace), then the response of man (personal righteousness that comes as a result of God's work).

You probably have noticed that Paul's epistle to the Romans has been a frequent source of quotations from the Bible in my discussion of salvation to this point. The reason for this is that the book is a thought-out, prepared presentation of the means by which God takes unrighteous, guilty sinners and through His mercy and grace creates righteous saints who have eternal life. Therefore, Romans provides us with some of the clearest arguments concerning salvation, and we would do well to heed the teaching found there. In fact, to present the biblical doctrine of justification, I would like to start in Romans chapter three and basically just "step back" and allow the Apostle Paul to present this doctrine to you.

After presenting his indictment of sinful mankind in Romans 3:10–18, Paul concludes the first section of the book in this way:

> Now we know that what things soever the law saith, it saith to them who are under the law: that every mouth may be stopped, and all the world may become guilty before God. Therefore by the deeds of the law there shall no flesh be justified in his sight: for by the law is the knowledge of sin. (Romans 3:19–20)

The first and most foundational concept to grasp here is that by deeds of the law, no flesh will be justified *in the sight of God*. The law, Paul teaches, was not meant to provide a way of salvation—instead, it was meant to give us a knowledge of our sin and point out to us our need of a Savior (Galatians 3:10–11, 19, 22–24). So no amount of legalistic keeping of rules and regulations can possibly bring about our justification. The law cannot mend our broken relationship with God, for it only shows us how far short we are of being truly righteous. A person can perform good deeds ("deeds of the law") forever and still not be righteous with God, for those deeds have no merit in God's sight. So what are we to do? How can we be made righteous? Paul continues:

But now the righteousness of God without the law is manifested, being witnessed by the law and the prophets; even the righteousness of God which is by faith of Jesus Christ unto all and upon all them that believe: for there is no difference: For all have sinned and come short of the glory of God; being justified freely by his grace through the redemption that is in Christ Jesus. (Romans 3: 21–24)

What is this righteousness of God that is apart from the law? It is the righteousness God gives men by faith in Jesus Christ. God does not give men righteousness because of works, or on the basis of works. God gives men righteousness on the basis of their faith in Christ Jesus. Yes, God gives them this faith, and on the basis of that faith He justifies those who believe in Christ. All men have sinned. All men have come short of the glory of God. There is no difference between one man and another with respect to the fact that all are sinners. So the way of salvation is the same for all as well—anyone who will ever stand in the Kingdom of God will stand there on the same ground. Each and every one will have been "justified freely by his grace through the redemption that is in Christ Jesus." Not justified because they believed, repented, were baptized, did good works, tithed to their church, were married in a temple, served a mission, or remained faithful to the end of their mortal probation—no, they are justified *freely* by His grace through the redemption that is in Christ Jesus! Not as a result of works, not as a result of merit—*freely!* Is this what the LDS Church teaches? Not if the following quotation from an LDS tract entitled *"Your Pre-Earth Life"* means anything:

By revelation, our Savior made known again the plan of salvation and exaltation. Resurrection comes as a gift to every man through Jesus Christ, but the reward of the highest eternal opportunities you must earn. It is not enough just to believe in Jesus Christ. You must work and learn, search and pray, repent and improve, know his laws and live them (p. 10).

Compare this with Paul's words:

Where is boasting then? It is excluded. By what law? of works? Nay: but by the law of faith. Therefore we conclude that a man is justified by faith without the deeds of the law. (Romans 3:27–28)

If I "earn" the highest rewards from God, then I can boast of my accomplishments. But Paul says that boasting is excluded. Why is it excluded? Because righteousness does not come by works, it comes by faith—faith in Christ Jesus. That is how he can conclude that a man is justified by faith without the deeds of law. Are you made righteous, Steve, by faith "without the deeds of law?" Or do you believe that there are certain legal works that you must do in order to gain God's mercy and grace?

Paul moves on from the great declarations of God's free grace to an example from the Old Testament—Abraham. The entire fourth chapter is an argument for the priority of faith over works based upon the example of Abraham, the "father of the faithful." Note how Paul opens his argument:

> What shall we say then that Abraham our father, as pertaining to the flesh, hath found? For if Abraham were justified by works, he hath whereof [something of which] to glory; but not before God. For what saith the scripture? Abraham believed God, and it was counted unto him for righteousness. (Romans 4:1–3)

Every Jew knew the story of Abraham very well. How, then, was Abraham made right with God? Was it by works of law? Was he made righteous by works? If he was, Paul asserts, he would have something in which to glory. But, Paul says, that's not what happened. Instead he quotes Genesis 15:6, and shows that it was Abraham's *faith* that made him right with God. He then goes on to say,

> Now to him that worketh is the reward not reckoned of grace, but of debt. But to him that worketh not, but believeth on him that justifieth the ungodly, his faith is counted for righteousness. Even as David also describeth the blessedness of the man, unto whom God imputeth righteousness without works, saying, Blessed are they whose iniquities are forgiven, and whose sins are covered. Blessed is the man to whom the Lord will not impute sin. (Romans 4:4–8)

He starts off by stating his premise: if we work for something, the wages given to us for our work is not considered a "gift" but simply what is owed to us. If you went into work on a Friday and your boss came up to you and handed you your paycheck and said "Here is a gift for you," you would probably be offended and say, "That's no gift! I earned every penny of it!" So in the same way, if we have to "work" for our salvation, work for our righteousness, then it is not a gift but simply a payment of what we have earned. On the contrary, Paul asserts, the one who does not work, but instead believes on him that makes the ungodly righteous, that man's faith is counted for righteousness. That is how one is justified—by faith and faith *alone*. A "faith + works" system doesn't cut it. That is not real faith. Faith is either totally and completely in Christ and not in any works, or it is not Christian faith. Can you see how Paul emphasizes this in Romans 4:5? He *contrasts* the one who works with the one who believes—one trusts in works, the other trusts in Christ, the one who did the works in our place! You can't hold on to works and claim faith in Christ. It just won't work. God imputes righteousness *apart from works* as David of old said (4:6).

Paul moves on to demonstrate his next point. When Abraham was made righteous before God in Genesis 15:6, where was the law? The law hadn't been given yet. In fact, the sign of circumcision had not even been given—Abraham was uncircumcised when he put his faith in God. When he did receive the sign of circumcision, it was but a *seal* of "the righteousness of the faith which he had" previously (4:11). Paul continues through the chapter showing the priority of the promise to the law, faith to works, and concludes by saying,

> Now it was not written for his sake alone, that it was imputed to him; but for us also, to whom it shall be imputed, if we believe on him that raised up Jesus our Lord from the dead; who was delivered for our offenses, and was raised again for our justification. (Romans 4:23–25)

Would you like righteousness to be imputed to you? Would you like the righteousness of Christ? You will never find it by seeking it through works, Steve. You may be sincere, and you may work very hard and be very "zealous" for your Mormon beliefs, but you will never be made righteous with God. Why not? Paul spoke of men who were very much like you:

> What shall we say then? That the Gentiles, which followed not after righteousness, have attained to righteousness, even the righteousness which is of faith. But Israel, which followed after the law of righteousness, hath not attained to the law of righteousness. Wherefore? *Because they sought it not by faith, but as it were by the works of the law.* For they stumbled at that stumbling stone; as it is written, Behold I lay in Zion a stumbling stone and rock of

offense: and whosoever believeth on him shall not be ashamed.

Brethren, my heart's desire and prayer to God for Israel is, that they might be saved. For I bear them record that they have a zeal for God, *but not according to knowledge*. For they being ignorant of God's righteousness, *and going about to establish their own righteousness*, have not submitted themselves unto the righteousness of God. For Christ is the end of the law for righteousness *to everyone that believeth*. (Romans 9:30–10:4)

Until you quit attempting to add to what Christ has done in His work, you will never know the peace of God. Paul spoke of that peace right after his discussion of Abraham:

Therefore *being justified by faith*, we have peace with God through our Lord Jesus Christ: by whom also we have access by faith into this grace wherein we stand, and rejoice in hope of the glory of God. (Romans 5:1–2)

The Greek text is very expressive in that it is plain that we *have been justified by faith*. In other words, Steve, I am already justified. I am not working to *become* justified—all that I do is based on the fact that I *already am justified!* Again, a little graph might help. As a Christian, I have been justified by faith in Jesus Christ solely on the basis of the free grace of God. That faith in Jesus Christ—which I freely admit was the gift of God Himself—is the sole basis for my justification. The life I now live I live empowered by the Spirit of God. I seek to "do good works" not to gain my justification, but because I already am justified, will remain justified, and desire with all my heart to glorify God. So, for me, it would look like this:

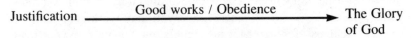

Justification ———— Good works / Obedience ————▶ The Glory of God

But you are seeking after full and complete justification. So in contrast with the above, your picture would look like this:

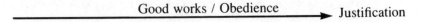

———— Good works / Obedience ————▶ Justification

I have believed in the all-sufficiency of the sacrifice of Jesus Christ, and because I have done so, God has imputed to me the righteousness of Jesus Christ. I do not stand before God in robes of righteousness of my own making. I stand before Him in the spotless robe of righteousness given to me as a gift of God's grace, a robe that was woven on the cross two thousand years ago. Because of this, I have peace with God. I cannot be condemned for I have been justified—the enmity that existed between myself and God has been taken away in my Lord Jesus Christ. That is the only way to peace with God.

A Brief Detour: James 2:20 and Paul's Teaching on Righteousness

It might be best right here, Steve, to address what seems to be one of the "favorite" passages of Mormon people who attempt to defend the idea that justification is *not* by faith alone, but by faith and works, that being James 2:17–24. I think it fits well here simply because both Paul and James refer to the same person as their example (Abraham) even to the point of quoting the same passage from the Old Testament (Genesis 15:6). Some have said that James and Paul simply disagreed on this issue and that their teachings are contradictory. But I think that is little more than a cop-out. A close examination of James' words reveals another story. Here is what he said,

> Even so faith, if it hath not works, is dead, being alone. Yea, a man may say, Thou hast faith, and I have works: show me thy faith without thy works, and I will show thee my faith by my works. Thou believest that there is one God; thou doest well: the devils also believe, and tremble. But wilt thou know, O vain man, that faith without works is dead? Was not Abraham our father justified by works, when he had offered Isaac his son upon the altar? Seest thou how faith wrought with his works, and by works was faith made perfect? And the scripture was fulfilled which saith, Abraham believed God, and it was imputed unto him for righteousness: and he was called the friend of God. Ye see then how that by works a man is justified, and not by faith only.

I've often commented that if the most "memorized" verse among conservative Christians is John 3:16, then the most "memorized" verse among Latter-day Saints is James 2:20, so often have I heard it quoted by missionaries and others. But does the verse teach that God's grace is insufficient without man's works to bring about full and complete justification? What is James talking about here?

As always, let's examine the context. First, James is not discussing how one is made righteous before God, how one finds forgiveness of sins. The whole book is not written to unbelievers, nor is it its purpose to discuss how unbelievers are made believers. Instead, James' book is primarily moral and ethical in nature. It is an exhortation to Christian living, directed solely to people who already name the name of Christ. We read in 1:18–21,

> Of his own will begot he us with the word of truth, that we should be a kind of firstfruits of his creatures. Wherefore, my beloved brethren, let every man be swift to hear, slow to speak, slow to wrath: for the wrath of man worketh not the righteousness of God. Wherefore lay apart all filthiness and superfluity of naughtiness and receive with meekness the engrafted word, *which is able to save your souls.*

James is talking to Christians (1:19) and calling them to a holy life. But in the process he "lets it slip" that he, just like Paul, believes that salvation is the work of God. It is God who "begot us with the word of truth" and it is the word of God that "is able to save your souls." This is exactly what Paul said in 1 Thessalonians 2:13,

> For this cause also thank we God without ceasing, because, when ye received the word of God which ye heard of us, ye received it not as the word of men, but as it is in truth, the word of God, which effectually worketh also in you that believe.

Part and parcel of this recognition of God's work of salvation is the idea that when God saves someone, they will be changed and will live a life that will demonstrate that they are truly Christians. This, too, is exactly what Paul taught as well. The famous passage in the second chapter of Ephesians that you have probably heard more than once in this debate is often not quoted completely—you may have read Ephesians 2:8–9, but how often did you hear verse 10 quoted along with it?

> For by grace are ye saved through faith; and that not of yourselves: it is the gift of God: not of works, lest any man should boast. For we are his workmanship, *created in Christ Jesus unto good works,* which God hath before ordained that we should walk in them.

We are saved by grace through faith. This salvation, and this faith, is not of ourselves, but is the free and undeserved gift of God. Our salvation is not of works, for if it were, then we would have something about which to boast. But Paul doesn't stop there. God saves us, but does He leave us just as we were? Does not God have a plan and purpose for our life? Indeed He does, for Paul goes on to assert that we are the creation or workmanship of God, created in Christ Jesus *unto* (not *by*) good works. God has before ordained that we should walk in good works, bringing glory to God. That is His purpose for us. Those good works do not bring about our salvation, they flow *from* our salvation. The salvation comes first—first we are justified. *Then* we do the good works, for only those who are right with God can even *do* good works! And this is exactly what James will be arguing for in his book as well.

So we see that James is addressing Christians and exhorting them to good works just as Paul did. Note Paul's words to Titus:

> This is a faithful saying, and these things I will that thou affirm constantly, that they which have believed in God might be careful to maintain good works. These things are good and profitable unto men. (3:8)

This is a common theme in all of Paul's letters. Never will you see the Bible saying "well, since God saved you, you can just go and have a good time." That kind of thinking is utterly foreign to the Christian, and is directly contradictory to the Word of God. In fact, many LDS people have made that very accusation against the gospel of grace, and I have often replied, "Do you know you just quoted a passage from the Bible?" They are normally taken aback by this, so I go on to quote the passage to them:

> What shall we say then? Shall we continue in sin that grace may abound? God forbid. How shall we, that are dead to sin, live any longer therein? (Romans 6:1–2)

A person who has died with Christ Jesus (Galatians 2:20) is a new creation (2 Corinthians 5:17). We have died to sin, and therefore cannot continue to live under its dominion. The desire of our heart is not to bring grief to God's heart, but to bring glory to His name. So we see that Paul and James are teaching the exact same thing. No contradiction here.

Next, we see that James does not believe that the law can bring a man into salvation—in fact, he is again in complete agreement with Paul. He writes,

> For whosoever shall keep the whole law, and yet offend in one

point, he is guilty of all. (James 2:10)

James asserts that it is not enough to simply keep *most* of the law, or to do "all you can" (2 Nephi 25:23). He says that nothing but perfection would do—and, since none of us keep the law perfectly, obviously that is not the way of justification, just as Paul taught (Romans 3:20).

And so we come to the second half of chapter 2, and the discussion by James of the relationship of faith and works. In verse 14 he tells us what kind of "faith" he is discussing:

> What doth it profit, my brethren, though a man say he hath faith, and have not works? can faith save him?

Now please note that the faith James is talking about is a faith that does not produce works. It is a faith that produces no fruit, shows no changed life. Is this the faith that Paul talks about in Romans, a faith that is in Christ Jesus and is the supernatural gift of God? Certainly not! So we see that James is talking about a "head faith," a faith that is nothing more than an intellectual acknowledgment of certain facts, not a true heart-changing, saving faith that is the work of the Spirit of God. Since Paul asserts that justification is based solely on *true, saving faith,* and himself denies that this kind of faith can exist *without* the resultant change in a person's life, then James' whole discussion here is directed not against Paul's teaching but against a completely different kind of belief—a belief that is still around to this day. James will attack the idea that a person can at one point in time simply acknowledge that Jesus is Lord and then go on to live a life of sin and debauchery, even to the point of denying the Lord (yes, believe it or not, some people actually teach that!), and yet still be saved! James denies that this is saving faith—and Paul denies this as well! But the important thing to grasp is that James is discussing a totally different concept than that we have seen in Paul. Let's go on and see how this is borne out by the text.

In verse 17 James asserts that a faith that does not result in works is "dead, being alone." Dead faith cannot save anyone. Mere intellectual assent to certain facts is not saving faith, and is surely not the work of the Spirit of God. He goes on to show the foolishness of this kind of "head faith" in verse 18, and in doing so gives us another *vitally important aspect* of his discussion in this chapter. James speaks of "showing" our faith, proving our faith before men. How can one show one's faith to other men? You certainly can't do it without works. Faith is a matter of the heart, so it cannot be seen by men other than in the *effects it has upon the manner of life of the person.* Why is this so important? Because when James will talk about Abraham being "justified" by his works, *he does so in the context of demonstrating his faith before other men, not before God!* The "justification" of which James speaks, then, is in a completely different context than Paul's discussion in Romans or Galatians. Paul says that no man shall be justified *in the sight of God* by works; James says that the only way a man can be justified *in the sight of men* is by works! Again, we see that the topics under discussion differ from Paul and James, and that in reality they are in perfect harmony with one another.

And so James asserts that while the demons "believe" and tremble, this does them no good, for the "faith" that is theirs is hardly the faith that is the work of the Spirit, but is just a simple recognition of the fact of God's existence. This kind of faith is of no use to them. As a result, faith without works is dead, and to that I say a hearty "amen" and say, "Paul taught the same thing in Romans, Galatians, Ephesians, Colossians, and all his other letters." But we need to recognize that James is *not* saying that true, saving faith, which always results in good works and is never "alone," is insufficient to save. Sadly, that is what most LDS try to say James is teaching, but he is not.

James then gives us an example: Abraham. He asks if Abraham was not justified by works when he offered Isaac upon the altar. Well, was he? We must remember, Steve, that the readers of James' letter would know the Old Testament story of Abraham by heart. How would they have understood his words? We know that Abraham "believed God, and it was counted to him as righteousness" in Genesis 15:6. This was at least twenty years *before* the offering of Isaac of which James speaks (Genesis 22:1–14). So James knew, as did his readers, that Abraham's faith had brought him righteousness *before* this act of obedience on his part two decades later. But as we have already seen, James is not talking about how one becomes righteous *in God's sight,* but how one *demonstrates one's faith.* So Abraham's act of obedience did not initially *make him righteous* but instead showed the *reality of his faith in God.* His works "perfected" his faith, showed his faith, and most importantly, *sprung from his faith.* In each instance faith is prior to, and foundational to, the works. James is saying what Paul said in different words in Romans chapter 12 and in Ephesians 2:10. When he says that a man is "justified" by works and not by faith only, the preceding discussion *prohibits* us from taking this to be a denial of Paul's doctrine of justification by faith alone. Rather, he is speaking of a different sense of justification (before men, not before God) and is still keeping before us the truth that real, saving faith will not be without works.

James' next example bears this out (James 2:25), for when he speaks of Rahab being "justified" by her works, we know that the reason Rahab did what she did was because of her faith. She told the spies in Joshua 2:9–11 that she knew of the true God Jehovah, and in fact said, "for the LORD your God, he is God in heaven above, and in earth beneath." Since she really believed that, she acted on her faith and hid the servants of Jehovah. Her actions showed the reality of her faith.

So we see that James and Paul are not contradicting each other. When the context of James and his whole teaching is taken into consideration, we see that he is emphasizing the importance of the demonstration of our faith by our works. He is *not* teaching us that our works bring about our justification *before God,* nor does he deny the fact that faith is foundational to, and gives rise to, real works of righteousness. So we see that Paul's doctrine of justification is not contradicted by James.

Back to Paul and Justification

Now this teaching is hardly limited to Paul's discussion in Romans. If you will sit down with Paul's letter to the Galatians you will find the exact same argument, only in much rougher terms! In fact, Paul is so adamant about the truth of justification by faith alone that he condemns any and all teachers who would in any way contradict this truth, so basic is it to the entire gospel. He opens his letter by saying,

> But though we, or an angel from heaven, preach any other gospel unto you than that which we have preached unto you, let him be accursed. As we said before, so say I now again, If any man preach any other gospel unto you than that ye have received, let him be accursed. (Galatians 1:8–9)

Those are very strong words, Steve, and I would like to ask you to read the entire book of Galatians and ask yourself this question: Are you preaching the message that Paul preached, or the message that his enemies in Galatia were preaching? Can you honestly preach the following words and say that they are Mormon doctrine?

> Knowing that a man is not justified by works of the law, but by the faith of Jesus Christ, even we have believed in Jesus Christ, that we might be justified by the faith of Christ, and not by the works of the law: for by the works of the law shall no flesh be justified. . . . I am crucified with Christ: nevertheless I live; yet not I, but Christ liveth in me: and the life which I now live in the flesh I live by the faith of the Son of God, who loved me, and gave himself for me. *I do not frustrate the grace of God: for if righteousness come by the law, then Christ is dead in vain.* (Galatians 2:16, 20–21)

The third "Article of Faith" in the Pearl of Great Price reads like this:

> We believe that through the Atonement of Christ, all mankind may be saved, by obedience to the laws and ordinances of the Gospel.

What laws and ordinances are there in the free gospel of grace? Where are they? When I read about the gospel in the New Testament, all I read about is the work of Jesus Christ and the sovereign grace of God. When Paul spoke to the Corinthians about the gospel, he didn't mention any laws and ordinances, only the work of Christ:

> For I delivered unto you first of all that which I also received, how that Christ died for our sins according to the scriptures; and that he was buried, and that he rose again the third day according to the scriptures: and that he was seen of Cephas, then of the twelve. (1 Corinthians 15:3–5)

That was Paul's gospel—the death, burial, and resurrection of Jesus Christ. Where are these "laws and ordinances"? They aren't there, because the gospel is the "gospel of the grace of God" (Acts 20:24) in Christ Jesus. It is not the gospel of the laws of God, or the ordinances of God, but of the *grace* of God. And as I already mentioned, grace is as far from meaning "obedience to laws and ordinances" as it is possible to get.

Paul confessed the true desire of the heart that has been changed and renewed by the Holy Spirit in Philippians 3:8–9:

Yea doubtless, and I count all things but loss for the excellency of the knowledge of Christ Jesus my Lord: for whom I have suffered the loss of all things, and do count them but dung, that I may win Christ, and be found in him, *not having mine own righteousness, which is of the law, but that which is through the faith of Christ, the righteousness which is of God by faith.*

I thank God daily that I do not have to stand before His awful throne to be judged for my own righteousness. I will stand before Him with the righteousness of God in Christ Jesus (2 Corinthians 5:17). I will not have to trust in a single meritorious action, a single act of obedience, because I know that no such thing can add to the work of Christ accomplished at Calvary. Will I therefore not be obedient? Will I therefore not do good deeds? Gracious no! The Spirit of God who indwells my heart has created in me a *longing* to serve God, to love God, to glorify God. I do "good deeds" not to *bribe* God or to *buy from God* His mercy or grace, but because God has already saved me, justified me, adopted me into His family. I love Him and wish to show my love for all He has done for me freely by His grace. I can't imagine what it would be like to think that I have to do this or that to gain God's approval, or even worse, once I have it, that I might lose it by not doing all the right things! I know many who are in that position, and my heart goes out to them. Are you in that position, Steve? If so, wouldn't you like to exchange that burden of continually striving after "worthiness" for the worthiness of Jesus Christ?

I will close this letter and allow you to reply by citing just one more passage, Titus 3:5–7:

Not by works of righteousness which we have done, but according to his mercy he saved us, by the washing of regeneration, and renewing of the Holy Ghost; which he shed on us abundantly through Jesus Christ our Savior; that being justified by his grace, we should be made heirs according to the hope of eternal life.

Justified by His grace, saved by His mercy, washed and renewed by the Spirit of God, all through my Lord Jesus Christ. That is Christian salvation, my friend. That is what the gospel is all about. I pray that you will consider these things, Steve, and that God will be merciful to you and grant you faith to believe. I look forward to hearing from you.

In Christian concern,

James

Questions From a Friend

Friday, August 3

Dear Steve,

Your letter was a welcome sight, and your questions and comments were a great encouragement to me. I appreciate your honesty and the fact that you are really examining the Scriptures and seeking to know what they really teach. I, too, have enjoyed our correspondence, and would be glad to meet with you a week from Tuesday. Till then, I will do as you ask and provide you with *brief* (yes, I know what the word means, I just don't utilize it much in my writing!) replies to your questions on the passages you listed.

First you asked about Philippians 2:12 which reads,

> Wherefore, my beloved, as ye have always obeyed, not as in my presence only but now much more in my absence, work out your own salvation with fear and trembling.

Note that Paul instructs the believers to work *out* their salvation, not work *for* their salvation. You can't "work out" something that you don't already have. So Paul is not asserting that the believers are to do works to *gain* their salvation, but they are to *work out* their salvation with fear and trembling. But don't stop at verse 12! Read on to the next:

> For it is God which worketh in you both to will and to do of his good pleasure.

So who is really doing the work, Steve? As we've seen, everything in the Christian life is dependent upon God. Even when we do good works, when we "work out" our salvation, we are utterly dependent upon God's power, God's Spirit! I like to say that we are "saved by grace, *and we are kept by grace!*" The Christian life starts by God's grace, continues by God's grace, and will be completed by God's grace. That is the message of Scripture.

The next passage you asked about was Matthew 7:22. Let's pick up the context by quoting verses 21 and 23 as well:

> Not every one that saith unto me, Lord, Lord, shall enter into the kingdom of heaven; but he that doeth the will of my Father which is in heaven. Many will say to me in that day, Lord, Lord, have we not prophesied in thy name? and in thy name have cast out devils? and in thy name done many wonderful works? And then will I profess unto them, I never knew you: depart from me, ye that work iniquity.

I believe very much in what the Lord Jesus says here. He speaks of those many, many people who have been deceived into thinking that their religious activities are evidence of their personal relationship with Jesus Christ. People of many religions will be standing there—I believe that nearly every LDS person will be in that group, because the Mormon Church teaches a false Jesus, so that there is no personal relationship there between the true Christ and the Mormon. But they won't be alone—there will be people from every Christian denomination who substituted religiosity for relationship. Did you hear what Jesus said to them? He didn't tell them that they hadn't undergone this ceremony or that ordinance—He told them that "I never knew you." That is the real test. Do you know Christ? I am reminded of the infamous "fireside" talk given by Bruce R. McConkie back on March 2, 1982. A book had been circulating at BYU that spoke about having a "personal relationship" with Jesus Christ. McConkie came to BYU to "correct" this kind of thinking. Here is some of what he said:

> I shall express the views of the Brethren, of the prophets and apostles of old, and of all those who understand the scriptures and are in tune with the Holy Spirit. . . .
>
> Now, it is not secret that many false and vain and foolish things are being taught in the sectarian world and even among us about our need to gain a special relationship with the Lord Jesus. I shall summarize the true doctrine in this field and invite erring teachers

and beguiled students to repent and believe the accepted gospel verities as I shall set them forth. . . .

Christ worked out his own salvation by worshipping the Father. . . .

Note it please, the Lord Jesus worked out his own salvation while in this mortal probation by going from grace to grace, until, having overcome the world and being raised in immortal glory, he became like the Father in the full, complete, and eternal sense. . . .

Our relationship with the Father is supreme, paramount, and pre-eminent over all others. He is the God we worship. It is his gospel that saves and exalts. He ordained and established the plan of salvation. He is the one who was once as we are now. The life he lives is eternal life, and if we are to gain this greatest of all the gifts of God, it will be because we become like him. . . .

Our relationship with the Son is one of brother and sister in the pre-mortal life and one of being led to the Father by him while in this mortal sphere. He is the Lord Jehovah who championed our cause before the foundations of the earth were laid. . . .

There are yet others who have an extensive zeal which causes them to go beyond the mark. Their desire for excellence is inordinate. In an effort to be truer than true they devote themselves to gaining a special, personal relationship with Christ that is both improper and perilous.

I say perilous because this course, particularly in the lives of some who are spiritually immature, is a gospel hobby which creates an unwholesome holier-than-thou attitude. In other instances it leads to despondency because the seeker after perfection knows he is not living the way that he supposes he should.

Another peril is that those so involved often begin to pray directly to Christ because of some special friendship they feel has been developed. In this connection a current and unwise book, which advocates gaining a special relationship with Jesus, contains this sentence—quote: "Because the Savior is our mediator, our prayers go through Christ to the Father, and the Father answers our prayers through his Son." Unquote.

This is plain sectarian nonsense. Our prayers are addressed to the Father, and to him only. They do not go through Christ, or the Blessed Virgin, or St. Genevieve or along the beads of a rosary. . . .

Now I know that some may be offended at the counsel that they should not strive for a special and personal relationship with Christ. It will seem to them as though I am speaking out against mother love, or Americanism, or the little red school house. But I am not. There is a fine line here over which true worshippers will not step.

McConkie's confusion comes from his polytheism, as we have seen. But it seems quite clear that unless God was in some way merciful to McConkie prior to his death, he will be one of those standing there saying, "Lord, Lord, did I not. . . ?" and Christ will answer, "I never knew you." And those words will echo throughout eternity in light of his telling people not to seek a personal relationship with Christ.

Then you asked about the LDS belief in three "heavens" (celestial, terrestrial, and telestial) that was based upon Paul's words in 1 Corinthians 15:40–41:

> There are also celestial bodies, and bodies terrestrial: but the glory of the celestial is one, and the glory of the terrestrial is another. There is one glory of the sun, and another glory of the moon, and another glory of the stars: for one star differeth from another star in glory.

The Mormon church has latched on to the terms *celestial* and *terrestrial* in its teaching of various levels of heaven. The third word, *telestial,* is not even an English word, but was created by the imagination of Joseph Smith by combining the first two letters of *terrestrial* with the last seven letters of *celestial.*

No Bible text can be understood outside of the context in which it is found. Such is also the case here. 1 Corinthians 15 is known as the "resurrection chapter." Paul is here discussing the topic of the resurrection of believers. Notice the two questions he has addressed in this chapter so far; verse 12 addresses those who did not believe in resurrection, and verse 35 asks the question, "With what kind of body do they come?" Paul is still answering this question in verses 40 and 41. What, then, is Paul's point?

Paul is here discussing the connection between our physical body and the spiritual body we will have at the resurrection. He maintains that there is definitely a connection between the two, but the future, glorified body will far transcend our current physical body in so many ways. To make his point, he brings in a number of illustrations. One is the seed and the plant (vs. 36–38), another that of the flesh of the animal kingdom (v. 39). When we come to the verses under discussion here, we see that he is continuing with the same train of thought—here comparing the glory of heavenly bodies with the glory of earthly bodies. This verse simply continues his comparison—there is no reason to believe that all of a sudden he decides to talk about different levels of heaven! The very next verse substantiates this quite well:

> So also is the resurrection of the dead. It is sown in corruption [a perishable body]; it is raised in incorruption [an imperishable body]: It is sown in dishonor; it is raised in glory: it is sown in weakness; it is raised in power: It is sown a natural body; it is raised a spiritual body. There is a natural body and there is a spiritual body. (1 Corinthians 15:42–44)

Notice the continued parallelism—perishable, imperishable; dishonor, glory. I would also like to point out with reference to the terms *celestial* and *terrestrial* that the *same* Greek terms are used in John 3:12, and are there translated by the King James Version as *heavenly* and *earthly*. Since it is obvious that Paul is here describing the nature of the resurrection body, and not different levels of heaven, what about the passage at 2 Corinthians 12:2? This passage reads,

> I knew a man in Christ above fourteen years ago (whether in the body, I cannot tell; or whether out of the body, I cannot tell: God knoweth;) such an one caught up to the third heaven.

Then, in verse 4, Paul identifies this "third heaven" as "Paradise." What is the third heaven?

The Bible does describe three heavens. The first heaven is that of the sky above us—the atmosphere of the earth. The second heaven is the abode of the stars and earth—"space" as we know it. The third heaven, however, was always the abode of God himself, what we would describe simply as "heaven." This was a common conception in Paul's time, and was a convenient way of describing things. Hence, Paul was caught up into the presence of God, into the "third heaven."

Next you asked my understanding of John 3:5–6 with reference to the necessity of baptism. The passage reads,

> Jesus answered, Verily, verily, I say unto thee, Except a man be born of water and of the Spirit, he cannot enter into the kingdom of God. That which is born of the flesh is flesh; and that which is born of the Spirit is spirit.

The vast majority of Mormons (and a number of other religious groups) interpret the phrase "to be born of water" to mean baptism by immersion. I have asked many Mormons if they knew of a single other place in the Bible where baptism is described in this way. There is no answer to the question, because there are no such other places. What does it mean to be born of water? Some feel that Jesus is referring to natural birth, picking up Nicodemus' words in verse 4 and carrying this through to verse 6. But I personally feel that Jesus is using the same kind of terminology that is found in Titus 3:5 ("he saved us, by the *washing* of regeneration, and *renewing* of the Holy Spirit") and that is found in the book of Ezekiel, a book that John was obviously very familiar with. Note this passage from Ezekiel 36:25–27:

> Then will I sprinkle clean water upon you, and ye shall be clean: from all your filthiness, and from all your idols, will I cleanse you. A new heart also will I give you, and a new spirit will I put within you: and I will take away the stony heart out of your flesh, and I will give you an heart of flesh. And I will put my spirit within you, and cause you to walk in my statutes, and ye shall keep my judgments, and do them.

Sound familiar? I believe this is what John is referring to, and, if we take the Bible as a whole, including all of what the Lord Jesus and the Apostle Paul taught about how one is forgiven and how one is made right with God, it is obvious that a human action of undergoing baptism cannot possibly be something that is *foundational* to salvation, for this would leave God utterly dependent upon the actions of men. Instead, baptism is an action of an obedient believer, a person who is picturing his death, burial and resurrection with Christ, *not* a person who is seeking after God's grace through a system of ordinances and works.

Speaking of baptism, you asked my opinion of 1 Corinthians 15:29: "Else what shall they do which are baptized for the dead, if the dead rise not at all? why are they then baptized for the dead?" Here it is in a nutshell: The Christian church has never practiced baptism for the dead in the sense that the LDS Church wants us to believe. They are forced to take 1 Corinthians 15:29 out of its context and force their own peculiar meaning on it. First, the Bible does not teach that baptism saves anyone (even 1 Peter 3:21, upon close examination, does not do so), hence it certainly would not be needed to "redeem the dead" as Mormons put it. 1 Corinthians 15:29 is found in the "resurrection chapter." The needed clue to its meaning is found in the language in which it was originally written, that being Greek. The word "for" is the Greek term *huper*. It refers to the taking of someone's place, or to substitution. Baptism "for" the dead is not baptism of a living person in behalf of or for the benefit of a dead person, but rather the immersion of a living person in the place of or into the former position of a now deceased person. It is the baptism of a new convert who takes the place in the church of one who has died. The baptism of a young child, for example, the day after an elderly saint of the Lord has passed away could be viewed as the younger person coming to "fill" the position of the person who has gone home to be with the Lord. This vein of thinking is carried on in the context when Paul says in the next verse, "And why stand we in jeopardy every hour?" Being a Christian in those days was a dangerous business. Paul's whole point in the entire passage has to do with the fact that if the dead are not raised (v. 12) there is absolutely no point in bringing new converts into this dangerous position through baptism when there is no future life to promise them, no reward in the future for their faithfulness. Why not just let everyone die off without filling their positions in the church, since, if there is no resurrection, "we are of all men most to be pitied" (v. 19). Belief in baptizing the living to somehow help in saving the dead demonstrates a complete misunderstanding of the New Testament teaching concerning the nature, extent, and purpose of salvation.

Well, I'm to your last question and have managed to actually stay "brief!" Not bad, huh? Well, your question centers around Acts 3:19–21. Here is what Luke wrote:

> Repent ye therefore, and be converted, that your sins may be blotted out, when the times of refreshing shall come from the presence of the Lord; and he shall send Jesus Christ, which before was preached unto you: whom the heaven must receive until the times of restitution of all things, which God hath spoken by the mouth of all his holy prophets since the world began.

This raises the entire LDS belief that the church went into a state of apostasy after the death of the last apostles, only to be re-established by Joseph Smith in 1830. The phrase "the times of restitution of all things" in Acts 3:21 is interpreted to refer to this restitution of the Church. In fact, as I recall, Steve, this verse is used on that little "17 Points of the True Church" card that you gave me when we first met. An examination of the text chosen to represent this claim will show just how weak this argument is. Acts chapter 3 is not in any way discussing the Church. This is seen in two ways. First, verse 21 says that the "restitution of all things" was "spoken by the mouth of all his holy prophets since the world began." As Paul points out in Colossians 1:25–27, the mystery of the church was not made known to the past ages and generations (see also 1 Peter 1:10–12), hence this certainly is not talking about the Church. Second, the prophets spoke of the restoration of Israel to its own land, and the restoration of the theocracy under David's Son. This is what Peter is discussing in Acts 3. Besides all of this, I must ask when it was that Christ returned, as verse 19 says this would happen at the "restitution of all things."

What is without question is that the Lord Jesus taught that the gates of hades (the KJV says hell, but hades and hell are not the same thing, so a better translation would be "hades") would not prevail against His Church (Matthew 16:18). If the Church ceased to exist for 1700 years, then Jesus spoke an untruth. And Paul, too, taught that the Church would not pass away:

> Now unto him that is able to do exceeding abundantly above all that we ask or think, according to the power that worketh in us, unto him be glory in the church by Christ Jesus *throughout all ages, world without end.* Amen. (Ephesians 3:20–21)

God is to be glorified in the Church by Christ Jesus for how long? For a few years before a gap of 1700 years? No, *throughout all ages.* To teach that the Church would cease to exist for nearly two millennia is to teach something that is contradictory to the Word of God.

Well, I actually kept this short. Surprised? I am looking forward to getting together with you next week. Please give me a call if anything comes up that would require us to reschedule. Thanks again for writing, and God bless.

In Christ,

James

LETTER 17

Grace, Grace, Grace

Monday, August 6

Dear Steve,

I enjoyed our phone call, brief as it was. I certainly understand your inability to talk freely in your situation right now. Hopefully we will have time to talk openly on Friday.

It's late, and the kids are in bed. (Oh yes, my daughter is feeling better, thanks for asking). My wife is in bed and, hopefully, is asleep. Sometimes the clicking of the keys keeps her awake. This crazy little desk lamp is flickering (why do they always do that?) and I've turned the brightness down on the computer screen so that I don't end up burning a rectangular green spot in my retina. It's late, and it's been a long day, but I had to write to you this evening.

Did you know that this makes the seventeenth letter I have written to you? I wrote my first letter on the twenty-first of May—eleven weeks ago. We've talked about testimonies, the Bible, God, Joseph Smith, the Book of Mormon, false prophecies, salvation—and a bunch of other things. But I want you to know that in the final analysis, all of that discussion leads up to only one thing: the gospel of God's grace. I told you that I didn't like talking about Joseph Smith, because I don't. The only reason I do is so that, Lord willing, I will be able to talk to you about God's grace. And I talk to you about God's eternity, His sovereignty, His holiness, and His wrath so that you will have a solid foundation upon which to understand His grace. And, in fact, once I have spoken to you about God's grace, there isn't much more for me to say.

Do you want to know what is so hard about accepting the Bible's teaching about salvation, Steve? I can't see into your heart, but if you are like me you have to struggle with pride and arrogance. It seems to be part of our sinful nature. We like to do things our way. It hurts us a great deal to admit we are helpless. We don't like to have to rely upon someone else. But when it comes to salvation, that is exactly where we are. As far as saving ourselves, or even starting the process, we are helpless. The best we can do falls so far short that it isn't even worth mentioning. Helpless.

To come to God on the basis of His grace, we have to give it all to Him. We can't hold anything back, can't trust in our works, trust in our goodness—nothing. God's grace is a hundred percent thing—He leaves no room for our little works. If He did, we'd boast about it anyway, wouldn't we? Of course.

I know the struggle in your heart—I can hear it in your words. Letting go of your "religiosity" would mean far more than just leaving Mormonism. I know how deeply involved your family is in the LDS Church, and you mentioned once a certain Linda back home. Believe me, I know what is going through your mind. I've never put pressure on you to make a snap decision—I don't believe that is the right way.

At the same time, realize that you are in a position that many others have faced during the past two thousand years or more. Following God normally costs a lot. The world hates those who give it all to God. But God is gracious, and He provides help in time of need. You can trust Him in that way.

And, aside from all that, you still have questions in the back of your mind about this or that, and it takes time to sort through all those things. But when you burn all the rest of the stuff away, the real question is this: Will Steve Hahn give himself solely and completely to the one true God, or will he continue to trust in his works, his religion, his own goodness? That is the real question. Will you accept God's grace on *His* terms? I can't make that decision for you. No one can. Indeed, you can't even make the right decision unless the Spirit of God works in your heart to enable you to do so. I am praying that He will do just that. But I am still to call you to Christ, call you to His grace. I have no greater gift to offer you, nothing more important to discuss with you. He is my all, His grace my strength. He has never let me down, He has always been faithful.

You are a good man, Steve. An honest man. But you are not good enough. You never will be good enough. And, you cannot try to get as good as you can, and then trust the rest to God's grace. His grace doesn't work that way. It is not the final rescue plan when you don't quite make it—the "heavenly net" in case you fall. Either you will be saved completely on the basis of God's grace or you won't. That's it. Quit trying to hold on to grace and works, Steve—you'll get ripped apart in the trying. Listen to God's Word, and believe what God has said.

You know I am your friend, and I am praying for you.

James

The Mission President Speaks

Friday, August 10

Dear Sir:

I am in receipt of your letter of Wednesday, August 8. I am sorry that you do not feel that you can allow the young men who serve in your mission area to make decisions for themselves or to examine the facts that would be relevant to their religious beliefs. I do not feel that your position is either scripturally defensible, or even logically consistent, and certainly your brusque tone was not required. I quote from your letter:

> Elder Hahn has been transferred to another area of service. Your correspondence will *not* be forwarded to him. I would like to ask you to not harass any of our missionaries any further. They are not here to carry on lengthy conversations with you, but to proclaim the message of the Church of Jesus Christ of Latter-day Saints.

I am sorry that Elder Hahn has been transferred elsewhere. I can certainly understand what someone in your position has to fear in allowing him to maintain contact with me. But in taking the action that you have, you have placed yourself in the position of taking responsibility for keeping a young man from examining the truth. And, since you are unable to respond to the information I have provided to him (and would gladly provide to you as well), you shoulder a terrible burden.

As to "harassing" Mormon missionaries, my desire to befriend them and share the gospel of Jesus Christ with them is hardly harassment. I shall take each and every opportunity God gives me to share the truth with all men, Mormon missionaries included.

Finally, sir, I would like to remind you that while you may think you have safely tucked Elder Hahn away in some remote corner of your mission area, you should remember that my God is not limited in time nor space. He knows where Elder Hahn is, and He knows that I, and many others, are praying for him. You cannot stop the Holy Spirit of God, sir. That is my confidence.

Sincerely,

James White

Conclusion

Some may not like the way I chose to end this work. Many continually ask me, "So, how many Mormons have come to the Lord in your ministry this month?" The "numbers mentality" is rampant in our country. If someone doesn't hit their knees and "pray the sinner's prayer," then somehow you have failed. The idea that we share the gospel solely to glorify God, and that it is God who brings the harvest *in His own time,* seems to be an old-fashioned concept. It would not have been realistic to finish the story in any other way. You have no guarantee that if you say "all the right things," and present "all the right information," that the person with whom you are speaking is going to respond positively. But even if Elder Hahn never came to Christ, would I be right to say that I wasted my time? Most certainly not. Whether our fictional Elder Hahn is ever saved is God's business, not mine. I pray, I care, I hope. God does the saving.

Leaving Mormonism is not like quitting a book club. It is normally a very long process. Mormonism is an entire culture that includes family, friends, schoolmates or co-workers. I have known people who have remained in the LDS Church long after they stopped believing it was true. But just because you might be called to invest hours of your time, and yes, even a good bit of your heart, in sharing with a Mormon *without the joy of seeing them come to Christ* does not mean that you should not do so. "Seed-planters" are desperately needed—people who care enough to share over and over and over again in faithful trust that the Lord will accomplish His will. It is not easy work—few would go along as far as Elder Hahn did. Some will insult you, some will try to ignore you. If you love God and the gospel, those things won't bother you. You just share with them anyway.

A word to the Latter-day Saint who reads this book: First, thank you. Thank you for reading this far and for considering what has come before. Some of you have read this book only so that you can be "prepared" to answer the objections that might be raised by the next Christian you encounter. I can only pray that God's Spirit will so convict you of the truth of what you have read that you will not be able to rest until you deal with the true God. Some others are really searching, really looking. I hope you have been helped by this book. I hope you have seen that it is not simply my desire to "tear down," but also to "build up." I have tried to take away falsehood but also to replace it with truth. I pray for you as I did for Elder Hahn—trust in God's grace. He is sufficient for you.

A word to the Christian reader of this book: I pray that you have read this book so that you can in love and tenderness share the truth with Latter-day Saints. I hope you will study it, memorize the verses used, and fearlessly share the gospel with Mormons. That is truly my desire. And I pray that if you are simply seeking information with which to "win a debate," you will think twice before befuddling some young missionary with your tremendous knowledge and then walking off victorious with your sword in the air. That accomplishes little. Christian truth demands Christian love, just as much as Christian love demands truth. They go together.

There are thousands of Elder Hahns pedaling their bicycles around the world right now as you read this page. One of these young men is probably close-by, doing his best to fulfill his "calling" in sharing the message of Mormonism with those around him. When he comes knocking on *your* door, what will you do? You might begin like this:

I wanted to write and thank you for the time you spent with my wife and I last Friday evening. . . .

Further information and a sample packet of tracts can be obtained from:

Alpha and Omega Ministries
P.O. Box 37106
Phoenix, AZ 85069

Or via Internet: Orthopodeo@aol.com

The books *The Changing World of Mormonism* and *Mormonism: Shadow or Reality?* can be obtained from your local bookstore or directly from the authors at:

Utah Lighthouse Ministry
P.O. Box 1884
Salt Lake City, Utah 84110

Scripture Index

Index of Basic Mormon Scriptures and Doctrinal Authorities

Index